DATE DUE

THE HUMAN IMAGE
IN POSTMODERN AMERICA

THE HUMAN IMAGE
IN POSTMODERN AMERICA

JOSEPH F. RYCHLAK

American Psychological Association • Washington, DC

Published by
American Psychological Association
750 First Street, NE
Washington, DC 20002
www.apa.org

To order
APA Order Department
P.O. Box 92984
Washington, DC 20090-2984
Tel: (800) 374-2721; Direct: (202) 336-5510
Fax: (202) 336-5502; TDD/TTY: (202) 336-6123
Online: www.apa.org/books/
E-mail: order@apa.org

In the U.K., Europe, Africa, and the Middle East, copies may be ordered from
American Psychological Association
3 Henrietta Street
Covent Garden, London
WC2E 8LU England

Typeset in Goudy by AlphaWebTech, Mechanicsville, MD

Printer: Port City Press, Baltimore, MD
Cover Designer: Naylor Design, Washington, DC
Technical/Production Editor: Casey Ann Reever

The opinions and statements published are the responsibility of the authors, and such opinions and statements do not necessarily represent the policies of the American Psychological Association.

Library of Congress Cataloging-in-Publication Data

Rychlak, Joseph F.
    The human image in postmodern America / by Joseph F. Rychlak.
        p. cm.
Includes bibliographical references and index.
    ISBN 1-55798-986-9 (hardcover : alk. paper)
    1. Psychology. 2. Human behavior. 3. Postmodernism. I. Title.
BF121.R93 2003
150—dc21   2002015069

British Library Cataloguing-in-Publication Data
A CIP record is available from the British Library.

Printed in the United States of America
First Edition

To my love,
to my life,
to my Lenora

CONTENTS

INTRODUCTION

There is an ill wind chilling the American consciousness today, stemming from a deep concern over the steady decline of decency in personal character and social relations. Some of us even think that we have a modern crisis here. What fascinates me about this crisis is its implications for the human image as we now move into what most scholars agree is a postmodern era in which life improvements have steadily taken place, including such things as better homes, advanced medical care, healthier diets, rising educational possibilities, increased job potentials, and improved communication and transportation systems. Community services are frequently aimed at righting various wrongs. A continuing string of "experts" has appeared to offer the unique service of motivating others, or instructing people to use self-help strategies in correcting life's maladjustments. Social sciences like psychology have over the years gradually shifted their emphasis from a disinterested scientific study of human nature to that of "how to" live better, happier lives through psychotherapy, counseling, and related "fix-it" strategies.

In fact, psychology as a helping profession has captured America's imagination across all economic levels. Psychology is one of the most frequent academic majors in American colleges and universities, and virtually everyone in the society spouts psychological lingo to characterize human behavior. And yet I have serious doubts that there is a clear and correct understanding of human nature involved here. I believe that traditional academic psychology has been excessively biased in its explanations of human beings. Psychologists have tried to stretch their scientific understanding of the material universe to cover human actions that simply cannot be captured in the same terms.

I do not raise this issue of erroneous psychological description to suggest that if we now "get it right" our understanding of human nature will necessarily allow us to help people live happier lives. I am not out to write yet another self-help book. In our eagerness to offer such books—in which readers are coached on how to gain confidence, develop greater insight—be successful in business, increase sexual gratification, or rear happy children, we have never really clarified the underlying human nature bringing about such satisfying events. Models borrowed from various engineering specialties have always been available to be used metaphorically in human description, as when the brain was said to be a telephone switchboard or the body a system of muscular pulleys and gears under direct manipulation by the environment. Currently, we have the computer model as the popular alternative, so that the individual is pictured as an input–output–feedback sequence of electrical signals. Do apparatuses like switchboards, pulleys and gears, or input–output–feedback signals really teach us anything about our human nature?

To understand real people we must proceed on the basis of a totally different image of humanity from that of the engineering models, or even the medical-model formulations of biology. This is not to deny the important role that mechanical and physical aspects of the human body play in life experience. But such automatic processes are not well suited—indeed, are specifically free of—the more evaluative and selective aspects of experience that people engage in daily. Understanding humanity demands something beyond the concepts to which engineering and medical models limit themselves. This realm of "something beyond" has been implied whenever people refer to topics like religion, mysticism, spirituality, emotionality, or simply faith. Such attributions suggest to me that there is a side to human nature that is impossible to explain in the hard sciences and materialistic philosophies of our time. But this side is there and needs to be properly understood if we are really concerned about humanity.

It is my intention in this book to clarify the as yet poorly understood essence of human nature. To do this properly we need special terminology, and this has always been a stumbling block for my readers, whose eyes tend to glaze over as I inconsiderately toss abstract philosophical concepts in their direction. Having gone through this unfortunate practice a dozen times I decided to do things a bit differently. In this book I take a more casual approach to the writing and also place my references and academic comments in the back of the book. I introduce the more technical terms in graded steps, first presenting them with clear definitions and appropriate examples and then gradually bringing them into the analysis of concepts as we move along. I have also tried to shift exclusive reliance on established scholarly works as my references to books and other media in which concerns over the human image are being analyzed (knowingly or unknowingly) in a more popular, everyday vein.

Among the first important concepts discussed is the changing view of causation in explaining how life events and personality styles come about. I then introduce several key contrasts, beginning with the fundamental difference between the meanings of *individual* and *collective*. Another important contrast is that of a mental process versus its content, from which flows the difference between a predication and a mediation or association form of reasoning. Other important contrasts include dialectical versus demonstrative logic and first-person versus third-person theoretical explanations. We gradually begin extending such background meanings to the clarification of what is meant by human nature. I continually contrast the machine image of human beings with an image that sees them as intentional agents of behavior.

At a broader level, I review America's ongoing development from a preindustrial to an industrial and then to a postindustrial stage focusing on the providing of services to the populace. I give this development major emphasis and equate its third stage with what is meant today by *postmodernism* (at least in certain quarters). I analyze deconstruction, which is often cited as a postmodern analytical tool, in terms of its unwitting support for human agency (self-determination, personal responsibility, etc.). At this point I rely on the Marxian argument, frequently applied to current analyses of collectives. A unique feature of the book presents Gary Kasparov's insightful views on why he lost his second chess match with the computer "Deep Blue." Human versus machine reasoning is clarified, and the point is made that in a postmodern age there is a change called for in the human image, moving psychology's descriptive efforts from the hardware to the software in the revamped machine metaphor. Many significant implications flow from this recognition that software requirements place emphasis on a new style of causal explanation.

A challenging analysis has to do with the complexities of collective versus individual reasoning. Can reasoning take place without biasing evaluations of what is being considered? Where does culture's collective influence come in? Can relativism in reasoning be avoided, and how can we tell conscious from unconscious reasoning? A significant chapter is devoted to the self-concept, which moves us into the role of autonomy, authority, and social rights in human experience. I introduce political correctness and also analyze morality. A chapter is devoted to various biological considerations in human behavior, which include not only the brain, genetics, and racism but also the emotional feelings of love and lust. I give detailed coverage to values, including religious and political commitments, as well as to relativism of both the cultural and the individual variety. I then analyze the postmodern era more specifically, with a summary of just how we may expect the average American person and family to behave in this societal and cultural milieu. The hope in all of this is to find an accurate image of humanity that encourages dignity and responsibility to one and all in the passing parade of life.

THE HUMAN IMAGE
IN POSTMODERN AMERICA

1

BEING HUMAN COLLECTIVELY
AND INDIVIDUALLY

Ask any American citizen today if he or she is an individual, and you are likely to get an affirmative answer. I doubt that this holds true everywhere in the world, but my questioning for many years has convinced me that it is certainly the case in the United States. Of course, precisely what is meant by the word *individual* and how it is being used on any specific occasion is not always clear. Quite often the concept is assumed to be another way of referring to a person living in the freedom of a democracy. The interesting aspect of the individual versus collective distinction is that it has so many ties to lifetime issues and experiences. I therefore selected it as a leitmotif for my perusal of various topics bearing on the human image.

Chapter 1 begins with definitions of important conceptions that are fundamental to the material that follows. I try to make them as straightforward as possible and relegate the more academic aspects to chapter endnotes. Chapter 1 therefore establishes a helpful terminological context for the many challenging issues covered in the remainder of the book.

BASIC CONCEPTS TO BEGIN WITH

The word *individual* refers to a single being, such as a person. I use *person* (or *persons, people*) as a neutral word signifying either individuals or members

3

of a collective. The word *individuality* has the meaning of setting a person off from others for some unique behavioral characteristic. *Individualism* has a broad range of meaning extending from a libertarian political ideology of self-sufficiency to a kind of egotistical lifestyle without regard for others. A *libertarian* ideology holds that the state—insofar as it is necessary at all— exists for the individual, and not vice versa. As used in this book, a *collective* is a gathering together of people. Any aggregation of people into identifiable groups, crowds, masses, societies, classes, cliques, and so on is understood to represent a collective. The word *collectivism* refers to an ideology favoring group ownership and the sharing of all resources as well as life decisions. The *collectivist* believes that the person exists for, or is an indivisible aspect of, the group (state, organization, union, etc.).

There are two kinds of individualism. One is the view that individuals must act alone on literally every aspect of life. Such individuals see no benefit in joining hands with others, even when help is called for ("I can do it myself"). They resist such cooperative efforts but may occasionally conform to reservations and suspicious expectations bordering on paranoia. Here is where we find so-called rugged individuals. We refer to this as *solitary individualism*. On the other hand, there are times when a person who advocates individualism accepts the need to join hands with others when there is a problem that would benefit from group action. This person is not viewing such mutuality as a collectivist solution but merely as taking advantage of the strength in numbers for a unique task of limited duration. We refer to this as *parallel individualism*. Critics have occasionally suggested that I consider this group action a form of *cooperative individualism*. It strikes me that such a phrase places too much emphasis on cooperation, thus detracting from individualism. Becoming cooperative is often a first step toward collectivism. Or, we find people here who are basically collectivists but want to believe that they are "really" individualists. In my usage of parallel individualism I want to convey the emphasis of the old saw "politics makes for strange bedfellows." That is, politicians sometimes join hands not because they are in a cooperative mode but because they have been forced to accept a certain negotiation, one that may not be entirely pleasant but with which they have to live. In like fashion, parallel individualists may not always see themselves as in the act of cooperating. They may see the group as "ganging up" to make things happen through force rather than cooperation. A coerced cooperation is no real cooperation.

Adding the "ism" to the concepts of individual and collective seems to turn their meaning in the direction of an ideology, a grounding belief in how things ought to be. A belief is something different from the act of believing. This involves a process versus content distinction. A *process* is something that is actively causing something else to come about, creating it or fashioning it in some way. A *content* is this "something else" that is acted on and produced. The process of gravity is continually at work forming the planets into their orbits or rolling teardrops down melancholy cheeks.[1] The planets and the teardrops are both contents of the same process. The process can be considered by itself, distinguishable from the content that it is processing. For example, a thought process may be studied independently of what it produces. Scott is thinking about being on time for the appointment with the doctor, while Suzy is thinking about the fact that he is driving the car awfully fast. Both of these people are using the identical thinking process, but the contents they are producing differ. Scott's content involves the meaning of "being on time," while Suzy's content involves "speeding dangerously." Such thinking produces certain content. Thus, we cannot say that the thought process is identical to the thoughts it produces. Processes remain essentially the same but content differs greatly.

A major challenge at this point is to ask, What sort of process causes human beliefs (thoughts, ideas, etc.)? This word *cause* is not as simple as it sounds. We tend to think of causes as cause–effects that impel things, as when a swinging bat or golf club hits a ball. But for 2000 years it was common to speak of a cause in terms of four different meanings. Aristotle (384–322 BC) developed this quartet of meanings after studying how earlier philosophers typically explained things.[2] The word he used was *aitiá*, which is translated from the Greek as "cause" and has the meaning "responsible for."

The first such responsibility is the *material* cause, or the stuff that things are made of and how they may differ as a result—like the difference between a cement and a gold brick. Biological influences such as genes or DNA would also represent material causes of certain influences on the body. The second responsibility is the *efficient* cause, which captures raw motions, blind forces, or signals. This is what we consider "the cause" today, as in the force that gravity has on things like orbiting planets and teary cheeks. The familiar "domino effect" in which a number of small rectangular wooden or plastic pieces click along, knocking over one after the other, is a perfect example of efficient causation at work. The thrust of motion and impact is from the first (*cause*) to the last (*effect*) domino to fall. A third responsibility is the *formal* cause, which involves the occurrence of patterns, outlines, shapes, rhythms, systems, and so forth. If we can, for example, identify our friend at great distances due to his unusual gait, this recognition is founded on formal causation. We just know his pattern of body language. Formal causes as patterns within and between patterns also comprise logic and mathematics, which are actually variations of the same calculation process.[3]

The fourth responsibility is the *final* cause, which addresses the purposes, intentions, or reasons "for the sake of which" things happen, including when things are avoided, created or destroyed, accepted or rejected, and so on. The final cause always includes the formal cause because a purpose is some kind of patterned plan or strategy that the person intends to carry out ("OK, here's what we do . . ."). Behaving for a purpose or intention is called *working toward an end*. The Greek word for "end" is *telos*, so any theoretical explanation relying on final causation is called a *teleology* (i.e., study of ends). I also use *telic* as a synonym of teleology (teleological, etc.). Because ends suggest something to work toward or achieve intentionally, a teleological theory is one advocating purpose, choice, or "free will." Sometimes this free-will capacity is called *agency* or *self-determination*. The opposite of a teleology is a *mechanistic* account. Mechanisms rely exclusively on efficient causation. The engines in our automobiles never intend anything. They are switched on by us and follow our orders—our intentions—completely. Problems can arise in the efficiency of the machine, of course, but it is never at fault for what goes wrong because it is never responsible for what takes place.

Although Aristotle believed that we should use all four causes in our explanations, the rise of science in the 17th century helped to drop final causation and weaken the use of formal causation. It was no longer acceptable to suggest that natural events had a purpose or were carrying out God's divine intentions. Thus began the era of British philosophy that relied on material and especially efficient causation to explain natural events on the basis of association.[4] The aim here is to explain all events, including human thought in terms of efficient causation, with final causation totally out of the account (formal causality was retained to an extent). Associations in thought work like the dominos, with an earlier mental content (*cause*) signaling a later content (*effect*) to take place without a genuine telic intention being involved. *Associationists* are therefore prone to be mechanistic in their view of bodily functioning as well as how thinking takes place. A word like *popcorn* might be associated (linked, connected, etc.) in one person's brain to a fireplace, in another a movie theatre, and yet another to painful gums. It all depends on the associated ideas aligned by the past experience of the person in question. This person would never intend to think of one or the other of such associated meanings. These associations would merely "happen" based on the frequency of past experiences flooding the mind in efficient-cause fashion. We characterize this style of theoretical explanation as relying on an *association model*. It can also be called a *mediation model* because the suggestion is that past experience mediates present experience without the identity of a person actually selecting or directing such associated sequences. A mediator has no identity and therefore cannot select or intend the meanings involved in its behavior. Thus, a robot is programmed to take in and store a certain number of mathematical signals ("information"), which then direct its ongoing mechanical responses by automatically mediating (combining, calculating, etc.) the past signals with those encountered in the present. There is no meaning expressed in such information processing. The actions of the machine are therefore under "blind" control.

Is there a comparable model that explains a meaningful act of human intention? Yes, there is: the *predication model*. Instead of picturing thought as a host of "one by one" external hookups under calculation and mediation, we can think of it as internal logical extensions from a broad context of meaning (e.g., the meaning of popcorn) to the specific (narrowing) realm of the targets to which this meaning will be logically extended (i.e., fireplace, movie theater, painful gums). Aristotle actually defined our model for us when he inquired "Why does one thing attach to [link or connect to] some other? . . . We are inquiring . . . why something is predicable of something . . . the inquiry is about the predication of one thing of another."[5]

Predication is not association. To *predicate* is to use one concept to envelop another in the formal cause manner of logic. When I say "Olivia is cool," I am extending the meaning of cool (as I understand it) to Olivia. She is my target to which the content of meaning known as "coolness" applies. In our example, popcorn is itself a sort of context within which any of a number of ideas might be meaningfully captured (framed, identified, etc.). The context acts as "the meaningful reason" for the sake of which an idea is formulated. In addition, the predication model enables the person to reject or discontinue the line of meaning extension from context to target. Because the person intentionally lays down the meaningful context from which thought extends, this person can willfully terminate the line of thought at any time. After a period of time has passed the person might decide "Olivia isn't as cool as I thought she was!" Of course, sometimes due to obsessions or addictions it is difficult for the person to stop certain meaningful thoughts at will.

Clearly, the fundamental difference between an association and a predication process is the role played by meaning. "To mean" is literally "to intend." For an example of the low value placed on meaning in association theorizing, we can turn to the exchange carried on between behaviorist (or associationist) B. F. Skinner (1904–1990) and humanist (or predicationist) Carl R. Rogers (1902–1987). This took place following one of their debates on the question of human teleology, which Rogers believed in and Skinner rejected. Rogers commented,

> A paper given by Dr. Skinner led me to direct these remarks to him: "From what I understand Dr. Skinner to say, it is his understanding that though he might have thought he chose to come to this meeting, might have thought he had a purpose in giving this speech, such thoughts are really illusory. He actually made certain marks on paper and emitted certain sounds here simply because his genetic makeup and his past environment had operantly conditioned [i. e., shaped] his behavior in such a way that it was rewarding to make these sounds, and that he as a person doesn't enter into this. In fact if I get his thinking correctly, from his strictly scientific point of view, he, as a person, doesn't exist." In his reply Dr. Skinner said that he would not go into this question of whether he had any choice in the matter (presumably because the whole issue was illusory) but stated, "I do accept your characterization of my own presence here."[6]

Skinner was assigning to himself precisely the same view his association theory assigns to all people.[7] We humans are not sources of personal control. Our environment manipulates us. No credit can be given to a person's individual achievements in the course of life, nor can we assign blame for individual shortcomings. Note the perspective or slant that Skinner took in framing his theoretical account of behavior. He looked "at" events the way that natural scientists do in the study of their subject matter. He thinks of himself as an object—an "it" or "that." This third-person or *extraspective* (i.e., on the outside looking in) account removes the observer from the objects or events under observation. This is like an astronomer looking at the heavens through a telescope or a histologist looking at tissue cells through a microscope. The natural inclination here is to think of causation in material- and efficient-cause terms for we can observe them taking place "over there."

Even if these scientists observe patterns (formal causes), reductionism in their theories pulls the explanation down from formal- to material- and efficient-causation as supposedly the "real" source of what is taking place. In line with the reigning British philosophy, the rigorous natural scientist is instructed to "reduce" all explanations to material and efficient causation. This is well-suited to an association process because here, too, events are molded into forms "from below" by the underlying efficient and material causes (stimuli, inputs, genes, DNA, stem cells) that presumably shape everything according to natural laws embedded in reality. This is not unlike reducing the patterns of dominoes toppling over to the first piece that toppled to get things going. An efficient-cause impulse kicked it all off and the course of events was blindly shaped accordingly. There is no need of intention in such accounts.

Teleological theorists like Rogers explain human behaviors from a first-person (e.g., I, me, we) or *introspective* theoretical perspective that approaches life from such internal identities looking outward. For teleological theorists the case above calls for the final cause with its accompanying formal-cause patterns framing certain ends, reflected in meaningful intentions and purposes. The predication process is required at this point because its purposes are not shaped *from below* via inputs but rather affirmed *from above* as conceptualized ideas. The predicating organism internally frames a purpose, such as "I could use a lucky four-leaf clover" and then sets about trying to find one on the front lawn. Spying this person "over there" pacing the lawn with head down, we might incorrectly assume from our extraspective (*third-person*) perspective that he or she has lost something. We misjudge because we have not asked this person what is going on introspectively (*first person*) and what is the predication framing his or her actions on the lawn assuming. As the old saying suggests, we cannot really understand some other person until we have walked a mile in his or her shoes.

The introspective perspective invites explanations founded on a predication model because it relies on the framing of assumptions through which meanings are expressed. This is like looking through glasses that act like predicating meanings. If the glasses are rose colored we see a happy world about us. If they are shaded black we see a gloomy world about us. But for me to know what another person's glasses portray I have to put them on, assuming thereby the introspective point of view with which he or she is confronting life daily.

SORTING OUT INDIVIDUAL AND COLLECTIVE PROCESSING

Skinner and Rogers were actually following a rich tradition of debate over how the human experience should be understood and explained. There have always been those who believe that the basic data are to be found within the collective relationships formed by a "body" of people.[8] As a working assumption I now claim that theorists who begin with individuals believe that predication is the basic process in behavior (even if they do not call it this), and theorists who rest everything on collectives are believers in the association process as fundamental to all human behavior. Occasionally, a third position is advanced in which the claim is made that individual and collective influences are equally important, or that there is a constant interaction at work between these two sources of experience. This means, in effect, that everything is ultimately connected to everything else, a claim that is hard to deny, much less disprove. And when things get difficult in the explanation, such a theorist can slip from one side to the other and back, appearing to be comprehensive but actually avoiding the need to take a consistent position.

I have found that, when pressed, the interaction theorists tend to be associationists after all.[9] Association theorists never really explain precisely where the newly created ideas being mechanically joined together originate.[10] Does the new idea assemble in the gray matter of an individual, or in the interactive bumping about of people in collective contact? I think it is always the individual person who through predicational examination—including vigorous exchanges with others—comes up with such innovative alternatives. Often this innovation is dependent on skillful evaluation and selection from a myriad of possibilities known "more or less" to all involved but initially chosen by one.

To say that the collective innovates a line of thought on its own is to imply a group mind, an identity initiating thought for those people living within its orbit. As this important question of a group process somehow creating thought independently of the individual's unique predicational processing crops up at several points in this book, I give it a formal title for ready identification and recall. Taking my lead from Thomas Hobbes (1588–1679), who pictured the collective state or commonwealth as an artificial person thinking for and directing its citizenry, I henceforth refer to the belief that collectives can think like an individual thinks as the Leviathan Assumption.[11] Hobbes limited causation to the material and efficient variety, denying teleology through final causation. Human beings were totally reliant on influences from external experience and never originators of actions from within their personal identity. I am departing somewhat from the precise Hobbesian conception of the collective as a Leviathan, but there is a strong parallel in the suggestion of a unifying group identity framing ideas for use among the members of a collective. The Leviathan Assumption therefore holds that some form of collective energy creates ideas supra-individually to be used by the masses in their ongoing reasoning.

I now bring together our basic concepts as elaborated by the terminology I have been gradually introducing into the mix. Let the concept of an *individual* refer to a person who is behaving according to the predication process. We can understand individuals only from their introspective perspectives, grasping the meanings of the various contents undergoing affirmation and extension into the course of their personal lives. Let the concept of *individualism* stand for one of these contents—an affirmed belief in the right of a person to self-select life's alternatives without necessarily conforming to the group (although parallel individualism allows for such occasional group participation). An *individualist* would be someone who embraces the ideology of individualism. It now becomes possible to speak of the individual (*process*) on the one hand and a belief in individualism (*content*) on the other. Furthermore, any one individual might reject individualism in favor of some other ideology—such as collectivism. Through the common process of predication, all manner of beliefs (contents) can be fashioned and carried forward depending on what William James (1842–1910) called the "cash value" for the individual, who seeks a payoff for the affirmation of worthwhile ideas ("If my idea works, the problem is solved").[12]

Just because individuals have a common predication process does not mean that they need to form a group consensus on the contents produced by this process. In the same way that a common digestive process is in effect though the food being eaten by different people varies greatly (including broad cultural differences such as French vs. Oriental cuisine), so, too, do the ideas of people who predicate via a common process vary greatly. It is in common ideas (contents) and not common processes that we find collective identities taking shape. Whether *pro* or *con* on some contested issue, the same predication process is involved in deciding where to stand on the plan being voted on, vehemently rejecting it, and then behaving for the sake of this rejection from then onward ("I will fight this plan to my last breath!").

We thus understand the term *collective* as a gathering of people into some form of group identity in which an association process is ultimately directing things. *Collectivism* could be one of the contents within this process, an ideology stressing the benefits of shared living like mutual support, diminished competitiveness, submergence of personal ego, and so forth. However, it is also possible for a person molded in the association process to advocate individualism. What distinguished Skinner from Rogers most fundamentally was a disagreement over the mental process that orients and directs human behavior. The position I am taking is that to presume humans are influenced by associated ideas mediating between either a stimulus and its response, or a response and the reinforcement to follow, is ipso facto to embrace collective theorizing. And to presume that humans are influenced by predication is ipso facto to embrace individual theorizing. Even so, regardless of which process we use in our understanding of people, it must be possible for the one selected to produce contents favoring either individualism or collectivism. Once again, contents stand apart from the process that produces them.

AN EXAMPLE LIFESTYLE

To put some life into the abstractions under consideration, I now compare an association and a predication explanation of the same lifestyle. Assume that we want to explain the behavior of a man in his early 40s who happens to be a social activist and an ardent communist. In explaining this person, an association theorist would probably think of both the pattern of behavior we call *activism* and the belief content we call *communism* (i.e., an ideology) as strictly the result of mechanical shapings in the past. These shapings would be observable, captured in the man's behavior from an extraspective perspective.

The man may have been reared in a family setting in which the values of communism were constantly preached. Possibly his parents were activists, or at least members of socialistic political organizations. As he matured through pubescence he may have joined left-wing organizations, formed friendships there with other teenagers, and even worked on several projects (e.g., public demonstrations) to improve the lot of the disadvantaged, or some such. These high-minded experiences were deeply rewarding, reinforcing his belief system all the more. He was frequently instructed in the tenets of communism, and as his input information increased so, too, did the number of associations in his behavioral repertoire. His level of mediating ideas or responses increased dramatically as he grew into a full-blown activist for the communistic cause.

But around his 40th year this man began to change his views, slowly at first and then more rapidly. Throughout his 30s he had found several problems with the ideology that had guided his life. He also discovered that many of his colleagues were not as altruistic in their motivations as he originally believed. He began to see merit in the political system that he had been trying to destroy. How do we explain this change in outlook using mechanistic association? Well, I think we would find the claim of new inputs somehow slipping in to mold the man in opposition to his long-standing beliefs. He presumably encountered a number of unrewarding or "negatively reinforcing" experiences during his 20s and 30s. His collectivist beliefs were aversively conditioned (e.g., ridiculed), or they might simply have begun to extinguish (disappear) because no one except his activist friends paid any attention to them. So, he began to be shaped in a new direction.

The association explanation does not hinge on a purpose or intention and in fact could be rendered without reference to the specific meanings used by the man in daily life. That is, we could simply refer to efficient causation on the *upside* (positive reinforcements) and efficient causation on the *downside* (aversive punishment or extinction). His strident tones were tempered and his manner diffident. Friends began thinking of him as burned out. He increasingly read the "propaganda of the other side." The associationist would point to such new stimulus inputs as shaping this man's behavior, acting as new cues to mediate (covertly direct) alternative courses of action that did not exist previously in his long-term memory system. Occasionally he is even seen conversing with opponents, and this, too, could result in a positive reinforcement for appearing to be so circumspect in looking at all sides.

A predication–process explanation would also begin in childhood, recognizing that early experiences always influence later experiences by acting as predicating frameworks for ongoing and upcoming life events. However, the point would be made that even these early experiences were under predication. The person as a conceptualizer was affirming and extending predicating meanings from the very onset of life.[13] The meaning of meaning is "to intend." He took influence from others but not like an efficiently caused machine simply registering inputs. Final causation was at work in his predicational processing. He emulated those he loved, took on their value system, and behaved for its sake. But in adulthood things changed. They changed not simply because life brought some unhappy inputs into his mechanical apparatus. It was not these new inputs that caused the changed outlook, but the context of meaning that he had used to frame life, and which with further experience under constant predication now turned sour.

I am assuming that all of these introspectively generated motives would be clarified through an examination of such third-person life assumptions. It would help if we had a real person under examination to support my guesses. Well, it just so happens that David Horowitz, in his autobiographical book *Radical Son: A Generational Odyssey*,[14] introspectively outlines a life much like the one I have been drafting. Horowitz was a radical communist in his youth and early adulthood but gradually changed his outlook for several reasons. I am not interested in these reasons per se but rather in what he had to say concerning the metamorphosis that occurred in his personality. As a self-described rationalist and a utopian, Horowitz believed that the environment "shaped human destinies" and that, therefore, human character could be formed through environmental manipulation alone.[15] But he was to learn, partly due to his personal experience as a father, that there was "something irreducible in human character itself that rebelled against efforts to direct it too completely."[16]

In time, he came to see that people are not so much victims of circumstances or fate but rather are willful contributors to what takes place in their lives.[17] This discovery moved him in the direction of individualism, away from collectivism, a fact he recognized when he noted that "As a Marxist, I was not used to thinking in psychological terms."[18] Horowitz found that the political left-wing "regarded people as objects of history, rather than as subjects who made the events happen."[19] Such introspectively framed insight permitted him to entertain a concept like free will, which he had previously dismissed out of hand.[20]

Horowitz moved from his early affirmation of collectivism (communism) to a form of individualism in which the person is seen as influencing politico–historical events rather than being manipulated by them. This strongly suggests that a predicational process had replaced an association process in his view of humanity. I could provide other examples of this change in process. We consider a woman who stopped her formerly all-consuming pursuit of art to study law or a man who quit a high-paying executive position to open a book store in a small town. All such examples can be cast by an association theory as moving from formerly positive to currently negative (and then newly experienced positive) associations. "One size fits all" in such explanations. But to really understand these people, we must look introspectively into their very souls and see how they are no longer influenced but are influencing. And in this pursuit of understanding, meaning is everything.

HUMAN AGENCY VIA DIALECTICAL REASONING

When people are thought of as making their own decisions and carrying out their own intentions (preferences, choices, etc.), we refer to this as *human agency*. An agent can believe or not believe what he or she is told, or even has seen for that matter. As with all of us, agents are pressured to conform in many ways, but they do so under the knowledge that they could be thinking or doing otherwise, all circumstances remaining the same. At least many agents have this insight. Many others never realize or accept that they have the capacity to accomplish things on their own. But most of us who believe in predication as a fundamental mental process also believe that agency is an aspect of this process. Here again, all of these people process meanings identically, but it is the content of these meanings that distinguishes them from each other.

The process of predication begins with the *affirmation* of a framing meaning, a premise (assumption, hunch, presumption, conviction, etc.) concerning whatever it is that we are thinking about. Affirmation occurs when we commit ourselves to what is intended, implied, surmised, and so on. We frame an initial or *major premise* about something and then extend this to whatever has been targeted for such meaning extension. A woman holds the major premise that she can tell if people like her by how much they talk to her in social contacts. This might be true in many circumstances, but if she now meets a shy person, who never says much to anyone, she will probably think this person does not like her when this is not necessarily true. It is all up to the major premise here, which frames a *pro-forma* context of meaning targeting some end. The associationist would doubtless consider such premises to be inputs from past experience and not intentionally framed (selected, patterned, projected, etc.). Association theory does not really have a way of conceptualizing agency because everything is molded into the person by the environment. How does predication theory avoid this major premise of the associationist that people believe and behave in ways fashioned by the environment and then input mechanically? It all comes down to *oppositionality*.

When Aristotle analyzed the predication process in detail he soon discovered that people in the act of reasoning by way of a predication process can arrive at their major premises in two logical ways.[21] The two forms of logic he named were *demonstrative* and *dialectical reasoning*. In demonstrative reasoning the major premises are affirmed predicationally as *primary and true facts*. A man looks out one early morning in January and sees 10 inches of snow on the ground. He begins preparing for the inevitable snow shoveling that this fact demands. He does not forget to put gloves on because snow is cold. Another fact!

Demonstrative premises cannot be self-contradictory or combine opposite meanings at the same time.[22] Demonstrative lines of thought are certain because they are either true by definition (all bachelors are unmarried) or they have been unquestionably proven by empirical evidence (smoking is harmful to physical health). They are always either–or, unipolar assertions. Dialectical lines of thought, on the other hand, follow a bipolar, oppositional course of thought in which contradictions and negations are quite welcome. The major premises are always open to examination on the other side of their meanings. Thus, a dialectically reasoning person may see an implication to the opposite of what is being intended. The Ten Commandments input by a machine intellect would have 10 courses of action open to it. But the dialectically reasoning human being would have at least 20! It is impossible to convey to a person that one should honor parents without thereby implying or "teaching" that parents can be dishonored. Many parents today believe that the emphasis being placed on sexual instruction in the primary schools has some such effect on their children, encouraging them to indulge in sexual activity by sheer implication to the opposite of the sexually abstemious attitude that the course instruction is supposed to convey.

Here then is the source of Horowitz's capacity to look over and evaluate what his significant others (parents, friends, teachers, etc.) were telling him. He could mull over the basic consistency of such teachings and judge their plausibility in relation to the other side of the picture. He could also judge the actual behavior of his radical colleagues in relation to the values espoused by them. There is another aspect of dialectical reasoning that should be mentioned at this point. I call it *affective assessment* or simply *affection*. This is the person's capacity to render opposing judgments of preference, such as good–bad or like–dislike. Evaluation is based ultimately on such opposites, which actually imply each other in the sense already noted so that it is impossible to know one without knowing the other (good is only "good" in relation to "bad"). Even as objects and events are encountered, avoided, learned, misunderstood, and so on, evaluation—expressed aloud or not—of the sort "This I like" versus "This I dislike" takes place.[23] Affective assessments appear to be emotional displays, but I do not agree with this equation. Emotions are involved with the physical equipment of the body and thus can themselves be evaluated affectively. Some people love to attend movies that are "tearjerkers." There are times when a sense of righteous anger seems called for ("I am outraged!"), whereas at other times feeling hostile anger is something to regret ("Sorry, I lost control"). It is clear that emotional feelings per se and the affective value that they convey are two different things.

If we put together the ability to select positions in dialectical contradiction to one's superiors and friends, affectively assess the merits of such opposing views, and come to a contradictory position having greater personal significance, we can understand how Horowitz's agency worked. I should also mention a few other concepts dealing with the introspection that goes on when agents tackle their views in this manner. One is *transcendence*, which simply means that the person can rise above a belief system to analyze and evaluate it. We transcend our experience when we back off and look it over circumspectly—up one side and down the other ("Let's see, what are my strengths with people, and what are my weaknesses?"). In doing this we turn back on experience in what is called a *reflexive* manner. The term *self-reflexive* is also used to capture this ability to turn the tables on our ideas and seek an alternative approach to things ("Face it, my self-assurance to this point is a phony act."). In doing so, we take full responsibility for the choices made in life. A thinker favoring free will would be likely to use some such explanation ("What is the moral choice now?").

CONCLUDING COMMENT

Chapter 1 establishes that there is more involved in answering "Are you an individual?" than was expected when I put this question to many Americans. On the one hand, I could be asking about a belief (mental content, idea) that the person has affirmed. On the other, I could be asking about the very cognitive process involved in arriving at such items. The latter question is more factually oriented, similar to asking if the lungs are involved in breathing and, if so, how? The former question is more like an opinion. We might even want to call it a *value*, as in "Do you value individualism?" Whatever the case, I have now introduced most of the basic terms called for in the chapters to follow. Chapter 2 takes us into a survey of some of the classic theories of personality that began on either a collective or an individual assumption (major premise) of the human image.

2

PERSONALITY THEORIZING AS DESCRIBING INDIVIDUALS OR COLLECTIVES

The human image does not carve itself into existence. We find it being framed in the various psychological explanations advanced over the centuries. In the field of psychology it is portrayed by the personality theories of our founding fathers, who did not always agree on such matters. In this chapter I go over some leading contributors to this image in psychology. I show that there have been dramatic shifts in how human beings have been described, whether as individuals or as members of a collective. I think this review will help us to appreciate that how we think about people is up to us. Surely, we will never identify "the" human image. There will always be room for dialectical alternatives, so that defining one image suggests its alternative through oppositional inferences of one sort or another.

The first attempts to describe human nature in what might be considered a psychological sense began in ancient mythological tales and religious writings. Modern psychology as we know it did not arise until the 19th century. During the introduction of modern psychology to universities in that century, personality study was not a major aspect of the field. The study of dynamic behavior played an insignificant role in academic centers but was adopted by medical specialists in their efforts to explain abnormalities that could not be traced to physical illness. Gradually, the academic centers took

17

an interest in what was to be called *personality*. The beginning efforts to create a dynamic psychology are usually credited to the psychoanalysts, and we begin our survey of theories with them. Although they made reference to collectives in one way or another, the psychoanalysts focused primarily on the individual client in their theorizing. We then move to collective interpretations of human beings with special emphasis given to behaviorism, a theory that effectively took the person qua individual out of personality theory altogether.

First, I have a few points to make about personality and theorizing in general. A distinction is sometimes drawn between *personality* and *character*. Personality is said to capture the person's style of behavior as a type, whereas character represents an evaluation of whether such behavior is righteous and admirable. In practice, these terms are usually used interchangeably. A *type* concept aims to capture the person "as a whole." For example, if we believe that people are either optimists or pessimists we are using a *typology*. On the other hand, when we see an array of some personality description in people's behavior we are said to be using a *trait* description. In this case we might say that Joe is very optimistic and Lindsey is mildly optimistic, suggesting that she has a touch of pessimism at times. Optimism and pessimism are being used dimensionally here, so that people can be said to have more or less of the trait in question. Type theories tend to become trait theories in time because people are rarely either–or in their total behavior.

PSYCHOANALYZING INDIVIDUALS

The three, universally recognized founders of psychoanalytical human description are Sigmund Freud (1856–1939), Alfred Adler (1870–1937), and Carl G. Jung (1875–1961). I am not interested in trying to summarize their theories in great detail. What I want to point out is their common tendency to—boldly or subtly—rely on teleological explanations of individuals. The basic aim of their analyses was to explain the individual's behavior, albeit occasionally influenced by the collective. Personal choice was always a legitimate alternative in these theories, and to capture this self-determination the psychoanalysts used the predication model.

Freud's Misunderstood Libido

In the practice of medicine it was *not* common for physicians in the late 19th century to think of people from an introspective perspective. Freud changed all of that. His concepts were based on the deeply personal premises of his clients (as well as recollections from his own experience). Freud believed that the medical model robbed his theory of its humanity by trying to reduce mental abnormality to the biological exclusively, such as to a germ or a blood chemical of some kind.[1]

Freud accepted Darwinian theory. He believed that the unconscious realm of mind is in closer touch with the human being's ancient animalistic tendencies than is the conscious realm. Indeed, Freud's entire theory is predicated on the premise that what is first or earliest on the scene in human development or maturation is basic to and determinative of all that is to follow. The first identity located in the unconscious realm of mind from birth Freud called the *id*. This is a wanton, totally hedonistic aspect of mind that sought pleasurable gratification without rational considerations. The id wants to have its cake and eat it too. It has many wishes, some of which are repugnant to the conscious ego's intentions (e.g., wanting to have sexual relations with a parent).

Freud said that the more rational aspect of mind, termed the *ego*, developed out of the id, but only because it could further the latter's pleasure seeking. Eventually, a *superego* aspect of the ego developed through contact with the external world. The superego or conscience reflects the moral teachings of the culture as conveyed by parents and other authority figures. The superego thus represents the collective, but it is not a primary determiner of all human behavior, for it, too, must accommodate the id's wishes. To be more precise, the ego serves as a sort of negotiator to get both the narcissistic gratification of the id satisfied and the ethico–moral demands of the superego met. Life in the Freudian manner is therefore a long line of compromise and self-deception.

Although he did not use the Aristotelian distinctions in causation, Freud clearly appreciated the impossibility of relying exclusively on material and efficient causation to capture the human condition. But he was forced to come up with some kind of quasi-efficient cause in his theory. The medical establishment had completely accepted the premises of Newtonian science, which rejected formal–final causation in the concepts used to explain "natural" structures or actions. Although Freud believed it reasonable to avoid concepts of intention and purpose in describing why rocks roll down hills (as Aristotle had done), he did not find it inappropriate to explain unconscious motivations in terms of such causation. However, the medical establishment was striving to be a member of natural science, and so Freud was called on to do something about it.[2] His answer to the challenge was the elusive libido theory.[3] *Libido*, or "psychical desire," is a strange concept, sharing the meaning of an energy that mechanically influences the organization of the psyche and also serves a purely instrumental role to meet the intentions of the personality identities called the *id*, *ego*, and *superego*.

Thus, on the one hand, Freud can speak of libido as becoming *fixated*[4] during certain psychosexual developmental stages of life (e.g., *oral, anal, phallic*) to bring about the adult character structure (e.g., *oral personality, anal personality*).[5] On the other hand, when Freud was in the throes of ending his friendship with Jung he could tell the latter "I took myself in hand and quickly turned off my excess libido [toward Jung]."[6] We see an immediate problem. The fixation usage of the libido concept "sounds" mechanical, a material- and efficient-cause sequence of automatic events taking place over the years of physical development. But if Freud can turn off amounts of libido formerly directed to Jung *at will*, we are no longer dealing with a force on the order of blind gravity or magnetic attraction and repulsion. We are dealing with a selective *instrumental* force used as a means to intentionally attain chosen ends. This makes psychoanalysis a teleology and not a mechanism. There are many points in Freudian theorizing in which a psychic identity uses libido in an intentional manner, as when the more conscious aspects of the ego *counter-cathect* (oppose, repress, etc.) *cathexes* (desired ends) being sent outward by the completely unconscious id. Freud and Jung had increasingly serious disputes over the nature of libido, with Freud wanting to keep it tied closely to the sexual realm, and Jung wanting to make it over into a broader force that represents both sexual and other kinds of life interests. Many believe this disagreement led to their eventual breakup.

Although Freud is frequently pictured as a biological reductionist, he is not actually of this stripe (see Chapter 6). He introduced concepts that sounded like traditional biological mechanisms without truly fulfilling this role. Libido is strictly in the mind. It is not a physical drive like hunger to be sated and perhaps used to imprint some line of behavior, such as giving children candy following some constructive action on their part in hopes of getting them to behave this way habitually. Biology is important to life, and we must all, as individuals, deal with our physical needs. But what makes Freudian theory uniquely "Freudian" is its characterization of the person as capable of intentionally influencing the course of events, at times reasoning quite dialectically to suggest an alternative never before seen or heard of. Freud conceptualized people as reasoning through a predication process and thus as being teleological organisms or human agents. It is important to appreciate that he felt it was necessary to explain the *process* of human reasoning and not just speculate on the *contents* of an unexamined process.

Adler's Teleology

Alfred Adler advocated both a human and a "within-nature" teleology. He believed that, at an early age, roughly between 3 and 5 years, every person frames a guiding *major premise* or *prototype* (also called a *life plan*) for the sake of which life is to be fashioned by the individual.[7] Final causation is the model here. Thus, a firstborn child with several siblings might assume the premised lifestyle of a "leader," looking after the younger children of the family and gaining recognition from the parents for such efforts. The youngest child in a large family might frame a premising prototype of the "helpless one," taking every advantage to be gained from being looked after by others. These styles or types of living would continue into adulthood, in which we might find the leader type with a large family also holding a political office and the helpless type still unmarried, out of work, and living with the parents. The latter sibling might be said to have an *inferiority complex*. I think we see that Adler has framed a teleological account of development here, shaped by the individual and not the group or external environment.

Adler also believed in what he termed a *progressive evolution*,[8] an innate capacity in all people to willfully bring about an evolutionary advance in the group. Here is where he used seemingly collective concepts like *social feeling* and *social interest*.[9] Adler held that if a large percentage of human beings made the intentional effort to empathize with others, given enough time in such an effort, "the power of social feeling will triumph over all that opposes it. Then it will be as natural to man as breathing."[10] Adler's views are frequently misunderstood because of his use of the word *social*, suggesting that he favored a collective view of personality. But Adler named his approach *Individual Psychology* because he wanted to explain things at this level of humanity. It is because of the intentions of individuals who consciously promote social feelings that humanity can advance through a higher form of evolution. We have a parallel individualism under description here. Adler was not sympathetic with those who blamed their cultural environment for having supposedly molded them in some negative manner (e.g., to be lazy). The young girl who points out that 99% of the females in her neighborhood end up as delinquents, and hence she is not to be held personally accountable for her delinquent behavior, would not be supported or comforted by Adler. He would remind her instead that, like her peers, she has personally chosen to be a delinquent and must assume responsibility for whatever flows from this fact.

Adler coined the concept of a *creative power* of the individual—a kind of willpower enabling the person to frame a goal of personal achievement that he called the *self*.[11] Along with developing social interest, it is our individual responsibility to grow and fulfill our human potential by moving toward and in time literally creating our unique self and thereby *compensating* for our weaknesses in a healthy manner. The role of predication in this self-realization effort is clear. Adler does rely on biological considerations, but not in the purely material- and efficient-cause sense of many psychological theories today. Adler is not thinking of a collective biological substrate that shapes or programs people to behave as they do. He is thinking of an active participation between the biological and the psychological. It is the latter and not the former that gets things under way. Social interest is not stamped into the human's consciousness manifesting itself thanks to the chemical dictates of DNA or some such. Social interest is a mere potential until the individual makes it into something of value by purposely working it into his or her daily living. Then, in time, its use will become embodied at a higher evolutionary level in all of humanity. It is up to us as (parallel) individuals to accomplish this end.

Jung and the Dialectical Mind

Jung was as strongly committed to teleology as Adler.[12] Jung believed that the human being is an intentional organism, infusing life with meaning from birth. He also believed that the psyche developed from a time when there was no personal consciousness. Thinking occurred in the *collective consciousness* of a human horde, precisely as the Leviathan Assumption holds. Gradually, however, a *personal consciousness* began to evolve out of the collective mass. Initially, the personal consciousness perceived the thoughts of the collective as if they were entities ("things") existing in external reality. In time the personal consciousness began to think for itself, but it never loses touch with the collective. In a true sense, the collective consciousness predicates the personal consciousness, offering it certain thematic meanings for consideration during times of need. Jung pictured the relationship of these two levels of mind as follows: "The conscious mind is contained like a smaller circle within a larger one."[13] This is a clear example of predication with meaning extending from the broader (collective) to the narrower (personal) realm. Recall the popcorn examples from Chapter 1, which depicted the predication process now under consideration.

The predicating meanings that the collective unconscious can send into consciousness are called *archetypes*. These are not exactly inborn ideas, for they have no specific form until the personal consciousness provides it. The point is that mind is not tabula rasa at birth.[14] The archetypes are *primordial images* carried forward in the psyche to play a role during times of need. A man who has been too crude with women might have his *anima* archetype—the "sense" of a female carried in the male's collective unconscious—take form in a dream. The dream figure of the anima would dramatically enact this man's crude behaviors to make him aware of them through a woman's eyes and, based on such understanding, be moved to correct things. But such corrections are not automatic. It is up to the person to choose what to do when prompted from the depths of unconsciousness.

Jung took the existence of archetypal themes as evidence that the psyche is *pro forma*, which in our terms means that it functions by way of a predication process. He spoke of life periods such as the presexual, prepubertal, and pubertal but did not adopt Freud's views on fixation, which he considered merely a failure to continue in development rather than an unresolved sexual problem. As noted above, Jung had great difficulty with Freud's concept of libido. He gave this concept a purely psychological definition, as "passionate desire, want, wish, or excited longing."[15]

Jung was not much drawn to collective reasoning for, as he said, "A hundred intelligent heads massed together make one big fathead."[16] He believed that collectives too easily succumbed to a herd psychology energized by excessive emotionalism. He felt strongly that improvements and corrective actions in the group begin with individuals who are willing to accept responsibility for taking a direction or setting things right.[17] He characterized individuality as a unique and unpredictable action. After decades of studying people, Jung concluded that, so far as their psyche (mind) is concerned, "I see in all that happens the play of opposites."[18] The organization and patterning of the human mind is therefore heavily dialectical, so that an *ego* identity in the personal conscious is opposed by a *shadow* identity in the collective unconscious. It is the shadow that encompasses all those behaviors that the ego rejects for itself as immoral. By ignoring these aspects of the personality the person can develop a *complex*. The devoutly religious person must recognize the lustful and hostile urges that have been confounding his or her daily life.

The ego must be made aware of this darker, shadow side of mind, and the way this is accomplished is for a *self* to be formed through therapy. In this activity the conscious and unconscious realms of mind must confront each other and the contradictions between them be resolved—or possibly merely accepted as such. If the complex is not resolved through a clash of opposite meanings, dissipating thereby its grasp on the psyche, the person will live out a narrowly *one-sided* outlook on life. This is like losing the ability to reason dialectically and becoming an exclusively demonstrative reasoning robot. Successful therapy means that the self does take shape as a dialectical balance is achieved between the light and the dark aspects of the psyche. The devoutly religious person now has a better grasp of sin, of how the bad is related to the good, and that the origin of sin is within and not shaped from without. We can learn from collective experience in the past, thanks to our collective unconscious, but the challenge of maladjustment problems confronting us in the present is solely up to us as individuals.

I think it is fair to conclude that, although our psychoanalysts may have disagreed over particular aspects of the human personality, they all favored theories that put the individual above the collective. The collective had its role to play in life, but it was the individual who initiated and directed events as an agent. People were described as intentional organisms who could take responsibility for their actions, but they could also deny their intentions through various mental maneuvers (repression, denial, one-sidedness, etc.). Biology was important and had to be dealt with, but biological urges were not simply mechanical nor were they always treated as necessary sources of influence. Behavior was conceptualized from an introspective perspective in which meaning played a central role as people carried out their intentions (purposes, choices, wishes, reasons, etc.) in behavior. From the analytical point of view, just because a behavioral motivation stems from unconscious sources does not mean it lacks intention. It is clear that our psychoanalysts viewed people as finally-caused "predicators" rather than efficiently-caused "associators" in their behavior. By the way, although Freud used a method of free association in the recovery of repressed memories, this therapeutic technique had nothing to do with mechanical association (i.e., demonstrative reasoning). Freud was not a mechanist.

BEHAVIORISM: FORGOING THE INDIVIDUAL

Behaviorism aims to describe the raw process that people have available as flesh-and-blood organisms. This activity boils down to behavioral *responses*, which in turn are triggered into action by antecedent *stimuli*. The antecedent–consequent sequence here is efficient causation par excellence. The physical structure—the body—put into behavioral motion is a material cause of what is under description and potential manipulation. Lawful forces guide what takes place in behavior just as they do in any natural event (e.g., rain, digestion, reproduction). Behaviorism is often called *stimulus–response* or *S–R psychology*. Many psychologists contend today that S–R psychology is "dead and buried." The new descriptive concept in behavioristic circles is the *input–output* sequence used by so-called *cognitive* (computer-based) psychology. This is heralded by many as a new and revolutionary way of looking at behavior.

In contradiction, I argue that the fundamental efficient causation underwriting S–R theory is alive and well in the input–output formulations of computer theory. It is old wine in new bottles, and I make this clearer as we move along. Behaviorism follows the strict limitations of Newtonian science, approaching the study of behavior in an exclusively extraspective fashion—studying behavior that is taking place "over there." Whereas the psychoanalysts looked deeply into the human mind to understand its inner workings from a uniquely personal point of view, the behaviorist's approach to the study of people is much like a mechanic reviewing the parts of a disassembled automobile engine before putting it all together. The mechanical process here calls for no assistance from the engine per se.

It is fascinating to learn that the father of traditional behaviorism, John B. Watson (1878–1958), once said that we should "try to think of man as an assembled organic machine ready to run."[19] Watson introduced behaviorism in a famous 1913 paper,[20] and, although there was an initial period of resistance to his views, this approach grew with increasing rapidity until, by the 1930s, it had totally captured the imagination of academic and research psychologists. Max Meyer (1873–1967) made the extraspective emphasis quite manifest in his behavioristic book, *The Psychology of the Other-One*.[21] By *other* Meyer meant "that one, over there," which lacked the introspective capacity of a "this one" to transcend and self-reflect. Behaviorists were encouraged to adopt the attitude of natural science, taking only observable efficient causation into the descriptions and analyses of behavior. This attitude is ready-made for the study of collectives, of observing the patterns of groups behaving en masse.

The material cause was eventually brought in to explain how an antecedent stimulus became associated with (or attached to) a consequent response. There were many such suggestions, but in the 1930s the behavioral theory of Clark L. Hull (1884–1952) won ascendance and for the next 20 years vied with the Skinnerian outlook for leadership among the behaviorists.[22] Material causation was pictured as a *drive stimulus*, a physical necessity like hunger or thirst that impelled the organism (usually a white rat being tested for speed of maze running, or some such) into action. The drive state was elevated as the rat became increasingly hungry or thirsty, causing it to seek relief. At this point the efficient cause also came into the picture as the animal ran about to learn its way down a maze (stimuli) so that it could be rewarded (or reinforced) at the goal box with food or water. The resultant *drive reduction* on eating or drinking (responses) cemented the S–R bond (connection, etc.). Presumably, there was no intention involved in this sequence of stimulus (drive) connecting to response (maze running) and eating. Only automatic behavior was involved and empirically observed. This general procedure was termed *conditioning* (conditioned reinforcement, etc.), and the assumption was that all behavior, from lower animals to humans was *shaped* in this fashion. This is what I call *association modeling*.

An important aspect of such associative conditioning is what I mentioned in Chapter 1 as *mediation* (mediating responses). This refers to the capacity that organisms have to turn their past responses into stimuli impelling their current responses. For example, an animal that has been put through the maze task several times records in working memory the cueing twists and turns its body has experienced in running the course. This is not an intentional recording, of course. It is believed that these automatically stored past responses serve as cueing mediators to facilitate the ongoing learning process. The more trials, the more cues recorded, the stronger the mediation, hence the better the learning of the maze layout. Mediation is simply an extension of the association concept. Even the use of language in humans is seen as a mediating action. Words are past responses, prompted by parents and others to be expressed by the person in childhood who then uses these past responses as stimuli today. The child learns to say *hot* (response) and that this word signals caution. A parent may have gotten the child to associate this word to danger connected with excessive heat, possibly using a raging fireplace as an initial example. The child learned to say the word (past response) and now uses it as a stimulus to avoid (current response) being injured by touching other dangerous items like a sizzling radiator or a steaming bowl of soup. All of this learning is automatic, although words like *intention, purpose, choice,* and so on can be learned through conditioning and used mediationally to make it appear the person is actually an agent when this is not true.

Skinner (see Chapter 1) changed the formula for how conditioning was to be understood.[23] Retaining efficient causation as the sole influence on behavior, Skinner suggested that responses were not stimulated by antecedents as traditional S–R theory suggested. Rather, they were *emitted* on a chance basis, to *operate* on the environment in some way. Such *operant responses* were then either *contingently reinforced* or they were not. If reinforced they increase their rate of emission over time (this is called *shaping* behavior). If not reinforced they gradually extinguish (stop occurring). For example, a bear lumbering through the woods might crush a log with its paw, luckily finding a nest of delicious ants within. He laps them up. The bear did not intend to find the ants. There is no purpose in this series of log-crushing operant responses. The environment can be said to actually "select" the outcome of the response for the bear, increasing the likelihood that such log crushing will take place. But even here the bear has no (final-cause) intention to crush logs. If no ants appear there is a trailing off of this response, until it extinguishes altogether.

Skinner eventually argued that this form of operant responding is actually what takes place in Darwinian natural selection but over a much longer period of time. That is, a change first occurs in (or is emitted by) the species that then either enhances or fails to enhance survival. For example, one species of deer might begin eating certain berries that another species of deer avoids. It turns out that these berries are health promoting, and the species that eats them survives drastic climate change, whereas the other does not. Once again, according to Skinner, the environment "selects" the survivors who had not planned things to come out as they did. It was survival of the fittest, but the lucky deer can take no credit for their good fortune, nor can the nonsurvivors be faulted for their bad fortune. Human behavior is the same (see Chapter 1).

In a true sense, this emphasis on environmental control of people turns every behaviorist into a social psychologist. That is, behaviorism has no need of a concept of individuality because ultimately everything that might be thought to be individual issues from group contact and is shaped into the person's behavior accordingly. Even so, the behaviorist does not have to accept the Leviathan Assumption because he or she makes no claims that there is a supra-individual intelligence purposefully directing people's thoughts. On the other hand, it is possible for someone who wishes to account for the ideology of a certain social class (e.g., proletariat) in conflict with another class (e.g., bourgeoisie) to rely on collective shaping to explain how such differences arise. Divergent economic circumstances are believed to force people into one or the other of these opposing classes.

But behaviorism is not without serious problems in its explanations. When experiments on conditioning theory were extended from lower animals (white rats, pigeons, etc.) to human beings, some interesting findings were reported, throwing cold water on the old beliefs that human beings could be blindly shaped like robots.[24] In fact, it is now pretty clear that people do not "get" shaped or conditioned unless two things happen: First, the person must have some idea of what is taking place in the experimental context (frame a relevant predication). Second, the person must be willing to cooperate with what is being implied in this context. Grasping the purpose of the experiment might be something like an experimental participant saying to himself or herself, "Every time that light flashes I get a puff of air blown into my left eye." Seeing the connection between the light and the puff of air, the person can then quickly close his or her eye when the light flashes to avoid having the annoying whiff of air blown into an open eye. Often the participant adapts to the circumstance without actually verbalizing the connection between the puff of air and the closing of an eye. But often enough such insight takes place. Furthermore, if for some reason the person is out to throw a monkey wrench into the procedure, she or he might *never* close the eye and sustain the air puff. If we are to understand fully the conditioning phenomenon, then we must see things introspectively, through the conceptual eyes of experimental participants. What is their understanding of the procedure being followed, whether right or wrong?

I once had an experimental participant scold my assistant and me for, as she saw it, trying to give surreptitious cues in the procedure. She mistook our administration of so-called reinforcements, such as saying "good" at various times in the procedure, as an unethical attempt to manipulate the findings. Affective assessment may also be involved in such decisions by participants, as in having to decide whether or not to cooperate with the experimental instructions. Some participants fail to cooperate out of a sense of humor. Others are simply hostile to the procedure, possibly irritated that they have to participate in such things to pass a course (most of the participants in psychological experiments are college students, either recruited or acting as volunteers).

What does this all mean? I think it is obvious that the interpretation being given to conditioning studies with adults as somehow a shaping or manipulation of their behavior is dead wrong. Such participants can and do exert significant control in the conditioning experimental procedure. It is not a matter of control between the experimenter and the participant but rather is one of cooperation. If the participants don't want to "play," all bets are off concerning experimental findings. And even if one does not go quite as far as I am doing here, the argument is surely convincing that the empirical evidence is just as supportive of a teleological understanding of human behavior as it is of a mechanical, S–R explanation.[25] In adapting to empirical results, I find that modern definitions of conditioning are written in ways that might accommodate predication modeling and its attendant individualism; but even so, the logic of "association of ideas" from an extraspective perspective still holds sway to keep collective explanations inviolable.[26] Traditions die hard. But nevertheless, the teleologist has been given a great boost in the experimental laboratory, which should encourage those who want to see the human image underwritten by agency and free will.

FROM INDIVIDUAL TO COLLECTIVE THEORIZING

Thus far I have discussed theorists favoring an individual image of humanity and theorists favoring a collective one. Carl Rogers, an opponent of Skinner (see Chapter 1), began his career focusing on the individual and ended it focusing on the collective. Rogers first attained prominence in the fields of counseling and psychotherapy by introducing what he called a *nondirective* and *client-centered* approach. Rogerian therapy is client-centered because the therapist believes that it is up to the individual client to frame the problem and then be in a position to effect his or her own cure. This is why the therapist is nondirective. The course of therapy is entirely in the hands of the client. The Rogerian therapist turns the direction of therapy over to the client again and again. For example, after the client has revealed something personally significant, rather than interpret this revelation in light of some arbitrary theory, Rogers would keep the client talking by posing the question, "And how did you feel about that?" The focus is always on the emotions and affections of the client's reality and not on the therapist's theoretical reality. Rogers placed more faith in feelings than in rational thinking. He distinguished between emotions and affective assessment as I am doing.

In his formal theorizing Rogers proposed that we think of people as behaving within a *phenomenal field*,[27] where they approach life in terms of their unique interpretations (e.g., as when seeing, touching, smelling, feeling). Rogers once referred to this as the person's *subjective reality*.[28] It is all that the person knows, experiences, or believes from a subjective perspective. As such, the phenomenal field is construed by Rogers introspectively and is essentially a predication process. It is possible for the person to know the meaning of a certain word mentally, such as what it means to experience hatred. But it is also possible to feel something physiologically and not be conscious that the feeling is hatred. Both forms of hatred are found in phenomenal experience, which lends meaning to ongoing experience in different ways.

Rogers placed great stock in the evidence provided by what he sometimes called *personal organic experience*, which is arrived at through an "*organismic valuing process*"—both of which are aspects of the phenomenal field.[29] He believed that, if we just trusted our emotions and allowed ourselves to look at our problems freely and without influence from anyone else (including the therapist), they would convey what we were truly interested in doing with our lives and why we might be in such a wretched state at present. Rogers found in his practice that people become maladjusted because they put too much stock in what others say and do concerning them. This implies an introspectively functioning identity within the phenomenal field that can find the meaning of feeling tones. To account for this individual identity Rogers introduced the theoretical terms *self* and *self-concept* (not to be confused with Jung's usage). The self-concept refers to the conscious self-definition that we give to our sense of identity when we speak of I or me.[30] The self-concept is an organization of hypotheses about life, which serve as guiding predications to meet our needs.[31]

The basic conflict that individuals have in life arises between the *needs of the organism* and the *needs of the self*.[32] Organismic needs are made known by feelings that indicate what the person finds satisfying or not. A young woman may take a position with her father's hardware business when she would really like to do something else. She does not quite know what this "something else" is, but her feelings tell her that, even though her father is pleased with her loyalty to the family business, all is not right with her organismic feeling tones. It would take some time in client-centered therapy for her to parse out her many feelings, look over her self-concept in light of these feelings, and then come to her own decision as to what to do about things. With successful therapy she would develop a *congruence* between her self-image and her organismic feelings. She would become a whole person once again, working now in her own small flower shop and surprised to find that her father is proud of her business initiative after all.

This focus on the individual in client-centered therapy shifted to the collective when Rogers became active in *encounter groups*. In this form of group therapy the client is assisted (some would say "pressured") to confront and deal with adjustment problems under personal denial but recognized by the group. What proved most interesting to those who had followed Rogers's early work is his willingness to trust the collective, as stated in the following: "In an encounter group I love to give, both to the participants and to myself, the maximum freedom of expression . . . . I do *trust* the group, and find it often wiser than I in its reactions to particular situations."[33] Whereas in his initial theoretical approach the therapist was kept in the background and the client was completely in charge of what took place, now the pendulum had swung to the control of the group. Rogers embraced and reassured encounter group members. At times he even revealed his personal attitudes and problems to the group. Occasionally, he expressed disappointment with the group's performance by walking out of a session that was going poorly.

In the final years of his life, Rogers thought of himself as a group *facilitator*, meaning that he promoted circumstances favoring change among group members. Here is an interesting excerpt from his later writings in which he uses a metaphor smacking of some kind of physical Leviathan Assumption to justify his faith in the collective as therapeutic agent:

> To me the group seems like an organism, having a sense of its own direction even though it could not define that direction intellectually. This is reminiscent of a medical motion picture which once made a deep im-

pression on me. It was a photo-micrographic film showing the white blood corpuscles moving very randomly through the blood stream, until a disease bacterium appeared. Then, in a fashion which could only be described as purposeful, they moved toward it. They surrounded it and gradually engulfed and destroyed it, then moved on again in their random way. Similarly, it seems to me, a group recognizes unhealthy elements in its processes, focuses on them, clears them up or eliminates them, and moves on toward becoming a healthier group. This is my way of saying that I have seen the "wisdom of the organism" exhibited at every level from cell to group.[34]

Rogers has thus replaced the heavy individual emphasis of his early theorizing with a collective emphasis. The metaphor of white blood corpuscles on the attack is powerful, but what it signifies is that during encounter the participants might surround one of their number and put great pressure on this person to admit to some sort of interpersonal difficulty or to acknowledge denying some problem in living. Rogers did not favor overdoing this, but encounter confrontations have been known to be brutal as the group members assault the targeted participant verbally and force the latter's dreaded concerns into the light of day. Note in the above excerpt that Rogers assigned a purpose to the group action, suggesting that he was accepting a physical or natural teleology in his theoretical speculations. He most assuredly accepted human teleology in the description of human beings. Whether he actually meant to apply the Leviathan Assumption, or something like it, we cannot say with confidence.

CONCLUDING COMMENT

Classical personality theorists, working with individuals in a therapeutic contact, favored individualism and parallel individualism over collectivism in their descriptions of human nature. As the field of personality was carried into academia, it confronted natural science and was gradually weaned away from clinical evidence and made over as a variant form of social psychology. This brought the collective into the limelight with its reliance on association and mediation modeling. Individualism was left in limbo as the field of personality gradually slipped into social psychology. People were the products of their heredity as molded by their environment. To find the person, find the sociocultural influences that shaped the person. Behaviorism became the theory of choice in psychology and, although there are those who claim that it is now passé, I believe the efficient causation at its base has merely shifted over to computer theorizing. I have more to say on this in Chapter 4.

Rogers's ability to move from individual to collective theorizing is remarkable, if for no other reason than that he either did not see the contradictory shift in his thinking or did not believe it was important enough to discuss. It is surely true that descriptions of human behavior (types, traits) are readily spun within either the individual or the collective framework. Often, whether intended or not, there is a combination of the two approaches in one analysis of personality. The effort has been made by some psychologists to bring the multiple theorizing about personality under one umbrella. In my experience, this effort has invariably led to a gobbling up of individual accounts by group accounts. This happens because the efficient causation of behavioristic accounts wins out over final causation. The former can be observed extraspectively without injecting verbal exchanges into them (as is done in psychotherapy contacts) and promises one day to trace every aspect of personality to its palpable roots in a hard reality moved by lawful forces functioning on their own without guidance by the person. The study of the individual is not even oriented to such behavioristic goals, which would substitute rigidly robotic actions for spontaneously chosen alternatives and thereby negate free will as a possibility from the very outset.

In my opinion, the science being practiced in psychology today remains predominantly a 19th-century Newtonianism, and none of the classic studies demonstrating the scientist's personal and intentional contributions to such study have seriously impacted the profession. Scientists give efficient causation primary consideration, whereas it is ever clearer to them that the formal cause takes precedence over the others.[35] As a result of this historical commitment to mechanism and its association modeling, little effort is spent in psychology trying to capture the human being's agency, even though it can be seen taking place everywhere—inside the laboratory or out. In the remaining chapters of this book I present evidence for this teleological claim, again and again.

3

COLLECTIVE THEORIZING
IN THE THIRD MILLENNIUM

As America now enters the third millennium it is reasonable to ask whether we have an appropriate human image in mind for the new era. If, as suggested in Chapter 2, association modeling continues to dominate psychological accounts of behavior, is the mechanism in human description that was introduced in the early 20th century still appropriate for today? Are all mechanistic associations alike? I want to put this matter off until Chapter 4. A more fundamental issue facing us right now is the need to identify any development taking place in American society. What collective identity have we been subject to, and how is it expected to change in the immediate future? Any questions relating to association modeling, or predication modeling for that matter, meld nicely into this analysis of the American collective.

Chapter 3 begins with an overview of Daniel Bell's influential three-stage model of collective society, focusing on the postindustrial period, followed by the historical roots and current applications of postmodernism and social constructionism. I then present the Marxian Argument, giving some background and a sense of the influence it can have on many aspects of collective social relations. I turn to a comparison of society and culture to discuss a process–content distinction before ending the chapter with a consideration of the root source of cultural relativism in human reasoning.

THE EMERGENCE OF POSTINDUSTRIAL SOCIETY

Three-stage theories are commonly found in the history of ideas. They have been used for centuries. Bell's theory of societal development is a recent example. Moynihan noted that Bell's theory, although still somewhat elusive on certain points, has been accepted and greatly enlarged on by several modern scholars.[1] Gingrich presented a three-stage model that paralleled Bell's theory, although the technical terminology was different.[2] Bell's first of three stages is the *preindustrial*, an agrarian society in which the economic base is that of extractive pursuits such as agriculture, mining, timber, and fishing. This is the period extending onward from the Middle Ages, overlapping into America during the era of large plantations and small family farms. Communities were located at relatively great distances from each other. Large families were highly desirable in the preindustrial stage, as children grew up to help on the farm and sustain the community. Little or no formal education was required to meet the needs of existence. Religious practices were taken quite seriously, from which developed a strong sense of individual responsibility and self-sufficiency.

The next stage in Bell's scheme is the *industrial*, in which there is a large-scale "application of technical knowledge to social affairs in a methodical, systematic way."[3] The artisan of the preindustrial period is replaced by the engineer. Industrial society seeks the coordination of men and machines in the manufacturing of goods. This is the stage of invention and the assembling of mechanical devices to fabricate various necessities. Fabrication replaces extraction as the major economic process. Although education for the worker has grown in importance, there are still many unskilled jobs available in the factories. Capitalism received a great boost during this stage. The family structure did not change dramatically, but greater mobility was introduced as many offspring left the farm to seek factory work in large urban areas, thereby weakening family ties a bit.

The industrial stage was the heyday of behaviorism in psychology. With the advent of the engineer it became common to think of the human being as a machine, moved along by mechanical devices that were under the shaping of the environment. The metaphor "Man the Machine" captured the imagination of many scientists.

Bell first used the term *postindustrial society* in 1959.[4] In 1973 he predicted that we would begin seeing this postindustrial period develop in the beginning of the third millennium,[5] which makes it the expected society of the 21st century. The postindustrial society is "organized around knowledge, for the purpose of social control and the directing of innovation and change; and this in turn gives rise to new social relationships and new structures which have to be managed politically."[6] Rather than extracting or fabricating, the key word here is *processing* (used slightly differently than my meaning; see Chapter 1). Processing of knowledge is central, calling for telecommunications and computers in the exchange of such information.[7] In an industrial society much attention is given to the managing of capital. In the postindustrial society the major concern is how to organize science as well as the institutions where intellectual pursuits will be carried out, such as universities.[8] The ideal of postindustrialism is to codify knowledge into abstract symbols so that such axiomatic systems can be used to illuminate many different areas of knowledge.

The professional class is the leading class of the new society; it gains significance from its level of knowledge rather than from the amount of property it owns.[9] The technology of this society shifts from the physical to the intellectual. Indeed, we can refer to it as an *intellectual technology*.[10] Along with the centrality of theoretical knowledge the postindustrial society places great emphasis on services, primarily human services such as health, education, and social aid as well as professional and technical services like research, evaluation, computer development, and systems analysis.[11] A service economy is also largely a female-centered economy "if one considers clerical, sales, teaching, health technicians, and similar occupations" as female professions.[12] The employment base for women expands during this developmental period. Summing up, Bell observed that, "The post-industrial society is defined by the quality of life as measured by the services and amenities—health, education, recreation, and the arts—which are now deemed desirable and possible for everyone."[13]

This expectation that certain services are possible for everyone soon leads to the claim that everyone has a "right" to receive them. To meet these aspirations, as well as those of the scientist–researchers working in universities, the government is increasingly called on for financial support. It is inevitable that in the postindustrial society an expanding government as funder of services generates increasing political activity, with people forming into sides on various issues. Bell did not believe that modern society could be divided into simply two classes, as in the Marxian Argument (see later in this chapter). There are classes forming into complex arrangements involving not simply financial considerations but also race, gender, religion, and even social attitudes (e.g., pro-life vs. pro-choice). There is also a huge government bureaucracy with a political agenda all its own to consider. As an industrial-based ideology, Marxism oversimplifies such complexities when it comes to postindustrial society.

Turning now to a major concern of our study, Bell concluded that, "The post-industrial society . . . is . . . a 'communal' society in which the social unit is the community rather than the individual."[14] There are many reasons why this is the case. Information, so vital to this stage, is ultimately a collective and not a private achievement.[15] In addition, "A communal society by its very nature multiplies the definition of rights—the rights of children, of students, of the poor, of minorities—and translates them into claims of the community."[16] Politicizing of decision-making in social affairs is a growing trend in postindustrialism, which becomes heavily involved with politics as more and more groups seek to establish their rights in an era of service to the community. Public policy involvements such as the problems of environmental pollution, health care, and education are also best cast in a collective light.[17] Finally, in the pursuit of human rights the question of justice inevitably arises, which then translates into various legal actions that turn the postindustrial into a rather litigious society.[18]

I find Bell's theory quite interesting and his predictions making sense. I am also impressed by his grasp of human reasoning, as when he observed that "Knowledge . . . is a function of the categories we use to establish relationships just as perception, as in art, is a function of the conventions we have accepted in order to see things 'correctly'."[19] The word *category* comes from *katēgorein*, the Greek word for "to predicate."[20] Here Bell presented the Kantian insight that seeing is believing only when the framework within which things and events are made known visually or intellectually makes sense to the reasoning individual. Thought is predicational, utilizing what is already known as the basis for assumptions used to know or learn more. People can project their course into the future and target desirable goals. Problems arise, but the fundamental truth for the predication theorist is that people are in control of their futures, singularly or in groups. In later chapters, we refer to this as an *existentialistic philosophical belief*. Bell did not make much of dialectical oppositionality, but I think this could easily be brought into line with his view of human beings as predicational reasoners. We want to keep oppositionality in mind whenever predication is under consideration.

The behaviorist would probably see in the rise of a service orientation the natural outcome of positive reinforcements impinging on the experience of everyone in the collective. That is, the suggestion would be that what we see here is a maximizing of positive reinforcements in the lives of people. In a sense, this result is inevitable if we take behaviorism seriously. The good life boils down to more positive than negative reinforcements occurring per unit of time-flow ("Life is a bowl of cherries"). The problem with this too-ready acceptance of hedonism is that we have plenty of evidence today that the pursuit of positive reinforcements by way of drugs and alcohol is tearing American society—or at least portions of this society—apart. A simplistic positive versus negative reinforcement distinction cannot therefore account for the postindustrial period's commitment to services and life improvements. I think Adlerian intentional efforts by way of predicated societal goals make better sense. Next I turn to a concept that has gained considerable visibility in recent years.

POSTMODERNISM

The word *post* that we have been using in Bell's formulation of postindustrialism has the ring of a fad replacing the even earlier fad of using *beyond* to introduce new ideas. We used to read of beyond this or that, and today it is post this or that. Such descriptors suggest a reaching across the present, which soon becomes the past as we read of postcapitalist, posttotalitarian, posthistoricism, postideological, and so on ad infinitum. We are now concerned with *postmodernism*, also called *poststructuralism*. This area of study has to do in large part with language, the knowledge that language conveys in various realms, and the supposed fact that there is no way to find certainty in linguistic expression.

Structuralism was proposed as a counter to so-called *essentialism*.[21] The essentialist believes that there is one and only one aspect of reality to be identified in the creation of knowledge—the freestanding "essence" of whatever it is that we are describing.[22] Aristotle would have considered this a formal cause. Essentialists are therefore *realists*. If an animal under observation has feathers, walks like a duck, and quacks like a duck, it's a duck. The defining characteristics here act as a precedent context that *sequaciously* (i.e., via logical necessity) extends to the animal under observation. *Structuralists*, on the other hand, point out that we have to use language to organize and convey our knowledge of anything. They claim it is easily demonstrated that we cannot actually locate a freestanding reality, for there is no "one" such thing in the first place. It all depends on how the item under study is captured linguistically. Structuralists are therefore *idealists*.[23] They believe that a tree chopped down in the forest does not make a sound in falling unless someone is there to conceptualize what happens.

As a matter of fact, structuralists do not even attribute authorship to the speaker who may believe she or he is conveying knowledge linguistically. We do not shape the language we use. It shapes us. We do not frame predications, which can be negated or accepted as we think along. It is the linguistic context patterned by culture that frames our predications for us, thereby providing us with the words we use socially without a willful intention on our part.[24] To speak of an individual in this theory is to speak of an illusion.

Although the structuralists believe that the individual is not the creator of what he or she expresses verbally there is still an assumption that the cultural context itself can be accurately identified, codified, and studied. The resultant account of things will always be relativistic, of course. Culture A's language system uses categories to understand reality that culture B's language system does not. However, within the constraints of these two cultural language systems, "truth" can still be identified and expressed—a truth for A and a truth for B. Unfortunately, a problem arises in that according to structuralism it is also true that, even within a given culture, disagreements over the truth being expressed can take place. Those who share a language system do not always read or understand a text the same way.

It has been appreciated for centuries that more than one meaning can be conveyed in a written text. In the Middle Ages, the theologians believed that they could "decode" such hidden meanings in biblical tracts. In the 17th century this form of biblical exegesis was termed *hermeneutics*.[25] The root of this word is from Hermes, the messenger of the Greek gods who conveyed the deity's wishes down from Olympus to the mortals below. The suggestion here is that the Christian God is also sending hidden, albeit discernible messages in the biblical text. This is the true message intended to be conveyed. The text as written is merely a smoke screen for this Divine Truth, which had to be covertly transmitted because of its uniquely esoteric nature. Analogical to the structuralist thesis, the writer of the relevant text was not author of this arcane truth. Writing under divine inspiration, the initial "author" was merely a conduit, entirely unconscious of the divine process taking place.

Gradually, hermeneutics expanded to mean any kind of textual interpretation, as in literary analyses that have nothing to do with biblical writings. And with the development of structuralism we find the two fields of literary analysis merging on such points as, for example, the nonexistence of individual authors, language shaping all thought, and the idea that "meaning is a matter of [culturally defined] context."[26] The removal of the text from the author's influence did not stop there. The so-called New Criticism of literary analysis claimed that the written text per se had its own "being" that could be analyzed "without the help of biographical, historical, or psychological background data."[27] This attitude sets the scene for yet another development taking place in dialectical (thesis–antithesis) fashion.

The new development was *poststructuralism* or, as more popularly known today, *postmodernism*. According to the postmodernists, not only are we locked into a language system, we are locked into an unsolvable exchange of dialogue, discussing all sides of conflicting issues without hope of achieving even a relative, arbitrary, culture-bound truth. A leading postmodernist today is Jacques Derrida, whose approach is termed *deconstructionism*.[28] In postmodern writings, anything that can be delineated for consideration (named, assigned a word value, etc.) is referred to as a *text*.[29] Derrida viewed words in a textual phrase as always dual in meaning, and this duality has a dialectical coloring. Thus, a word–signal is never without a trace of meaning to its opposite (negation, contradiction), which is a meaning that is not mentioned in the text but which functions as a *trace* nevertheless. Such meaningful traces can and invariably do unhinge what is being conveyed to suggest the reverse. Thus, to *deconstruct* a text is to find such traces and note how they influence what is being meaningfully formulated. A close reading of the text invariably shows that the distinctions being drawn fail because of the inconsistent and paradoxical use being made of the concepts within the text. This obvious use of oppositionality as fundamental to deconstruction strongly suggests that we are now concerned with a predication and not an association process.

A well-known deconstructive effort is Friedrich Nietzsche's (1844–1900) analysis of efficient causation.[30] Nietzsche challenged the view that such causality is a basic principle of our universe. He deconstructed *cause–effect* to show that, even though we tend to think of the thrust of efficient causation from the former to the latter, we overlook the important role played by the latter (effect) to the former (cause). I feel a pain, look about my person, and discover a pin pricking my hip region. Instead of following the phenomenal truth, in which effect (pain) preceded cause (pin prick), we reverse the sequence and arbitrarily give the initiative to the cause. This deconstruction of the cause–effect construct is not done to dismiss this concept. In fact, we have now used the notion of cause to deconstruct the very notion of causation—the experience of pain causes us to discover the pin and frame our conception of the pin causing pain. We have settled on a formal-cause pattern consistent with our predicating assumption of causation. The central role played by dialectical reasoning in all of this is clearly evident.

Often in an oppositional alignment of things there is a hierarchy suggested, so that we know that tall is better than short or fast is better than slow. Of course, this preferential alignment can be reversed in specific situations (e.g., slow cooking is sometimes better than fast, tall people can find riding in certain automobiles a cramping experience). Note that an oppositional contrast is still present albeit reversed in the special circumstance. Derrida claimed that such a hierarchical influence is always implied in oppositional arrangements of meaning such as cause–effect (the cause is better), and so another form of deconstruction is to "overturn the hierarchy at a given moment."[31] The concept of cause is normally hierarchically superior to the concept of effect, but Nietzsche succeeded in having the effect switch places with the cause, thus overturning (deconstructing) the hierarchy. I must again emphasize that it is the patterning power of dialectical oppositionality in meanings that makes all of this possible.

But this does not mean that deconstructionism or other forms of postmodern theorizing embrace a predication model of mind. We find no concepts of purpose or intention in such models. The role of meaning in language boils down to the associations between language terms mouthed by people in discourse. Texts converse only with other texts under the constraints of the language in which they are framed (written, recorded, etc.).[32] Because any meaning has its opposite trace, there is no way in which to escape the fact that nothing stands textually free of anything else—including its negation—nor can any text be proven better than any other. The result is a frozen gridlock of alternative points of view known as *intertextuality*, that is, an "endless conversation between the texts with no prospect of ever arriving at or being halted at an agreed point."[33] The obvious irony here is that we have a method of overturning meanings dialectically, yet supposedly there is no way in which to overturn the intertextuality. This paradoxical circumstance is supposedly due to the fact that postmodernism lacks teleology. However, I take issue with this position and claim that, thanks to the use of dialectical reasoning, the postmodernist is actually relying on a predication model of human reasoning, which always involves teleology.

What the postmodernist who claims there is no teleology in the human condition is attempting to do is explain things through language systems in an extraspective manner, so that words come down to mere efficiently caused signals rather than finally caused expressions of intentional meanings. At the level of the printed word per se we can think of the process as associative, as being exclusively demonstrative (third-person). Words assemble together, and what they mean at any point in time depends on how they relate to other words in a strictly "chance" manner, like a kaleidoscopic rearrangement of bits of colored glass tumbling through efficient causation into an unintended pattern signaling something or other. But the recognition of oppositionality in this mix clearly establishes that not everything in this pattern is a chance occurrence. A predicating person who can grasp dualities by way of opposites has options built into the cognitive process that a robotic machine does not (a point we return to in Chapter 4). The person can always exercise these options just as Nietzsche exercised his option to deconstruct the conceptual understanding of efficient causation.

SOCIAL CONSTRUCTIONISM

Yet another area of human experience that is much discussed and debated today is *social constructionism* (or *constructivism*). I find that the concept of a *construct* is used in both an association-process sense and a predication-process sense, which leads to confusion when considering this term. The association usage interprets a construct in the sense of assembling parts or pieces together as when we build something out of bricks. We assemble brick on brick to construct (build) a wall and can describe its progress extraspectively. The predication usage, on the other hand, interprets a construct as intentionally forming meanings through such mental efforts as framing, conceptualizing, interpreting, deducing, and analyzing. To construe on this view is to introspectively lend meaning to events in the precedent-sequacious sense of extending predicating meanings to frame what can then be known (learned, understood, etc.). We construe life events when we predicate them, lending them meaning and in this sense doing—or at least contributing to—our own shaping.

On the other hand, according to social constructionism, people are solely what their society shapes them to be. People model one another and absorb what they say to each other as a collective. This fits neatly into the behavioristic ideology and its associative processing conceptions. Once again, the person is disregarded in favor of the group. As the eminent German sociologist Émile Durkheim (1858–1917) once urged, social scientists must "avoid reducing the social world to the psychological."[34] He believed that "what we take to be knowledgeable propositions about the world are essentially the outcome of social relatedness. What we take to be knowledge bearing propositions are not achievements of the individual mind, but social achievements."[35] We have staunch advocates of this view today. Thus, Harré suggested that "we should begin with the assumption that the primary location (in both a temporal and logical sense) of psychological processes is collective rather than individual."[36] Sampson, relying on an association-process meaning of construction, next brought in Derrida's hierarchy distinction that "every [social] construction has a dominant group—the constructors—and its others, those who are constructed."[37]

Language as a mediator comes to play a major role in social constructionism. For example, Gergen argued that language is a form of interpersonal relatedness in which the individual is collectively immersed and therefore continually influenced by what is conveyed verbally.[38] As certain postmodernists have contended, the person merely reflects the language moving through his or her associative processes in the manner of what the behaviorists called *mediation*. This formulation pictures the individual as unable to reverse meanings dialectically in the manner of Derrida or Nietzsche. In other words, some postmodern theories support social constructionism, and others provide alternatives that demolish its claims. Once again, the key here is oppositionality. I think that there is a hint of the Leviathan Assumption in the social constructionist viewpoint. Such theoretical explanations never really make it clear what the process is that keeps the collective in power over the individual. We naturally add behavioristic conceptions to make up for this lack. Maybe a group mind (Leviathan) explanation would be better.

Not all social constructionists are ready to dismiss the role of the individual in society's progress. In fact, they find this role taking place at the very birth of collective belief.[39] Berger (with Luckmann) defined *social construction* as follows: "All social phenomena are *constructions* produced historically through human activity."[40] There is an ongoing social content of belief available to the person, who in turn modifies and contributes to such belief so that it changes meaning over time. The initiating source of this change is the individual, for at no point is there a group mind consciously framing events. The individual human being frames an idea and then announces it for consideration by others. If it is seen as meaningfully relevant, this idea is then *objectified* and *internalized* by others in the collective.[41] An example given by Berger describes how a religious genius might introduce a new mythology—taken as the truth, of course—that will become part of the cultural lore (objectified) and then used as grounds for social action (internalized) by succeeding generations of human beings living in this culture.[42] This is obviously a predication process at work, in which the precedent context taken by the genius floods everyone's predicating understanding with new meanings to be internalized and used in the future as framing assumptions.

But the individual member of the collective is not a mere pawn to such internalizing of belief. Berger added that, "Rebellious constructions of the mind 'can' liberate the individual to a considerable extent from the definatory system of his society."[43] People as individuals can "say 'no' to society and often have done so."[44] Much to my satisfaction, Berger, unlike most social constructionists, appreciated the important role that oppositionality plays in human reasoning and the behavior to follow. I can readily endorse a Bergerian form of social constructionism.

CLASS IDENTITIES AND THE MARXIAN ARGUMENT

I now detail Karl Marx's (1818–1883) theory of society and culture because it has in various ways played an important role in how we view human behavior today. To fully appreciate the argument of Marx concerning class collectives, we must begin with Georg W. F. Hegel (1770–1831), an idealistic philosopher–theologian whose ideas were revised by Marx to turn this idealism into a realistic materialism. In the course of this revision it is interesting to see a reinterpretation of dialectical reasoning taking place— from an individual to a collective process. We should also keep in mind that "dialectics" did not begin with Hegel, nor with Aristotle. We can trace dialectical analyses to ancient Eastern and Western philosophies that existed centuries before the birth of Christ.

Hegelian philosophy analyzes the gradual working out of consciousness by an individual (albeit divine) mind or spirit. History for Hegel is not an unfolding of impersonal, efficiently caused laws but is more like a reasoning process—a succession of premises under affirmation and their negation leading to conclusions, which in turn suggest new premises to be negated until such time as a perfect understanding or fully enlightened consciousness is reached by the deity.[45] Hegel therefore stated that "the essential movement of thought is dialectic."[46] Hegel spoke of the dialectical flow in Aristotelian terms as a *thesis* (initial meaning affirmed), *antithesis* (opposite of the initial affirmation), and *synthesis* (combining the best meaning of the opposed sides). Presaging the later view of Derrida, Hegel believed that each idea affirmed has within it the seeds of its own contradiction.[47] Resolving such contradictions enables progress in ongoing thought.

Hegel believed that human history is a record of the deity's progression through successive stages of spiritual development carried out as a form of dialectical reasoning. For example, he traced these stages of development from the spirit of Egypt (thesis) to its contradiction in Persia (antithesis) leading to an entirely new Greek spirit (synthesis). Even though Hegel is talking about collectives like Egypt and Greece, his analysis is basically that of an individual—namely, the deity! As he put it,

> The principles of the successive phases of spirit that animate the nations,
> in a necessitated gradation, are themselves only steps in the develop-

ment of the one universal spirit, which through them elevates and completes itself to a self-comprehending *totality*.[48]

Hegel found this self-comprehension of the deity—presumably achieved via divine self-reflexivity and transcendence (see Chapter 1)—in the Prussian monarchical state, which he took to be the last word in the historical development of humanity.

Marx accepted the dialectic as a world principle, a law of nature manifested in historical advance, but he conceived of it as a play of opposites within a society's means of material production and the distribution of wealth that it adopts. Ideas do not carry the oppositionality of dialectic; they do not create social institutions or distribute economic rewards. Ideas are the *result* and not the cause of such dialectical aspects of material reality. Marx therefore said that Hegel had set dialectic on its head. Social institutions, political attitudes, philosophies, and religions are merely the superstructure of society that has been built on the soil of its own material production. The entire purpose of this superstructure is to retain the status quo, which involves the material advantages of some groups and the expropriation of others. In the England of his time, Marx observed the worker, the *proletarian*, getting a meager return for the amount of actual production he or she contributed to the material rewards enjoyed by society, whereas the capitalist, the *bourgeois*, who like a leech did not work at physical labor to produce wealth, reaped greater and greater rewards nevertheless. Capital is therefore not a personal but a social (collective) power.[49]

Borrowing the Hegelian concept of dialectic, Marx saw in this uneven distribution of wealth a *class conflict* taking place, reflecting the formation of a triad. One class (bourgeoisie) that had been the synthesis of a bygone era was now facing its antithesis in a new class on which it must prey (the proletariat); consequently, what would most certainly issue from this "tension of opposites" was a revolution (a negation) and the establishment of a classless society (synthesis). Class conflict would then no longer occur following this final "negation of a negation" because the expropriators (i.e., the bourgeoisie) would disappear from the face of the earth, and peace with plenty for all who actually worked to produce capital would be achieved.

For this communistic revolution to occur it is vital for the proletariat to attain self-consciousness as a group identity. This is what *class consciousness* means. Instead of a Hegelian divine spirit coming to self-consciousness for freedom's sake, a self-conscious class of people must attain its freedom through such collective awareness. Only then can it marshal its forces against the oppressor. Marx therefore stressed that "The proletarian movement is the self-conscious, independent movement of the immense majority, in the interest of the immense majority."[50] Ideas are class linked: "The ruling ideas of each age have ever been the ideas of its ruling class."[51] The class struggle always directs things—including highly intellectual pursuits such as philosophy, art, religion, law, or medicine. No aspect of the social life of a people escapes this class logic. Furthermore, "every class struggle is a political struggle."[52] The very notion of individuality has a class-linked meaning because, as Marx challenged his readers to appreciate, "You must . . . confess that by 'individual' you mean no other person than the bourgeois, than the middle class owner of property."[53] Although he referred to the person in the singular (i.e., bourgeois), Marx is here thinking in class terms. This is what I mean by the *Marxian Argument: the charge that the individual is a product of his or her class background, and can never break free of this collective shaping.* Political maneuverings for power and advantage must therefore always be viewed in class terms.

How do members of a class acquire their class-linked beliefs? Is there a social mind á la the Leviathan Assumption to think for the individual? Something like this seems necessary to frame the bourgeoisie and proletariat ideologies at the outset, so that people can absorb their class identity. Or might it be possible for each person to reason individually and thereby arrive at the same ideology anyhow? Predication processing would hold that each person individually affirms a belief held in common by all members of a class—some of whom may well act as teachers. This would be the way Berger would explain things (ref. above). The close friend and collaborator of Marx, Friedrich Engels (1820–1895), once implied that predication might be involved in such class consciousness. Thus, he said that "each person follows his own consciously desired end" and occasionally that might even include "purely individual whims of all sorts."[54] Comments like this suggest a human teleology. Even so, Marx gave such great emphasis to the class concept that it became common to think in collectivist terms when discussing his views on human reasoning. This collective emphasis invited the use of an exclusively extraspective process of association in describing human events. Engels eventually settled on an equally mechanistic formulation. In an unfinished book he suggested that dialectical materialism might be an aspect of physical reality per se.[55]

The Marxian Argument has been extended over many comparisons other than strictly economic distinctions like bourgeoisie versus proletariat. For example, we might now distinguish rural from urban residents of our nation on the basis of certain opposing values in their respective worldviews. Such contrasts can be seen as a smaller version of the dramatic clash that Marx had drawn out on the basis of economics, involving alternative factors such as gender, race, and religion.[56] Whether or not all of the contrasts drawn along the Marxian dichotomy are truly opposite is an open question. Quite often the clash is drawn along cultural lines, so that simply being in "this" or "that" collective of any sort—or even in some minority within either subdivision—qualifies as a reason for framing "opposite" outlooks on some issue. Marx's logic of class-linked ideas has now been transformed into cultural-linked ideas.

An alternative phrasing is "cultural relativism" of ideas, which invariably comes down to some kind of association explanation in which people are shaped in different cultural settings and hence have no clear way to understand each other or agree on important matters. We constantly hear the following statements today: "You can't really understand me, you come from a different culture." "All truth is relative, so who can say (choose, accuse, conclude, etc.)?" "There is no reality, only cultural contrasts." Marx's claim that every class struggle is a political struggle stems from such a basis, for what is sought is the power to frame the mores by which to live. And when it comes down to male versus female, Black versus White, Northern versus Southern, and even young versus old, we have a real mess on our hands. There seems to be no way in which to relate trustingly and unselfishly within a myriad of "opposite numbers." Life has been politicized to the hilt.

SOCIETY IS PROCESS AND CULTURE IS CONTENT

Although they are regularly equated, there is a clear difference in function between *society* and *culture*. The former is a process, and the latter is a content being produced and utilized in this process. Social forces in the societal process are the active side of events, making things happen through the efforts of its citizenry who aspire, create, solve, produce, challenge, reject, invent, revise, introduce, file, record, manufacture endlessly, and so on. *Culture* refers to whatever is produced and retained as important to the identity of a social collective or society,[57] including language systems, political organizations, mores, dress, customs, records of achievements, belief systems, artistic styles, scientific knowledge, religion, values, myths, and so on. The social constructionists analyze such contents without specifying the social process that creates and retains them as knowledge.

Cultural products or artifacts can be written down in books and stored in libraries for later generations to draw on. This would be called a *print culture*.[58] A society's cultural output can set a group apart from other groups who have different beliefs and behavioral styles. If there is no way of recording the knowledge in print, it must be passed on by word of mouth, resulting in an *oral culture* in which much is lost to forgetting and biased recollection. A culture could not exist if there was nothing to pattern meaningfully and thereby pass on to others across generations. Nor would we have such cultural contents without the energy and power of the people acting as a society. Culture is inherently collective, although a portion of the entire collective may choose to create alternatives to live by, making up what is usually termed a distinctive *subculture*.

Both the Leviathan Assumption and Marxian Argument take root from the presumed power of the culture, as a whole or as classes within, to influence individuals. There is a kind of Durkheimian reification of cultural contents taking place in which the individual is descriptively swallowed up by all that is input from experience. Anything that might be said about a person is ipso facto a cultural content. But, as we have noted, what is "said" about the person culturally is not "produced" by the culture. Cultures do not produce; they are not the creators but rather the created—used by people as individuals or collectives to learn, enjoy, resent, deny, or create even more.

Association and predication theorists agree that collective experience is heavily involved with cultural content. The associationist would see these contents as items that either are or could be linked together through a shaping process (reinforcements, mediation).[59] Associative bonding of this type would be conceptualized extraspectively, so that the social realm would account for a person's views and behaviors completely. Forces of nature "out there" are moving things about "in here." A predication theorist, on the other hand, would suggest that the individual selectively affirms the cultural contents intentionally as frameworks through which he or she makes experience meaningful. Forces of logic "in here" are moving things about "out there." This is how I understand the Bergerian form of social constructionism.

What about beliefs and attitudes known as *norms* or *class consciousness*? The associationist would claim that such group convictions are simply another manifestation of conditioning, albeit on a grand scale. Conversely, the predication theorist would refer to these joint outlooks and assumptions as "predications held in common" by a vast number of people. It is not necessary for all members of a society to agree with every meaningful belief supported by its culture. Parallel individualism is an example of people getting together based on a limited range of predicated agreement ("This is the one deal that we see eye-to-eye on").

RELATIVISM AND EVALUATION IN REASONING

It is readily appreciated that people are influenced by cultural beliefs, so that a person brought up in the East may have quite a different notion of what life is all about than a person brought up in the West. We all know of this as *relativism* or *cultural relativism*. Such convictions are not simply selected by organic evolution to be embedded in the material substances of a person's constitutional makeup. At the least, it seems difficult defending such a biological viewpoint when we find that people of one genetic heritage (race, family, etc.) can be removed from a given cultural influence by being reared in a different cultural milieu (e.g., moving as a child from a rural to an urban environment, or vice versa). There is a *nature* (inborn) versus *nurture* (learned) issue here that has been debated in science for centuries and remains a lively issue today. Just what is "relativism" anyway?

For the association theorist, *relativism* refers to the kinds and frequency of conditioned bondings that have been cemented to the outlook of the person in a collective. Someone reared in a traditionally religious (e.g., rural) culture will probably live a more restrictive lifestyle than someone reared in a highly sophisticated (e.g., urban) culture. There is always a range of religious commitment in any society, of course, but a comparison of two or more cultures can legitimately be made. The differences between the cultures of two collectives (societies) are understood by the associationist as due to the connective bondings made by the shaping of behavior in the group. And the relativism comes in when we compare the contents of any two cultures. A slight moral indiscretion may be easily overlooked in one culture, whereas in the other it would be taken quite seriously. Hence, any religious practice has more than one meaning "relative to" the practice of a comparison group.

Note that the locus of relativism for the associationist is in the extraspectively conceived cultural content. There is nothing internal or introspectively conceived in the association process per se that involves relativism. The associationist needs contrasting cultural contents to speak of relativity. The cultural items that are conditioned (or tabulated) into this or that level of processing determine the relativism. Thus, to find out the relative importance of anything (such as religious conviction) in the culture we must tabulate the number of times the item has been wound into daily events and behavioral practices, directed choices, resulted in punishment when abused, and so forth.

The greater the number of times such cultural manifestations take place, the more important is the religious conviction under consideration. We can then contrast this level of importance with similar measures taken of something else—like science—and conclude that "relative to" one item (science), the other item (religion) is more (or less) important depending on how many times it was recorded over the period of time during which such counting was done. There is no point in discussing relativism in the *process* of tabulating such factors. We must have the numerical findings of these cultural *contents* to speak of relativism. The tabulations of such content will give us our relativism with an empirical precision.

When we turn to a predication theorist the locus of relativism shifts to the *process* per se. That is, in framing a predication the person is always in the position of extending meaning from the assumptive context selected and affirmed to the target (see Chapter 1). This is a final-cause affirmation in which a target's meaning is relative to—or, "for the sake of"—the meaning being extended from the context in precedent-sequacious fashion. This leads to an astonishing suggestion: *All thought is relative, all of the time!* This is due to the fact that it is always dependent on a framing major premise of some sort. Change the premise and the course of meaning extension (i.e., reasoning) changes accordingly. But how is it possible to change a premise without necessarily having to add more and more inputs on one side or the other of the issue under consideration? This is the kind of question raised by an associationist who is ever looking for the extraspectively observed crucial tabulation that can decide the relativism.

Suppose a person hates a certain food. The usual example here is some kind of vegetable like broccoli. How might a change of mind on the palatability of this food take place? The associationist would argue that more positive inputs must be made to the person's memory reserves. For example, we might convey how this food is good when cooked with other kinds of vegetables, deep fried rather than boiled, smothered in appetizing sauces, and so on. We would also see to it that the person would hear of these recommended improvements again and again (repetition thereby searing an influence into the habit system). The solution here is purely mathematical, of adding to one side of an issue with more and more inputs on the other side until a change occurs. This is like adding only red marbles to a 50/50 mix of red and white marbles in a glass jar and mixing them about until there is a deep red caste to the jar as a whole. If these colored marbles were individual items of thought we could say the frequent inputs of one type of idea (red) is believed rather than an alternative idea (white). There is no internal search here, no transcendent effort to look deeply into the implications of the meanings encompassed by the ideas, ending in a decision to think one way rather than another.

But when we seek such changes in a predication process these internal searchings and evaluations leading to intentional decisions are what we see taking place. The predication theorist appreciates that *all* reasoning depends on relativism, on the framing of the target *relative to* the grounding context of meanings. Hence, to change one's attitude toward a certain food there must be an internal examination of projected alternatives or possibilities for the future. In a sense, the effort to change relies on a reevaluation of one's eating pattern, reasoning through until a confident position is taken in favor of the benefits to be achieved from the change, relative to the lack of benefits for one who does not change. The self-reflexive processing of predication now makes it possible to look into the future and evaluate what it might hold for the person who would move in one direction rather than another ("Lower your cholesterol and you lower the chances of heart trouble"). In the final analysis, it is up to the person to make an enlightened choice of what to do. Here is where *values* may be said to influence the course of events.

Evaluation is always somehow involved in thought. Thinking and evaluating are two sides of the same coin. This *metaphorical* allusion to sides of a coin serves as a good example of the predication process and its contents. Metaphorical meanings are precedents. Something already known (a coin) is used to enrich our understanding of another item of experience: This could be expressed as a *simile*: "Thought is like a two-sided coin." In fancier garb, we might even think of the precedent framework as a *model*. Whether metaphor or model, the premised content is framed either tautologically ("A rose is a rose") or analogically ("Sally is sly like a fox").

If we think of metaphors and models as examples of the predication process, the formalization here makes it appear that a thinker is always cognizant of such efforts to stretch the meaning of one thing to learn about another. But in most thinking we are unaware of the precedent meanings (frames of reference, etc.) guiding our thought. But here is the source of many guiding thoughts, including *stereotypes* and affective preferences. Our thinking is always relative to such—often highly personal—predications, which is why I believe that we must know in order to know further. Lacking a precedent frame of reference (i.e., a final-cause "that") extending thought sequaciously ("for the sake of which") means that no further knowledge is possible. Many of these reference frames (i.e., meanings) are provided for us by our culture, but we must process them for ourselves, or they will have no effect. It's true that our parents teach us right from wrong, but as Adler has taught us, this does not take hold unless we personally believe it.

Thought is also relative to the affective assessments under way at any moment. It is easily overlooked that our likes and dislikes are ubiquitous evaluations influencing the course of our thought. We cannot always say "why" we like some things and dislike others. But we act on our grounding affections nevertheless or struggle against them at times. Many people believe that they are the master of their affections, that they can come to like what is good and dislike what is bad simply by putting their will into high gear while aiming it in the right direction. On the basis of 40 years of empirical research, I have some reservations regarding this belief.[60] It is quite difficult to change our affections. This usually comes over long periods of time. Sometimes a sudden affective change seems to occur because a person has been trying to deny a positive or negative affection of a target, only to suddenly "give in" to the true circumstance. Whatever the case, affective assessment is an extremely important aspect of cognitive evaluation.

CONCLUDING COMMENT

I have decided to take Bell's analysis of American society seriously and use it as a predication on which to draw for various discussions in the remaining chapters of this book. Realizing that there are as many different postmodern theories as there are postmodern theorists I, with trepidation, adopt the term *postmodern* as essentially a synonym for Bell's *postindustrial* stage. This is a Derrida-like postmodernism, in which dialectical oppositionality plays a central role. The social constructionist view of Berger is also wound in here so that I recognize both collective and individual factors in the postmodern (postindustrial) era or stage.

I have no intention of speculating on what sort of social era will follow postmodernism. But what I see happening in the present is an effort by psychologists to retain the human image used in the industrial stage, when a different postindustrial or postmodern image is called for. Reasoning per se is always *relative* due to its reliance on various major premises bringing its thought forward sequaciously from a precedent meaning to what can then be grasped in the knowledge to follow. Affective assessments are also important influences on thought. Such aspects of thought do not occur as efficient causes but are rendered as final causes, as behaving for the sake of a precedent evaluation. In Chapter 4 I look more deeply into the claim made by social scientists that the computer can account for such human performances as reasoning, choice, and free will.

4

A MISSING LINK IN
THE HUMAN IMAGE

In this chapter I ferret out some major—albeit overlooked and unappreciated—involvement of dialectics in American culture and society. This enables us to bring closure to the issue sketched in Chapters 2 and 3 regarding the changing type of association processing that has occurred in mechanistic explanations over the years. With the supposed demise of behaviorism (which I do not agree has actually taken place) there has been much time given over to the computer model, which supposedly provides psychology with all that is needed to account for human reasoning, including free will. But, as I show, the dialectical aspects of human reasoning have continually eluded psychological theorizing. And the progression of machine modeling of behavior from a fixed system of pulleys and gears to electrical computers directed by carefully reasoned, adaptable programs demands a terminological change in how we represent the human image. This is another way of addressing the changing process of association in mechanistic formulations.

Chapter 4 begins with an in-depth study of the computer analogue, taking up what such nondialectical formulations of the human image have meant in psychology. The interpretation of free will that computer advocates have promoted is found seriously wanting. Two major examples of overlooked dialectical reasoning in human description are presented. A consid-

51

eration is given to the role that existentialism and its derivative value system has played in propounding oppositional behaviors among postmodern Americans. I then review the contribution of oppositionality to the difference in mental functioning between consciousness and unconsciousness. Chapter 4 closes with a call for a change in the human image based on what we have learned from our modeling of people's behavior via both pulley and gears and computer machinery.

THE COMPUTER MODEL: STRENGTHS AND LIMITATIONS

Computers are one of the major contributors to the service economy of the postmodern or postindustrial society. We can buy things, sell things, and find all kinds of assistance or knowledge by clicking onto the World Wide Web. Even more interesting in some ways is the "about face" made by engineers today. In the industrial era the aim was to turn people into machines, but now the challenge is to turn machines into people (robots). The well-known Turing test has this goal, whereby the computer "enacts" a human being so perfectly that we cannot tell the difference.[1] Actually, what makes this enactment possible is a clever program (i.e., *software*) written by an expert programmer who anticipates what might be involved in a dialogue between two people and sets up such exchanges through the operation of electrical machinery (i.e., *hardware*).[2] The machine simply mediates these programmed signals without intention. In the actual test, a volunteer participant types certain observations and questions on the computing machine's keyboard, and the program not only answers these as if an unseen person in another room were doing so but also poses observations and questions of its own. Can the participant at the receiving end tell if it is a machine providing the exchange of ideas, or is it a real person? Some people find it impossible to make this decision or do so incorrectly, but others decide fairly easily and can even think of ways to confound the program directing the machine's "verbal behavior."

Computers process *information*, which the average person thinks involves meaning, like the understandable statements "Snow is cold" or "Bob is dependable." But Claude Shannon (1916–2001), one of the primary founders of information-processing theory, made it perfectly clear that information has nothing to do with the meanings of the message being transmitted.[3] The basic unit of information in a digital computer is the *bit*, short for *binary digit*. This refers to the number of signals (information bits) required to select one electrical impulse from two equally probable alternatives. A bit involves halving (i.e., cutting in half) the total complex of signals ("information") available in the sense of either–or. Thus, if there were four equally probable alternatives open to a course of electrical signaling, it would require two bits of information to decide on a singular course of action. One bit would reduce the four alternatives to two, and another would select one of the two remaining possibilities.

If we think of information processing as halving electrical signals in this fashion, it is possible to equate a decision such as "true or false" with the electronic switch that is either *on* (true) or *off* (false). This was Shannon's insight.[4] Later, McCulloch and Pitts[5] demonstrated that the all-or-none firing properties of nerve cells were essentially constructed in this binary fashion. An active or firing neuron was *on,* and an inactive neuron was *off.* McCulloch and Pitts perfected the neural network conception and tried to map the binary logic of the machine onto the structure of the central nervous system. Note that the logic here is exclusively demonstrative. Information is either–or, and never both. Once it was realized that a person could assign meaning using these electrical signals, a new opportunity arose. Information encoded for meaning could be attached to the electrical signaling. The process of encoding the signals did not actually create this content of meaning, so it would be incorrect to claim that computing machines were thinking meaningfully. In other words, computer processing is *not* predicational.

Those who use computers soon learn how demanding of accuracy they are in what is being typed into their programmed instructions. Make a slight typing error and the program will not work. But this has nothing to do with precision as such. It is due to the fact that computers *match* on a one-to-one basis; they do not grasp contexts or subtleties in the communication process. There is no moving from a broad range of meaning to a targeted end (see Chapter 1). Either we are in perfect matched alignment with the program demands, or we are out of luck. When we make an error in typing on our keyboard our machines are never cognizant of what we were intending to type, although they may seem to be when "correcting" our misspelling. Actually, they are automatically matching the words we type with a bank of stored words. If the matching does not occur an automatic signal is triggered. The lesson to be learned here is that "Machines match, people predicate."

As nonintrospective processors computer machinery does not know the contrasting difference of *me–you,* so it never grasps the outlook of the *non–me* or *you* (i.e., the other person) with whom it is "relating." I am forced into anthropomorphizing the computer to convey my points, but I have found over the years that everyone does this, including some of the most rigidly behavioristic types who do not believe that people are freely reasoning organisms. Computers "reason" in a literal, precise, or demonstrative fashion. They never reason dialectically and cannot judge affectively as to their likes and dislikes ("no preferences please"). They cannot deal in analogies, frame metaphors, or understand spontaneous similes—all those capacities that we humans use routinely. Computing machines can be programmed to *simulate* oppositional reasoning. But the hardware processing is never itself dialectical in nature, and the content of simulation is notoriously poor.[6]

COMPUTER EXPLANATION OF FREE WILL

Many social scientists believe that computer technology can account for human agency or free will (see Chapter 1). To understand this claim I must first clarify certain terminology used to describe computer processing.[7] *Output* is any change produced in the surroundings by the machine, such as when a robot lifts a block of wood or a missile strikes its target. *Input* is any event external to the machine that modifies its actions, as when the approach of an oncoming train signals the crossing gates to be lowered. Note the ease with which we can slip into efficient-cause terminology here, so that input can be thought of (and usually is) as a stimulus and output as a response. This is why I think the cognitive revolution, which relies on the computer analogue to explain reasoning, is not revolutionary. Behaviorism still lives! There is great similarity between computer and behavioral theories. But computer technology did add a third concept to behaviorism—that of *feedback*. There are actually two types of feedback. On the one hand, we can speak of *positive* feedback, which is a fraction of the output from the machine returning as input.[8] On the other hand, feedback is called *negative* when the machine is being directed by the margin of error obtaining between its movements and a specific goal that its program is targeting.[9]

For example, if a spacecraft is aimed at the moon, it will continually monitor its position relative to this target from which it can bounce off signals. As the spacecraft strays off course this disparity or negative feedback is entered and adjustments automatically made in its rocket firings to correct its course. As it does so, positive feedback can also be used to signal that certain adjustments are being made in flight putting the spacecraft on course. In their famous paper on machine agency, Rosenblueth, Wiener, and Bigelow argued that primitive machines (e.g., pulley-and-gear types) could not be interpreted as goal oriented, but "purposeful" machines, which directed their movements (like the spacecraft mentioned above), did orient their actions to attaining a goal. The goal is "a final condition in which the behaving object reaches a definite correlation in time or in space with respect to another object or event."[10] If the goal is not giving off a signal (input), then there is no negative feedback possible. After dismissing teleologies based on final-cause explanations as "illogical," Rosenblueth et al. offered an alternative view: "Teleological behavior thus becomes synonymous with behavior controlled by negative feedback. . . ."[11] What we have here is an extraspective formulation of an introspective concept—referred to variously as agency, purpose, or free will. There are several rebuttals to be made here. Probably the obvious one is the fact that the machine behaving under negative feedback and hence adapting to circumstances cannot just get "fed up" and "chuck it all" as people often do in dealing with frustrating tasks. There is no such freedom to quit. Nor can the missile decide on the goal to engage in the first place. Indeed, the machine cannot even try new ways of adjusting its path to the goal ("No shortcuts allowed"). It is just as locked into the program here as if it had no influence on events at all—which, of course, it doesn't.

I find that the concept of feedback is frequently misused by professionals and the general public alike. People use it informally to refer to any kind of input that is requested by one person of another, as in asking someone to "Please give me your feedback on this matter as soon as possible." Actually, this is an introspectively framed request using the extraspectively framed feedback concept as a metaphor (albeit inappropriately). What this person is asking for is not feedback but new input. The (positive) feedback here would actually be a repetition of the request for something called feedback. If we take a little liberty with the phrasing of this request, and pretend that this meaning is involved here, we might say that the positive feedback would be something like, "You have just requested new input on the matter at hand." The output request would return in part to signal the ongoing computing process as to what is taking place. This process never frames a predicating request as is implied in the misuse of the feedback concept. Computers do not "think up" what they do and then carry out the action required. They might be said to learn about what they are doing *after* they have done it.

Here is an example of computer intelligence assuming that people were really such machines: As Mary Helen slips behind the wheel of her automobile, she is continually informed by both positive and negative feedback, as follows:

> You have just turned the car engine on. You are pulling into traffic. Your speed is a little high. You slow down a bit. You just turned left. You are looking for a parking spot. You turned to the right and parked the car. You locked the car.

I don't think this series of feedback reports even remotely conforms to what takes place in Mary Helen's thought processes, but it is something like what takes place in our spacecraft ("You are drifting off course [negative]. You added thrust [positive]," etc.), assuming we are willing to agree that a machine really does think.

A major problem faced by the theorist using negative feedback to explain free will is the fact that not all goals in human experience exist. People will work for goals they know will never be reached, such as in striving for "self-perfection." The person knows introspectively that there is value in the pursuit of perfection even though it is naïve to expect that this goal will literally be accomplished. But the extraspectively processing machine has no such imagination. Its goal must be a literal "something" to target and then be told about this targeting after the negative feedback adjustment has been accomplished. If there is no actual goal for signals to be bounced off, there is no negative feedback possible.

I conclude that there is little support for teleology in the control through negative feedback interpretation of agency. It is not possible to capture an introspective concept like free will extraspectively, but for some reason such pretenses are widely embraced in the social sciences. I think that the most important role for dialectical logic is this capacity people have to transcend, oppose, and even negate what experience is forcing them to accept. Here is where people truly can break free of shaping founded on a dialectically generated evaluation to behave otherwise "all circumstances remaining the same" (i.e., final causation underlying what we call free will).

OVERLOOKING DIALECTICAL REASONING

In this section I take up two often overlooked examples of dialectical reasoning in association theory. These include B. F. Skinner's behaviorist theory and the explanations surrounding the defeat of chess champion Gary Kasparov by an IBM computer. Whether it be these two participants in the incidents under consideration, or just about any psychologist reviewing what transpired, the role of dialectical reasoning is almost certain to be overlooked. After I have clarified the lack of employing opposition in the theorizing of Skinner, I will extend this dialectical understanding of human nature to the remarkable behavior that is emerging in postmodern times.

B. F. Skinner and Behaviorism

I have referred to Skinner previously (see Chapter 1) as a premier example of a behaviorist, even though he was to drop this self-description in later years. Skinner brilliantly framed, developed, and defended a school of thought regarding human nature. He had no appreciation for, and little knowledge of, dialectical logic or the possibility of something like dialectical reasoning actually taking place. Skinner told of an exchange he once had with the eminent philosopher and mathematician, Lord Alfred North Whitehead (1861–1947). The occasion was a banquet at which Skinner was seated next to Whitehead and naturally fell into conversation with him concerning the role of science and how it could be practiced in psychology. This was in 1934, and the youthful Skinner was admittedly flushed with the excitement of behaviorism, arguing that in time the thinking and behavior of people would be completely accounted for by the environmental factors that determine it. Skinner did not use our technical language, but he was clearly viewing all such explanations as dependent on efficient causation. Whitehead apparently found some things lacking in this program for a science of behavior. Skinner gave us this account of their closing positions:

> He [Whitehead] agreed that science might be successful in accounting for human behavior provided one made an exception of *verbal* behavior. Here, he insisted, something else must be at work. He brought the dis-

cussion to a close with a friendly challenge: "Let me see you," he said, "account for my behavior as I sit here saying 'No black scorpion is falling upon this table'."[12]

What sort of analysis could explain this statement? I suggest that there is a strategy here of Whitehead selecting an improbable something—a black scorpion—falling on the table, but *not* to affirm its presence. The verbal statement negates that which is not happening and is highly unlikely to occur in the first place. Even so, its meaning is completely accurate. Whitehead was posing a convoluted argument that might be expressed as follows: Only a human being, with dialectical reasoning capacities to affirm or deny any proposition expressed, would consider it logically reasonable to say that something highly improbable was not taking place. Your (i.e., Skinner's) theory of behavior cannot account for such odd but strangely logical and accurate observations.

A dialectical formulation of this sort is not what Skinner's demonstratively framed logic was to make of this exchange. He had no reply at the banquet, but after a day or so he came to a demonstrative (i.e., nondialectical) interpretation of Whitehead's challenge. Skinner decided to interpret the remark on the basis of what he presumed *was* said by Whitehead and not on what *did not* need saying. He thus analyzed the sentence to find the probability in it that the black scorpion response was a metaphorical allusion to behaviorism.[13] This assumption established a context from which further meaning could be extended. Skinner found Whitehead saying something like, "I am afraid that behaviorism just isn't going to be accepted at this table today."

Either the dialectical or the demonstrative interpretation of Whitehead's intention can be used, of course, but the point to be made for present purposes is that a dialectical formulation cannot arise as an explanation by a theorist if he or she does not accept it as a possibility (i.e., a premise) in the first place. This is another example of needing predicating knowledge to create further knowledge (or understanding). Having no sensitivity to this alternative, Skinner cannot use it as a precedent context within which to target the black scorpion example. Whether it be Nietzsche's deconstruction of cause–effect or Whitehead's challenge, all such maneuvering is fair game in dialectical logic. Such logic also occurs in mundane circumstances, as in the case of the drunk who rings our doorbell at 3 AM to offer congratulations because our house is *not* on fire—which is the happy truth, but why mention it?

Silly or sound, we can see in such dialectically driven evaluations and logical analyses the sort of human being that a postmodern age has actually encouraged to develop—that is, a being who is more than willing to be different or unusual. I will have much to add to this in later chapters. Indeed, this postmodern person is virtually obsessed by the need to deconstruct anything traditional and to create instead some kind of alternative.

Oppositionality via dialectical reasoning is a first step in this effort to be different (unusual, etc.)—frequently characterized as being an "individual." The developing postmodern generations have adopted a bewildering array of alternative behaviors and lifestyles, such as open cohabitation of the unmarried. The traditional family structure has been severely weakened and even rejected by many, often in the name of providing greater freedom, equality, and independence for women. People, especially young people, seem to be competing over the distinction of being considered "most shocking" in personal appearance and behavior, searching for a high-point dramatic scene to enact on the spot, framed by a deconstructive array such as eccentric dress, vile language, and rude manners.

There is also an interesting pattern of behavior to be seen in some postmodernists that takes on a "righteous" quality in defense of the deconstructive efforts underway. I refer to such a person as a socially oriented *scenarist*—that is, a creator of imagined scenarios that are aimed at rectifying and sometimes castigating the behavior of others in the collective. The scenarist hovers about, waiting to "show up" and lecture those who prove vulnerable for such an attack, no matter how accidentally and superficially their supposed misstep (e.g., using a social slang) came about. Scenarists also police the collective in a self-appointed effort to protect the disadvantaged and make certain that everyone possible receives the same cultural acceptance and benefits. But there is a strong hint of righteous hostility in their zeal to existentially reduce everyone to a common denominator.

New cultural heroes have emerged in recent decades, such as narcissistic rock stars leaping about a stage with painted faces, beating suggestively on their guitars held at hip level in a flagrant effort to advance sexual expression. The lyrics of the music frequently dramatize the plight of minority outgroups and deliver a (scenarist) criticism of traditional racist and other demeaning social practices, albeit in a crude manner that has turned away many who might benefit from them. I believe that only a dialectically reasoning organism could possibly concoct the universally deconstructive—or is it destructive?—pattern of rejection that we see taking place in today's emerging postmodernism. There are, of course, both collective and individual features of such an emergence. But to cover the field adequately we require the insights of both a demonstrative and a dialectical process. I now move to another oversight of dialectical reasoning in human thought processing.

Gary Kasparov and Deep Blue

One of the more fascinating incidents concerning computer processing occurred when the IBM computer "Deep Blue" engaged the greatest living chess player of the era, Russia's Gary Kasparov. It was the classic human versus machine confrontation. I think we can learn a lot about human reasoning by looking carefully into what took place.

Deep Blue is actually a group of 32 linked computers, each attached to eight special-purpose processors. Thus, there is parallel computing taking place when Deep Blue swings into action. In the 3 minutes allocated for the participants to examine the chess board positions before making a move, Kasparov is capable of framing 2 per second, whereas Deep Blue is covering some 100 million chess moves per second. Thus, before making a move Deep Blue, through sheer "brute force," has surveyed about 36 billion different board possibilities and "selected" the best one (as identified by the directing master program). The builders of Deep Blue claim that it is not, strictly speaking, a computer designed to test or represent artificial intelligence. But given what took place, I am not sure that Kasparov would agree.

There were actually two chess contests held, one in February 1996 and a second in May 1997. Six games were played on each occasion, with the winner awarded over a half million dollars in prize money. It is very interesting to compare Kasparov's attitude following each of these matches. In Game 1 of the 1996 contest, Kasparov was shocked when Deep Blue defeated him in only 37 moves. He rebounded well to take Game 2. There followed two draws, and then Kasparov took Games 5 and 6 with strong victories.[14] He remarked that the last game was fairly easy, because by that time he had learned what to do in adapting his game to his "opponent." Incidentally, Kasparov freely admitted that he had anthropomorphized Deep Blue, dismissing the image of the machine early in the match and replacing it in his mind with a humanoid image of a very strong opponent. This opponent would have a style of play (formal-cause pattern), and he expected to figure it out and then intentionally use this understanding to his advantage (final cause behaving "for the sake of" knowledge).

Fortunately, he did locate a weakness in his imagined opponent's style of play. Kasparov found that when he rapidly used certain atypical shifts in strategy during the contest, the machine would not readily adapt its style to such modifications. I would suggest that, in devising these rapid shifts, Kasparov was clearly bringing dialectical reasoning into play. Deep Blue required its programming team to go back to the laboratory and find out what to do about these unusual moves. And in their analyses I have no doubt that they, too, relied on dialectical reasoning. A brute-force approach can be negated through finding the right strategy during the match, and this Kasparov said he was capable of doing, as follows:

> At one point, for example, I changed slightly the order of a well-known opening sequence. Because it was unable to compare [i.e., "match"] this new position meaningfully with similar ones in its database, it had to start calculating away and was unable to find a good plan. A human would have simply wondered, "What's Gary up to?" judged the change to be meaningless, and moved on.[15]

Thus, after losing the first game, Kasparov adopted the strategy of avoiding giving Deep Blue any concrete goal on the basis of which to calculate its moves. All the computer could do at this point was to drift planlessly and fall back on brute-force surveys of its memory bank to "look" for the best possible matchings but never really organize a winning strategy. Summing up, Kasparov boasted that he

> could figure out its priorities and adjust my play. It couldn't do the same to me. So although I think I did see some signs of intelligence, it's a weird kind, an inefficient, inflexible kind that makes me think I have a few years left [to compete and win].[16]

We now know that the inflexibility stems from the fact that the computer is limited to reasoning demonstratively. Dialectical reasoning is the way human beings drop literalness in favor of possibility through shifting perspectives to an opponent's likely intentions ("Is he serious or just running a bluff?").

During the 1997 match something happened that disturbed and even astounded Kasparov. Deep Blue won the match 2 to 1, with 3 draws. During the tie-breaking Game 6, Kasparov made a simple misplay at the opening and could never recover. But this was not the disturbing incident. Indeed, Kasparov's state of mind leading to the Game 6 error could well be traced to the incident that he confronted in Game 2. In this game Deep Blue seemed to sense the danger in making a move that Kasparov "gave" to it, ensuring a short-term advantage. The machine had an opportunity to shift its queen to a devastating position, which on the face of things was a very intelligent selection. It was a "no brainer" for a brute-force program to select. But instead, the machine (i.e., its program) "negated" the enticing move being exposed and followed a subtler but superior tack that proved to be nearly decisive in defeating Kasparov.[17] Negation is a major form of dialectical reasoning. Apparently, in the year between matches, the programmers of Deep Blue had corrected for the tendency to always take seriously Kasparov's unusual modifications in play. The programmers explained that they had developed software that enabled the machine to change the style of the program in mid-match play as well as its "judgment" capacity from game to game.

It was this flexibility and seeming understanding of Kasparov's strategizing that dislodged him intellectually and emotionally. He began to play defensively and later stated that "I lost my fighting spirit."[18] He also suggested that the programmers must have altered Deep Blue's instructions in mid-game. Although the programmers did admit that they had fine-tuned Deep Blue's program *between* games (e.g., at one point making it play less aggressively with its king's pawn), they deny influencing the machine's decisions *during* actual play, which is where Kasparov believed that he had encountered something of the sort.[19] Whatever the case, it is clear that Kasparov was upset by what we might term the *dialectical strategizing* that the machine carried out, assessing when a move was good or bad, or possibly had long- or short-term potentials for success. It seemed as though the machine was aligning such oppositions and drawing a decision between them, exactly as a human being would do. Kasparov wondered if the program was tailored exclusively for his style of play and demanded to see the printout. He has since challenged Deep Blue's programmers to a tie-breaking match in which 10 games would be played over a 20-day period. He wants first, however, to have the log of 10 Deep Blue games played with a neutral player or another computer. To the best of my knowledge, this challenge has not yet been accepted. And the apparently dialectical features of the computer's play that upset Kasparov in the first place have never been recognized for what they are.

We might now ask, Was the computer actually reasoning dialectically? I would say "no," but that the programmers did a good job of simulating such oppositional mental processing. If I am wrong and the programmers stumbled onto a truly oppositionally reasoning machine program, it would surely herald the onset of a genuine cognitive revolution. The closest program of this sort that I am familiar with was drafted by Douglas Lenat, entitled *Automated Mathematician* (AM). This program was designed to "learn" through discovery. It made use of frames and was instructed, among other things, to look for inversions in certain data. Although highly creative initially, in time AM was described as going "off the deep end into strange investigations about numbers that would be at the same time odd and even."[20] This finding strikes me as a marvelous *synthesis* of the *thesis* (odd) and its *antithesis* (even) in classical dialectical logic as used for centuries to underwrite such historical analyses as Hegelian and Marxian philosophy. Such dialectical machinations have also been used to bamboozle.

The capacity to think "off the deep end" is typical of human beings, who can move from such strange predications as uniting the non-unitable to a creative innovation drawn from the depths of such unthinkable and demonstrative processing. When ideas that are unconventional pop into mind (via dialectical ties in meaning), they can be rationally (i.e., demonstratively) judged, refined, and then put to test in experience. It is the dialectical capacity to reason transcendentally, free of logical rules dictating solely unidirectional steps, that proves human beings are not machines. There is a marvelously creative, eccentric, eternally unusual side to the human mind that should never be dismissed as mere hoax or an error term to be explained away or ridiculed. Dialectical reasoning sets us free even as it sometimes leads us up a blind alley.

One last point: Kasparov may have anthropomorphized the hardware of the computer as if it were the flesh and blood of a human being. But what he actually confronted was not a material-cause substance at all but rather a logical pattern (formal cause) called a *software program*. It is in the logic of the software program that we find the chess game taking place. Software has been growing in importance as computer circuitry has expanded into the huge networks of today. Thanks to this shift in emphasis from mechanical hardware to the logic of software, it is difficult to pinpoint the actual source of a computer's reasoning qua calculating. Some computer experts believe that the software so influences the hardware that once newly drafted, unique software has been loaded into the memory of a certain machine it literally becomes a different machine.[21] The changes in the software create new machines in the circuitry of the same old hardware! This leads to questions about whether it is possible in every instance to actually distinguish hardware from software. We hear of so-called *firmware* today in which logical steps are available as ready-wired inserts to be plugged into the circuitry of many different programs.[22] Be this as it may, the fundamental fact remains that, wherever this reasoning takes root from, the resultant virtual reality is entirely demonstrative in nature. Computing machines reflect only half of the human image—the "button-down" and not the "breaking-free" side.

EXISTENTIALISM, OPPOSITIONALITY, AND BEHAVIORS THAT SHOCK OR INVITE BIGOTRY

In 1959 I was invited by a student group at my university to give a talk on existentialism. Little did I realize that in the next decade most of the social changes that occurred were to be rationalized in terms of this very existentialistic philosophy, as interpreted by the pop culture of that era. Critics have informed me that there has been a rejection if not a backlash against existential philosophy in recent decades. But as I listen to the rationale for various deconstructive behaviors (like those cited above), I hear core arguments taken from the existential philosophy touted in the 1960s and 70s. Maybe what has occurred is that certain existentialistic beliefs have been transformed into a sort of "street smarts" value system, and that is what I hear. In any event, having "missed the boat" once with this philosophy, I do not plan to do it again.

I took the position in my talk that existentialism was not, strictly speaking, an actual school of philosophical thought and hence that it would not have a lasting influence. I described it as a passing criticism and rejection of traditional philosophy of any sort and that it had no direction to offer for the future. I had personally been impressed by the emphasis on dialectic in many existential writings, which is always a good source for negating other points of view. Existentialists essentially believe that we all live within a sort of Rogerian *phenomenal field* (see Chapter 2), a context of meaningful understanding that sets the grounds for the sake of which we intentionally create our lifestyles. This *pro forma* view of mind is consistent with the predication model.

Existentialism as a philosophical outlook has two basic demands, both of which can be seen as emphasizing individualism in human affairs. First, it asks the person to take responsibility for his or her life's decisions and actions. Second, it provides a host of arguments to be used by those who wish to challenge the authority of public institutions such as the state government— a need increasingly felt in the 1960s by the opponents of the Vietnam War.

I did not realize when I gave my talk how important an existentialistic outlook would prove to be in the rise of postmodernism (see Chapter 3). The spirit of freedom that it engendered, matching up with the footloose writings of Jack Kerouac and others of that period, readily captured the "rugged individualism" imagination of younger Americans.

Two of the generally recognized fathers of existential philosophy are Nietzsche (see Chapter 3) and Sören Kierkegaard (1813–1855). Personal choice is a prominent theme in Kierkegaard's writings. He spoke of the willful choice an individual must make to follow God's spiritual lead rather than the mundane trappings of a clergy who had long since traded their spiritual zest for a lifeless religiosity.[23] Kierkegaard stressed the role of dialectical logic in the person's internal searching. The collective cannot do this searching for the individual, who must transcend the routine aspects of life, reflexively explore various alternatives, and then choose the best course to follow. Nietzsche agreed with Kierkegaard that one must actively "leap" into making life's choices, taking full responsibility for them, and eventually achieving authenticity in self-realization.[24] Such life rewards are individually earned.

The admonition by Kierkegaard and Nietzsche to actively engage life, and to assume personal responsibility for such willful action, was transformed from an individual to a collective concept by various groups in America during the tumultuous 1960s. For example, the radical group Students for a Democratic Society (SDS) took the personally responsible attitude as a sort of credo. Each supporter of SDS, by the very fact of having embraced this organization, was prepared to assume such responsibility. Unhappily, personally chosen actions were eventually taken by the SDS activists to destroy property as a way of demonstrating or publicizing their commitments. This resulted in fire damage and an unintended death of a student at the University of Wisconsin. But what comes to mind each time I think back to those days is the fact that Nietzsche was known to rely on a dialectical style in his writings,[25] and Kierkegaard actually said of himself "with me everything is dialectical."[26] Is this paralleling of dialectical philosophers with daring and even criminal acts of personal choice merely an accident of history? Or is it possible that the encouragement received from such dialecticians to think and act beyond the constraints of society facilitated the rise of willful action, even as it also led to dramatic changes in traditional behavioral patterns such as sexual relations, gender roles, and family structuring?

I was very wrong about existentialism. It has proven to be, in its various manifestations, a highly influential philosophy of the 20th century, and I think this will hold true for the 21st century as well—at least in the general public if not among the academics. It therefore puzzles me that the obvious role of dialectical reasoning in all of this continues to go unnoticed by the social scientists of our time. Oppositionality in human affairs is vastly underestimated. I do not know exactly why this is the case, but as a first guess I would suggest that the meaning of the word *dialectic* has been so demeaned by modern science as a sophistical strategy in discourse (which it often is!) that the possible functioning of an actual process like this in human reasoning is not taken seriously. But there *is* such a process and—borrowing a page from Jung—it seems that, the more we emphasize only demonstrative reasoning in human thought, the more the dialectical side of thought struggles to balance the scales. When such oppositional demands break through to consciousness, we invariably have a problem. Everything that is sacred and settled is threatened by negation. The "old" is under attack as never before. Out with the old and in with the new, delivered in as shocking a manner as possible. It is as if modernity seeks to stretch the difference between "then" and "now" by introducing ever more shocking changes in values and customs along the way. The notion that there is no such thing as certainty is central to the postmodern view of existentialism (see Chapter 8). One wonders why there is no scenarist politically correct reaction to this, because scenarists surely think they are correct in what they champion.

There was also a concomitant weakening of respect for traditional authority in America during the 1960s, spurred on by the negative reaction of young adults to the Vietnam War. Demonstrations against the war were extremely emotional displays of negation, at times bordering on religious fervor. There was also a claim of "mind expansion" advanced by advocates of ingesting certain drugs (see Chapter 6). As a result, a growing number of people in the 1960s unleashed their dialectical reasoning capacities as never before, tearing down in hopes of rebuilding a better world (precisely what kind of world remained unclear). The rejection of tradition literally extended the logic of opposition from fashionable attire to faded and torn jeans, well-trimmed hair to frequently unwashed and uncombed hair, neatness to sloppiness, and common courtesy to the ignoring of traditional manners altogether.

In typical existentialistic fashion, all such changes flowed from *negation*. In fact, as we see in later chapters, the former aspirations of existentialism to take individual command of life, assume personal responsibility, and direct things to a better ending have themselves come under negation and rejection. It is suggested that to take on such idealized personal goals in life today is to repress other people who cannot compete with equal confidence and sense of purpose. One is made to feel guilty over pursuing individual success. Individualism by way of personal achievement is literally made out to be a form of bigotry, a theme not lost on the scenarist, who is quick to criticize the noticeably ambitious person. The ironic result here is that a philosophy of individual negation has turned itself into a philosophy of collective negation that denies the individual freedom to excel.

OPPOSITIONALITY AND LEVELS OF CONSCIOUSNESS

Precisely how to understand consciousness is not yet settled. This concept is widely debated in the social sciences today.[27] The most frequent term used in definitions of consciousness is *awareness*.[28] A conscious organism is presumably aware of circumstances taking place and especially any potential implications thereby. Actually, consciousness is not a useful concept in association theorizing, which presumes that various inputs mediate and control behavior. Neither is it useful in computer explanations of behavior. There is really no need for a concept like awareness in such accounts. Awareness in association theorizing is simply the result of additional inputs shaping the person into believing that he or she knows something or is in control of personal behavior. As we have learned from our encounters with Skinner, such beliefs are said to be illusory. Consciousness is therefore seen extraspectively by the associationists as a process that intervenes[29] or mediates[30] between the stimulus input and the response output. There is nothing unique about this processing. It is like all of the other efficient-cause processing in the associationist's explanations.

The predication theorist has a distinct need for the concept of consciousness due to the fact that such processing can take two forms. On the one hand, a framing premise can be affirmed as absolutely correct and therefore not open to challenge. Thus, a person might affirm that "My account of what took place is the only one possible" and confidently refuse to consider alternatives. According to predicational theory, this is the logical stance of a person reasoning demonstratively. Aristotle traced this sense of conviction to the belief that one's major premises in the predication process are presumed to be indubitably "primary and true."[31] On the other hand, it is possible to reason predicationally and at the same time be aware that major premises other than one's own may be substituted. In this case, the position taken would be something like "My account of what occurred is based on my preferential assumption, and although I greatly favor it, there is always the (unlikely) possibility that other accounts I am aware of might be considered better than mine." In this formulation we see the transcendent capacity of dialectical reasoning making a contribution to individual thought.

I propose that we refer to *consciousness* in predicational terms as *transpredication*.[32] To *transpredicate* is to realize through the transcendent capacity of dialectical reasoning—in which thought turns back on itself analytically—that premises other than the one we favor can always be brought to bear in framing our target. When we transpredicate we reason for the sake of not only what is being affirmed but of what is being implied, inferred, rejected, contradicted, or contrasted in ongoing thought. Here is the source of awareness that can enrich our understanding of events through the sequacious extension of such dialectically conceived alternatives. Consciousness is thus dependent on this capacity to be aware of alternatives, a capacity that Kasparov sensed in Big Blue. The more genuine alternatives the person is aware of— whether pro or con—the greater is his or her level of consciousness.

Unconsciousness, on the other hand, may be understood via the predication model as *unipredication*. To *unipredicate* is to take no cognizance of a realm of possible meaning outside of the meaning currently expressed by the affirmation of one unilateral premise. This demonstrative, "a rose is a rose" form of processing tautologically can reduce the chances of creative thinking because it discourages imaginative flights of fancy ("stick to the facts"). Unconsciousness is also typified by the rigid unipredicating premises that make the person literal and thus vulnerable to influence from others, as when hypnotized or under the emotional pressure of a crowd. The unipredicating or unconscious person is unable to transcend ("back off") and critically analyze what is occurring so that countering the suggestions of others becomes impossible.[33] The person is robot-like because of this loss of consciousness (i.e., limited to unipredication). Of course, sometimes it is good to unipredicate. With the innovator in particular a unipredicated conviction is often necessary so that others cannot influence her or his creation through negative analyses or pointless recommendations. Judicious unconsciousness obviously has a role to play in sound and confident reasoning. Creative people are often stubbornly committed to a single idea and for a good reason. They see merit in what others have not yet grasped.

It is important to keep in mind that any one person can switch dialectically from transpredication to unipredication and back again, depending on the intentions being brought to bear in ongoing reasoning. The same capacity to intentionally shift from one premise to another in transpredicating is what we have named *relativism* (see Chapter 3). The reason for shifting about in this manner has invariably to do with the meaning of the content under processing. That is, the meaningful contents of the reasoning processing have much to say about why there will be an emphasis on transpredication or unipredication. The racially prejudiced person may unipredicate rigidly in dealing with certain minority group members but transpredicate widely when carrying on business dealings.

A NEEDED CHANGE IN THE HUMAN IMAGE

It is clear that computer technology is *not* capturing the full range of human reasoning and intelligence. The computer, as the earlier pulley-and-gear machines, deals in mechanical associations that limit it to demonstrative reasoning. However, unlike the earlier machines, the computer relies on various programs to influence its course of action and, some would say, its very essence. If we use the earlier machines and the computer as contrasting models for human reasoning, what might we find?

Because the program is an integral part of the computing machine, the programmer who designs and directs this program must be given special consideration. The programmer has an ongoing influence in the association process that is not true of the older machines, which were built in a fixed design and did not require the continual interaction with human beings that is true of computers. We have thousands of years of evidence that human beings engage in dialectical reasoning. The programmer can be expected to fall in line here. He or she has used and is using dialectical reasoning to direct the course of program design, which means the computer is sharing in this self-adjusting process (as Kasparov learned!). This results in a strong analogy between computer and human—so strong, in fact, that we could say that there is no longer any reason to limit ourselves to explanations of human behavior in traditional mechanistic (i.e., efficient-cause) terms. What is called for is a new human image, one that includes teleology by way of dialectical reasoning rather than being limited to the blind mechanism of old. Postmodernism supports this change in image for it has openly embraced dialectical formulations. So why not adopt formally what is taking place informally—human behavior as a teleological process in which formal and final causation plays a role? Psychology would surely blossom as new insights would burst on the scene with the advent of a teleological human image.

CONCLUDING COMMENT

Dialectics continues to be a missing link in human description. The technical lingo has changed from *stimuli* to *inputs* and *responses* to *outputs*, but the basic human image of efficiently caused organisms moved along as intentionless beings under the mediating shaping of their environment remains the dominant model guiding psychology in this third millennium. I suspect that most psychologists are aware of this problem but are not yet willing to take on what it implies for the future—namely, a change in the human image embracing teleological factors like agency, intention, self-determination, choice, personal responsibility, and so on. The service emphasis of postmodernism has influenced things to the point where psychology seems to consider itself a helping profession and no more. Touchy questions like the nature of humanity have been put on the back burner and may soon be taken off the fire altogether. Psychologists seem increasingly prepared to let biology answer such questions (see Chapter 6). And yet, as noted above, computer technology has given us a clear suggestion of where to take the investigation of human nature. Instead of viewing computer technology from an exclusively extraspective perspective, focusing on the hardware machinery to draw metaphorical allusions to people, we must appreciate the vital importance of the software, and especially those humans who write it.

Comparatively silent for the past few centuries in which science and its demonstrative reasoning was dominant, the as-yet-unrecognized and hence-unnamed dialectical side of human reasoning seems to be flooding human awareness to the point of a Jungian one-sidedness. This is not exactly something to celebrate. Not all of the dialectically generated changes strike me as for the better, and I do not mean simply the dress codes and flesh adornments that many of the "old timers" find unattractive. We also find that the rigors of demonstrative reasoning are under challenge today, and this is more serious for it challenges rationality per se. Thanks to deconstructive arguments, *right* can be made into *wrong* and vice versa. The tearing down of convention through negation, contradiction, and denial is obviously exhilarating to many postmodernists, who seem to be taking a kind of adolescent pride in toppling long-standing beliefs and practices. Shock value is fun, but where is all of this leading us?

5

THE SELF TAKES OVER

With Chapter 5 I begin a review of various human life developments and occurrences that use explanations founded on either an association or a predication model. The latter model is the one I take to be underwritten by the teleological human image called for at the close of Chapter 4. In the remaining chapters of the book I touch on many of the important issues facing the American public today. I seek to determine how well our two models help us to clarify things that people find themselves embroiled in. Chapter 5 begins with a consideration of the concept of self and whether it is best interpreted as a content or a process. Association and predication theorists differ on this point. I also examine important aspects of selfhood, such as self-reflexivity and self-esteem. The discussion then moves on to an array of topics widely debated today, such as personal responsibility, autonomy, political correctness, diversity, multiculturalism, authority, and morality. Through them all I assess whether a telic view of human nature helps us to achieve a genuine understanding of such human manifestations.

SELF AND SELF-REFLEXIVITY

If a person refers introspectively to his or her singular identity, the term likely to be used is *self*. The suggestion here is that a certain uniqueness exists in behavior, for not all selves are alike, and some people even seem to have more than one self-like orientation (Jekyll–Hyde) in the same personality system. There is an interesting distinction to be drawn in this concept between self as *mediator* and self as *predicator*. The association concept of self is as a collection of mediating cues, mechanically processed into personal identity as received or input from the external environment.[1] The predication theorist has a more dynamic understanding of selfhood. Although much of what the person comes to learn about selfhood stems from the attitudes and impressions of others (i.e., as contents), there is also a significant contribution made to this knowledge by *self-reflexive* examination and evaluation of ongoing behavior (this was touched on in Chapter 1). We can keep tabs on our ongoing thoughts and even challenge their validity. This brings predication into the picture. We come to know our selves through the fact that we sense a difference between what is taking place in actual experience and what might have taken place otherwise had we intervened or contributed in some way.

The historical record supports the tying of such reflexivity to selfhood. In Europe during the 13th century, the noun *self* actually stood for the reflexive capacity of mind to turn back on itself and examine acts of sin and feelings of guilt ("I am sorry that I stole from him"). As a result of such personal examinations, the concept of self had a negative connotation to Europeans of that period.[2]

SELF-ESTEEM

The negative connotation of self gradually gave way to a more positive meaning during the medieval Italian Renaissance (14th–16th centuries), during which it became acceptable to seek personal improvement and even excel in the realms of philosophy, art, literature, and music. Currently, there is considerable effort being spent to raise the self-esteem of Americans, with particular emphasis given to children. The nondirective therapeutic approach of Carl Rogers and the existential philosophy that flooded America's pop culture in the post–World War II era both have contributed significantly to this effort to increase self-esteem in this country.[3] *Self-esteem* in the many studies conducted on this subject is usually defined as "a deeply felt appreciation of oneself and one's natural being, a trust of one's instincts and abilities."[4] It is widely believed today that children benefit from a positive *self-image* (self-concept, etc.) derived from a feeling of self-esteem that should never be contaminated by negative feelings. But the steps taken to increase self-esteem in children have greatly annoyed some critics, particularly in the field of education. Such practices as giving social promotions, inflating grades, replacing the pursuit of knowledge with the pursuit of good feelings, allowing students to set classroom standards, and emphasizing political correctness (see later in this chapter) have led to much criticism of the American public school system.

There are many reasons why such practices have been instituted, of course, and the motivation is always well intentioned. For example, teachers are disturbed to see that children of poorer families are refused advantages that are routinely given to their wealthier peers, such as newer and better equipped school buildings, small classroom sizes, exceptional teachers, and so on. There have been thousands of studies conducted on the relationship among a rising or falling self-esteem and educational achievement, sexual promiscuity, delinquency, and substance abuse. A frequent criticism leveled at the purveyors of esteem enhancement is that they presume achievement will follow rising self-esteem rather than vice versa.[5] I believe that this theory of "give them more esteem and they'll do better" dates from the old drive reduction theories of the associationists that dominated in psychology during the 1930–1950 period. The idea here is that as a "good" drive level increases, "good" things will happen. But the chicken–egg problem remains: Does the higher self-esteem really impel the better performance, or is the rise in performance impelling the rise of self-esteem? Here again we have a process versus content dispute. Association theorists view self-esteem as a content driving things hence capable of being increased through additional input ("Kick it up a notch"). Predication theorists view the person as gaining esteem through transcendent self-evaluation ("I can't believe I did it!").

The research findings on self-esteem as a quasi-drive are not exactly clear and simple. In some studies we find, as expected, that positive self-esteem enhances classroom performance. The offspring of abusive parents have low self-esteem and do poorly in school. But other studies have found that abusive parenting does not reduce self-esteem. There is a weak tie between teenage pregnancy and low self-esteem, due primarily to the fact that girls who become pregnant are more likely to ignore contraceptive protection. Teenage girls with high self-esteem take greater precautions in the use of contraceptives and therefore do not become pregnant as often as do girls with low self-esteem.[6] So, if we consider just pregnancies, the girls with high self-esteem merely appear to be less promiscuous than their peers with low self-esteem. There is some evidence that low self-esteem can induce participation in delinquency, although several studies are inconclusive. There is no reliable evidence that delinquent behavior raises self-esteem.[7] Welfare participants have not been studied sufficiently for reliable conclusions to be drawn. The evidence to date suggests that the long-term reception of welfare lowers self-esteem.[8] Self-esteem has not yet been clearly linked to substance abuse. Reports from Alcoholics Anonymous suggest that if the person with a willful intention to do so conquers substance abuse, a certain rise in positive self-evaluation takes place. But there remains an underlying recognition of a lasting personal vulnerability, which makes the level of self-esteem difficult to assess.

Self-esteem shaping can apparently be overdone, resulting in an unrealistic bias on the part of those who are being shaped. One study reported that 68% of the 13-year-old American students sampled believed that they were "good" in mathematics when in fact they were doing poorly.[9] They must have had some pretty encouraging teachers who drew on the old pump-priming assumptions of drive theory. Unfortunately, they were pumping air. I think it is fairly evident that affective assessment plays a huge role in the establishment of self-esteem. It is the individual, beginning early in life, who evaluates his or her circumstances and then proceeds over the years according to this initial premise. As Adler taught us, people with adjustment problems have already framed negative predications regarding their life—both accurately at times and inaccurately at others. Increasingly disliked meaning-extensions follow as the person works her or his way through life on the basis of such negative self-fulfilling expectations.

Freeman[10] has noted how a person's recalling past inadequacies often motivates a desire for self-knowledge. Our personal development must be gauged by comparisons between recollections of past failures and corrective developmental efforts that we have made beyond them.[11] This development is aided by our imagination via the dreams we have for self-enhancement: "We . . . literally, would not exist, save as bodies, without imagining who and what we have been and are: kill the imagination and you kill the self."[12] Imagination is a major aspect of the predication process. According to association theory, to evaluate oneself positively is to be shaped to evaluate oneself positively. There is no role here for a conceptualizing mental process that evaluates intentionally and thereby shapes inputs rather than being shaped by them.

A common criticism of the predication model is that, because it is oriented more to the individual than the collective, it must inevitably breed selfishness. I have touched on this possibility previously. Those social analysts who have discussed selfishness at some length, such as Fromm[13] and Riesman,[14] have pointed out that a selfish person is really not a true individual. Selfish people are not actually interested in themselves per se but instead only in what others think of them or notice about them. They shine in the reflective light of others, which is why they are always seeking more from them (or more *than* them). They need others to survive. The selfish woman must know what people are saying about her lately. The selfish man wants to make more money than other people in his social circle so that others will have to take notice of him. He cannot wait to see the faces of his competition when he tells them about his latest financial killing. This man and woman are not people with self-esteem. They are selfish people who have an obsessive self-involvement. We must also not overlook the fact that there are selfish aspects of collectives. If we think of long-standing social barriers—other than the "big three" of ethnicity–race, gender, and religion—we have clear evidence for selfishness in collectives of the following sorts:

exclusive clubs and organizations, "old-money" identities, secret societies, noblesse oblige, labor unions, residential location (e.g., northsiders), gangs, and so on.

Even if self-esteem comes from achievement, and not vice versa, the task achieved has to be a truly challenging one that is not necessarily viewed by others as important or proper. We all want to be liked and recognized to some extent, but there are times when we take the ire of others and live with it. There is strength to be gained from seeing good when others see bad. The teenage boy, who for the first time stands against a parent to do something he truly thinks is the right thing to do, can gain self-esteem as he marches away from parental orders to carry out his chosen albeit insubordinate alternative. Even if he has misjudged and things go wrong, so long as he admits the error and learns something from the experience, he can gain what no teacher could give him by "positively reinforcing" his mediocre performances in the classroom. We do learn from our mistakes, and our self-esteem can be raised accordingly. So, the very concept of achievement depends on our personal sense of what is taking place in life. The question arises: Can and will people take responsibility for what they have done, even when it proves to be a bad (foolish, etc.) mistake?

PERSONAL RESPONSIBILITY THROUGH AUTONOMY

Responsibility is a challenging concept taking meanings from many precedent assumptions. Being personally responsible would seem to require something like *autonomy*, the ability to govern oneself through the use of reasoning, evaluation, and choice. As fundamentally teleological in nature, these concepts must be framed introspectively for them to make sense. The range of one's personal reasoning, evaluations, and choices can be affected by certain rights (i.e., fair and just claims). For example, Thomas Jefferson's (1743–1826) concept of individualism was grounded in the *natural rights* of human beings.[15] He meant by this the freedom to live self-sufficiently within a society. Samuel Adams (1722–1803) believed that the sole end of society was to safeguard the natural rights of its citizens to be free.[16] But in addition, there were *civil rights* to consider. Civil rights derive from a mutual compact among citizens in the sense of parallel individualism. It was understood that the individual would have to give up some personal freedom to the group, as in obeying laws that maintain order in the society. I do not interpret this as the group shaping the individual. Such laws, like *normative values* of any sort, are actually predications held in common by the individual members of the group—a further reflection of parallel individualism.

If one uses terms like *individualism*, *autonomy*, *natural rights*, and *civil rights* in a discussion of personal responsibility, and regardless whether one is politically a liberal or conservative,[17] a stereotyping of one's social views by others is likely to take place. And it is a virtual certainty that anyone who uses factual data that are also used by bigots, no matter how accurate and reliable such data typically are (e.g., citing federal crime statistics on various groups), is likely to be charged with or at least strongly suspected of being a bigot by the nearest scenarist. It would follow that such attributions of bigotry flow from the associationist view that people are always shaped and hence to use information that known bigots have been shaped into using implies that one must also have been comparably shaped ("If the shoe fits, wear it"). As I have suggested earlier, speaking one's mind freely and openly is becoming increasingly risky in the postmodern era.

POLITICALLY CORRECTING RESPONSIBILITY

It is difficult for me to see how we can speak of personal responsibility without also speaking of evaluation (see Chapter 3). The very meaning of responsibility involves accountability, the capacity to judge right from wrong, and the obligation to acknowledge when one is personally the agent or cause of some outcome.[18] Even our affects and emotions are tied into evaluations of our circumstances. Appreciating that the reasoner must affirm a predication for the human thought process to proceed, and that evaluation is always involved in such affirmations, leads us to an interesting if perplexing problem. There are collective versus individual ramifications of this problem. I refer here to *political correctness*, a concept that is related primarily to the issues of *diversity* or *multiculturalism* in postmodernism. As we noted above, political correctness is well intentioned, with the aim being to change stereotypically negative assessments and behaviors by rewording all possibly derogatory references to descriptions and behaviors of others, especially racial and ethnic minorities and people with physical disabilities. Someone, somewhere evaluates a verbal usage deemed socially harmful and then proposes a correction in the language. This revision is then pressed on to the general public by others (scenarists, etc.) as *politically correct*, or *PC*.

To give a familiar example of PC, instead of referring to people with physical limitations as *handicapped*, we are encouraged to describe them as *differentially enabled*. We move dialectically here from a negative to a positive emphasis. The phrase is obviously quite loose or nonspecific, for highly developed physical specimens in various forms of athletics would also fit the designation of being differentially enabled. I think we can see the influence of deconstruction here, for it is understanding the motivation for recommending a PC adaptation of the language that matters, and invariably it is something moving from the negative to the positive, a simple dialectical flip-flop.

The political aspects of PC are to be seen in certain changes that occurred in how to achieve social assimilation of racial and ethnic minorities in the United States. Initially, the goal here was termed *multiculturalism*, which was derived from the even earlier metaphor of America as a *melting pot* in which cultural differences blend into each other. The "multi" in multiculturalism was not then understood as difference. Quite the contrary. School children were to be put through a common curriculum and instructed in the English language. But as persistent difficulties were confronted under the multicultural assumption, a change seemed to be in order.

For example, for those minority children doing relatively poorly in school, it was posited that their self-esteem was the problem. The PC innovation was therefore introduced to redefine assimilation in terms of diversity. As Bernstein has noted, the idea now was that "different children should learn different things, each group of children having what is presumed to be their own culture reflected back to them, thereby giving them self-esteem and cultural legitimation."[19] In 1968 the U.S. Congress passed the Bilingual Education Act enabling school children who did not speak English to learn in the language they did speak (Spanish, Cherokee, etc.).[20] Bilingual education has fostered a growing emphasis on diversity in school subjects, including topics targeting racial–ethnic and gender differences, extending from the elementary to the college level. Whether this is appropriate is much debated today.

Some believe that PC recommendations place social problems ahead of education, turning schools into psychotherapy clinics and allowing a serious decline in academic performance to take place. We also cannot dismiss the fact that it is possible for people to conform overtly to PC recommendations and diversity maneuverings yet maintain private objections to these practices. People may be forced by their employer or a court of law to attend what are called *sensitivity* training sessions if they fail to adopt PC recommendations in their language usage. It would be easy to train them if they were exclusively demonstrative reasoners. But they are not. They reason dialectically as well. So no matter how many times they are told and shown what sensitivity involves, it fails to sink in unless they find personal meaning in the grounds for such practices. Personal responsibility demands a conscious examination on all sides of the issue under consideration, so that, even if some people view sensitivity training as enforced conformity, they will have a rounded and honest grasp of why it exists and how it is expected to improve things. Such insight affirms the fundamental humanity that we are all after.

THE MYTH OF INDIVIDUALISM

The third millennium now under way is a period in which the freedom to express behavioral alternatives in America is greater than ever before. Diversity has won out over the melting pot image of multiculturalism. Apparently there is now a suggestion afoot that we refer to America as a *salad* rather than a *melting pot*. Salads have distinctly different pieces even as they constitute a totality without needing to blend identities. I believe that diversity is a form of difference within bounds, largely influenced by the younger generation of this country. I say "within bounds" because it is still apparent that there are certain vogues in effect to delimit what will and what will not be accepted as reflecting true diversity. Individualism has been equated (or confused?) with how much difference can be shown by a person's attire, hair style and color, tattoos, bejeweled body punctures, and so forth. The greater such difference, the greater the supposed individualism manifested. One does not win much credit for individualism nowadays by carrying on intellectual discussion and debate, particularly in defense of traditional beliefs and values. Unless one carefully distinguishes tradition from past oppression and injustice, it may evoke for the scenarist nothing but memories of persecution, discrimination, or domination. The continuing need to be different in some way has also combined with the existentialistic and postmodern desire to cast off tradition (see Chapter 4). This violation of tradition is therefore considered by many to be a way of achieving individuality.

It is in the violation of tradition where the oft-cited deterioration of culture is likely to be found. One of the most apparent signs of cultural decline is in the loss of good manners. *Manners* have been referred to as the *grammar of society* because its rules of proper behavior bring society into patterned order in the same way that the grammar of language patterns the noise of speech into something meaningful.[21] Good manners identify the individual as having been raised in a civilized fashion.[22] But the foul language in public, the selfish disregard for others in social contacts, the sloppy attire, unkempt personal appearance, and the often brutish attitude in general unquestionably signify that American civilization is experiencing a cultural decline. And I am forced to admit that these losses in civility have issued from—or at least have been greatly encouraged by—the pursuit of the individualism supposedly gained by breaking free of as much tradition as possible (see Chapter 4 on this point).

What we have here is a *myth* of individualism, a false attribution of internal self-sufficiency to externals such as dress and a phony attitude supposedly distinguishing one person from another when there is no true individuality in the picture. Difference is confused with individualism. The person is unconsciously being influenced by the group to conform to a certain value structure (see Chapter 7). A true individual might consciously accept these values or not, rejecting some as faddish attempts to manipulate and direct. Not that there are no true individuals walking around with eccentric attire and rings dangling from various body parts. But such externals alone cannot capture this individuality and the chances are that the more this is undertaken as a competition with others ("Who is coolest?") the more it is a charade. The person who rejects such group pressures is not always given credit for a truly individualistic lifestyle. A more insulting appellation is likely to be leveled at the person who refuses to join the blue denim parade ("dork")—that is, the intellect it represents. But if one knows the latest gossip, understands the newest slang, adorns oneself in the "coolest" attire, styles one's hair a certain way, or uses the leading consumer product, there is a reassuring sense of acceptance offered by the collective. This lifestyle has some interesting implications for morality and authority, to which we now turn.

MORALITY, AUTHORITOPHOBIA, AND THE AUTHORITY WITHIN

In the 1960s, America was engaged in a controversial war that eventually came to be defined by many citizens as immoral. As opposition grew, people participated in demonstrations and civil disobedience to resist what they claimed was a repressively immoral social order (see Chapter 4). When key government leaders were shown to have falsified war statistics, trust in their authority faltered. This trust took a further nosedive during the political scandal of Watergate. The ideal thus became avoidance of authoritative direction in the name of individual freedom ("Do your own thing"). In time, a veritable *authoritophobia* developed. I do not mean by this a fear of authority figures such as police. I mean a fearful unwillingness to identify with or assume an authoritative stance of any sort. This fear of becoming "the" authority in a situation even extended to the private family scene, where authority was questioned rather than blindly upheld. In addition, child-rearing advice from specialists encouraged an egalitarian structuring of the family in which an offspring's attitude had equal weight to that of the parents. The concept of a *universal*, an authoritative belief (content) that transcended and corrected the individual's subjective views, was no longer sought much less cited as a moral or ethical aid. Authoritophobia actually turns anti-authority into a positive sense of morality.

In this vacuum, "feelings" displace morality, where the person evaluates his or her behavior to "feel good" as often as possible. We sometimes forget that feelings are themselves evaluated by both affective assessments and the weight of logic. The possible lack of doing good in our continuous efforts to feel good does not go unnoticed when we bring to bear the transcending process to evaluate our behavior. Such transcendent evaluations can be a source of internal discomfort known as *guilt*. Guilt conveys that we have violated a respected law or rule, or that we have fallen short, through laziness and excuse-making, of where we should be functioning. It is this capacity to move from selfish concern with one's own feelings to concern for one's actions in relation to others that typifies mature moral development.

It could be that the ultimate authority is some form of *authority within*, a suggestion that scholars have advanced for centuries. Among the first was

Thomas Aquinas (1225–1274), who asked people to "Trust the authority of your own instincts."[23] Five centuries later, Edmund Burke (1729–1797) observed that "Society cannot exist unless a controlling power upon will and appetite be placed somewhere, and the less of it there is within, the more there must be without."[24] A century later, Hippolyte Taine (1828–1893) suggested that, in the final analysis, "Every man is his own constable."[25] In an ideal society, people would be guided by their inner capacities to evaluate and follow chosen principles, experiencing guilt when violations occur. Many people argue that such internal evaluations are rarely practiced with sincerity today, even by those who attend religious services. Authority must therefore follow Burke's rule and shift to the external realm, where what is needed is more police enforcement, bigger and better prisons, and the end of plea bargaining for felons.

Sigmund Freud can probably be blamed for much of the questioning of authority today, although I am not suggesting that this was his intention. In his tripartite division of the personality into id, ego, and superego, Freud succeeded in making the superego (or conscience) repressive, restrictive, and punishing. The superego contributes greatly to the problems of adjustment. It is formed while the person is experiencing extreme fear of possible physical abuse during the Oedipal-complex phase of childhood development (castration, beatings, etc.). At this time the boy is said to lust after mother sexually and fear father's retribution, and the girl has the same attraction to father while fearing mother accordingly.[26] In reaction to this fear, the child internalizes parental values, and the Oedipal conflict is thereby resolved. This does not always come off smoothly, however, and Freud was to find an unresolved Oedipal complex at the root of *every* neurosis that he treated.

In contrast to Aquinas, Freud thus made the conscience the unreasonable aspect of mind, born of fear and hence obeyed blindly. Even normal people were influenced by how their superego formed in development. If the superego was well formed, with a great deal of psychic energy (i.e., libido), we witnessed a rigid, guilt-laden person whose life was guided by the socially dictated one-and-only way to behave with demonstrative reasoning predominating. If the superego was poorly formed, with insufficient mental energy for a healthy maturation, we witnessed a person with no conscience to speak of, one who might manipulate others ruthlessly and never suffer a qualm of conscience by dialectically redefining what is good or bad as circumstances allow.

AUTONOMY AND THE POLITICAL SPECTRUM

A person guided by the authority within could very well become autonomous, which has to do with independence or the capacity for self-government. The word *autonomy* comes from the Greek *autos* or "self" and *nomos* or "rule" (governance, etc.).[27] To govern oneself immediately suggests *individualism* when we are thinking of a single person, but we might also use this descriptor for a collective—as when we speak of the self-governing independence of a nation. Gaylin and Jennings have contended that the terms *freedom, liberty, autonomy, choice, personal rights, voluntarism,* and *endowment* are currently the "most often used and revered words in our moral and civic discourse."[28]

Actually, I suspect that there is a danger here of seeming to define these terms when in fact all we have done is to substitute one of these words for another. I think here is where a causal analysis helps. All of these terms fall under formal and final causation, and their specific meanings doubtless tie into certain contexts where they were used to capture teleological events. Although Gaylin and Jennings did not list *authority,* we could readily find this meaning sweeping through concepts like *autonomy, empowerment,* and *personal rights.*

What such words provide is a context of meaning from which we can establish our major content-assumptions to predicate what we might then learn, enact, reject, overlook, and so on, as our life proceeds. Note that Gaylin and Jennings referred to the *moral* without mentioning authority. I find it difficult to avoid using a concept like authority in discussing morality. Even if we reject the classical distinction of right from wrong, the concept of *morality* is still tied meaningfully to some universal rule or principle guiding its applicability. There is no way around this, even though there are those who would deny that moral imperatives are anything more than social mediators, handed to people rather than derived via self-reflexive examination.[29]

There is an interesting contrast to be seen in the political atmosphere of the United States. I refer here to the difference in perceived self-determination of the liberals (on the left) and conservatives (on the right) of our political spectrum. One might frame this difference in terms of individualism, but I think it is better thought of as contrasting interpretations of autonomy. The autonomous person is self-governed, living by his or her own laws or at least putting each common law to careful examination and evaluation before accepting its restrictions.[30] This pattern is not precisely the same thing as individualism. Autonomy deals more with the force of law (rule, etc.) on the person. Some people who are not drawn to individualism as a total life pattern are nevertheless prone to be autonomous in their more legalistic endeavors, involving such things as civil liberties, human rights, or constitutional interpretations. People like this can be collectivists, and they often take on positions of leadership in the group because of the sagacity with which they promote their autonomy. Parallel individualism can also be found in those people who provide leadership for the group. Great leaders of others can be attracted to individualism. Here is where political differences can be observed.

That is, as I have found in my surveys over the years, people with a liberal political outlook consider themselves individuals, just as those following a conservative political stance think of themselves as individuals. The significant word here is *freedom*. Both political devotees emphasize that they have the right to experience individual freedom. It is in the interpretation of what such freedom involves that we find a difference emerging. Liberals interpret freedom as liberation, as continually developing so that they are not bound by an ironclad tradition, open to alternatives, ever searching for those aspects of collective living that need repair, change, and improvement. Whereas 18th-century liberalism was suspicious of any inroads made by the government to the individual,[31] by the 20th century a friendlier attitude emerged in this political stance toward government intervention.

For conservatives, on the other hand, the definition of liberalism reflects a suspicion of what they take to be excessive government intervention ("Government is too big"). They see government programs as limiting or choking off opportunities to succeed, as in placing limitations on land use, introducing minimum-wage laws, increasing taxation, and so on. Conservatives do not want to introduce government programs to right every wrong in sight. They do not see changes in areas like sexual mores, family structure, or religious belief as inevitable developments for the better. They favor tradition and view the past as a source of helpful knowledge. They want to strengthen what they see as the long-standing American family structure. From their perspective, an individual is someone who is free to take personal responsibility for things rather than always counting on the government to do so.

People also take influence from both ends of the political spectrum at the same time, thereby thinking of themselves as independent voters. For example, their stand on abortion (pro or con) is a common reason for crossing over from one side to the other on a single issue. Note how this highly sensitive issue touches on the very content meanings that we are discussing, with a "freedom to choose" position for the liberals and a "right to life" (i.e., "freedom to live") position for the conservatives. Highly traditional religious beliefs are identified with conservatism (e.g., the "Bible belt" or "old-time" religion). There are awkward confrontations between many religious conservatives, whose faith teaches that homosexual behavior is sinful, and members of the gay community, who consider their sexual preference as simply an alternative lifestyle. Once identified, both sides are immediately subjected to unfortunate stereotypes (pervert, bigot, etc.). It is difficult getting around these predicated images of each other so that tolerance can be practiced. No one likes to be called such names. Life-threatening problems arise when the extreme ends of our spectrum produce collectives like terrorist groups or individual "mad bombers" seeking to disengage or destroy the government.[32]

HOMELESSNESS AS AUTONOMOUS LIVING

An interesting attribution of autonomy is to describe people in the so-called *homeless community* as living autonomously. It is difficult thinking of such people as actually living in a community. They are more like a random collection than a structured community. The term *homeless* is said to have been coined by the political activists Mitch Snyder and Mary Ellen Hombs.[33]

In the 1950s, a government-sponsored study group recommended that the patients in mental hospitals be gradually released into the community, where they might be more readily socialized. As a psychologist, I was opposed to this from the beginning. I also believed my colleagues in the social sciences justified this recommendation in their own minds in large measure on the basis of a mechanical image of humanity. Their predicating assumption was that, because all people are blindly shaped into behavioral patterns by society, the best way to reshape these patients would be to put them out in the real world—rather than isolating them in closed hospital wards—and then let nature take its shaping course.

There was a saving grace projected in all of this. The completed program was supposed to have a community-based treatment aspect in which the discharged mental patient would be enrolled in an ongoing training— that is, reshaping—program until reasonable normalcy in behavior would be achieved.[34] Due to lobbying by the mental health professions for more patient autonomy qua liberty, in 1963 the U.S. Congress provided federal funds to help establish such mental health centers in the community.[35] This halfway-house training aspect of the program was never realized, thanks in large measure to financial demands as well as the discovery of new psychotropic drugs. Rather than shaping them back to normalcy, psychotropic drugs made the patients less agitated, more tractable, and hence easier to handle. A fair number of psychotherapists felt that the medications essentially served as "chemical straightjackets." As for the dream of shaping people back to reality, this proved a total failure.[36] With the introduction of Medicaid in 1965, the care of mental patients—as well as those patients with an alcohol or drug addiction—who live in residential nursing homes has been reasonably successful, at least insofar as management of the disturbed person is concerned. Whether this involves an actual "cure" is disputed by professionals.

Those people who are not signed into a formal program or shelter, often living through an alcohol- or drug-induced haze, are described as *homeless* rather than *normless*. Because they can find a night's shelter when needed (e.g., at the Salvation Army) or get an occasional meal, not to mention panhandling to feed their drug habits, they are routinely described by caretakers as living in a sociologically legitimate manner. There are even romanticized versions of their lives picturing them as filling a necessary slot in the community's diversity.[37] Such "street people" seem to be living autonomously under their own rules, often rejecting opportunities for jobs or a return to family life. They hustle their way through a pitiful day-by-day existence, making us wonder if they are ever truly free to take full responsibility for their lives.

CONCLUDING COMMENT

The only way to understand human beings as selves with more or less self-esteem is to think of them introspectively, as predicating and enacting their lives on the basis of personally significant meanings. Those social critics who champion PC seem to believe that self-esteem can be manipulated by decreasing the internal hurt that people experience when insensitive remarks are voiced or actions are taken in regard to their disabilities, ethnicity, gender, religion, and so forth. Dignity comes from the capacity that people have to achieve autonomy, to confront life experience with an intention to shape it rather than being shaped by it (which includes getting people to stop making insensitive remarks about others). We cannot avoid being influenced by our experience, but neither do we have to succumb to every external shove. We can follow our authority within or reject all such ethical–moral prompting. We can also be ground under by drugs or alcohol. I believe that self-determined victories over even much smaller things in life are extremely important. I do not think the collective can provide this sense of personal victory. We have the mental capacity (process) to do it ourselves. It is not easy, but it is in achieving such difficult goals that we raise our level of self-esteem or self-evaluation.

We see cultural trends today suggesting that it is wrong to assume leadership or claim authority (authoritophobia), much less behave in a well-mannered fashion. Aggression is equated with hostility and achievement with authoritarianism. These collective influences, well-meaning in the sense that they are aimed at keeping everyone in the collective at ease rather than in competition with one another, weaken or suppress the very desire to excel that leads to individual self-esteem. There is also the tendency to deny the essential characteristic of human thinking as an evaluating process. Are we to do away with the necessity of rendering evaluations in living?

We need a better understanding of our evaluating process so that we can both benefit from our innate ability to further what we consider right and to put restraints on what we consider wrong. This does not happen automatically. It calls for personal effort, internal examination, and at times a willingness to admit the inadmissible. At such times it may be necessary to set PC aside for a while because it is then essential that we confront the "unvarnished" truth, say what hurts, and absorb what is dispiriting. But now, coming full circle, these are precisely the kinds of challenges that, when mastered, ensure the raising of one's level of self-esteem.

6

BIOLOGY AND BEHAVIOR

I have noted previously that a biological explanation of behavior is framed extraspectively, drawing on material substances and electrochemical reactions to make its case. The mechanic who lays all of the disassembled parts of some inanimate object like an automobile's engine before us to explain "how it works" is accounting for things extraspectively. There is no agency in the assembled machine, just parts supporting and impelling one another into an unintended motion. Biological and medical accounts follow a similar strategy. We study the parts and how these elements can be corrected if something goes wrong.

This style of explanation is actually collective in that there is no opportunity for the mechanism to change itself, direct its course, or halt its actions "at will." Biological concepts like *genus* and *species* derive from group uniformities in physical structure and are effectively collectivist in nature. If a psychotropic drug makes a mental patient more tractable, this is taken as evidence that mental illness is biological in origin. This proves to be a great hindrance to dynamic psychological explanations of the sort that Freud, Adler, and Jung introduced (see Chapter 2). The latter theorists were viewing the mental patient from an introspective perspective, in which it was assumed that there was something in addition to just material and efficient causation making a host of mechanical parts move about blindly. There was also an inner—introspectively situated—identity (self, ego, etc.) intentionally making things happen through formal and final causation at both a conscious and an unconscious level (see Chapter 1). Eventually, it was necessary to combine both the physical and the psychological into a *psycho-physical* account because both automatic mechanism and teleological intention were proven to play a role in most human illnesses, mental and otherwise.

The majority of psychologists and psychiatrists today believe that Freudian theory is entirely biological, particularly because he referred to the energy of libido in his accounts. Actually, as noted in Chapter 2, the medical establishment pressured Freud into using a pseudo-physical concept like libido.[1] In a letter to Jung, he once accused his medical colleagues of waiting for the discovery of physical causes of mental illness as if for the messiah, "who must after all come some day to all true believers."[2] Jung was no more pleased with the limitations that biology placed on psychology. He wrote to Freud that some of their medical colleagues "squeeze the flexible and fruitful psychological approach into the crude schematism of a physiological and biological straitjacket."[3]

Even so, biological explanations of behavior are the fastest growing alternatives in psychology today, aided no doubt by the fact that they place emphasis on material and efficient causation, which are presumed to be the "basic" influences in all human action. Therapeutic contact with the client is no longer the source of dynamic human insights that it was for the founders of psychoanalysis. Curative motives relying on medicines have eclipsed the analytical and philosophical motivations of the classical therapists. Indeed, a growing proportion of clinical psychologists today are seeking licensing to administer psychotropic drugs in their practice. We have many human behavioral problems in our current society. Is it reasonable to expect that an exclusively physical analysis will increase our understanding and help to solve such problems? And if so, does this mean that teleological aspects of behavior have no place in the understanding of human behavior?

Chapter 6 is tailored to shed light on the role of teleology in what are supposedly strictly biological aspects of human behavior. I begin with a look at the human brain and then consider what brain imaging and genetic transmission have taught us. I then move into a consideration of emotions before taking up the biological basis of addiction. Our final topic is that of racism, an attitude that biases human relations in a negative direction on the basis of physical differences in appearance.

BRAIN STRUCTURE: SOME FACTS

For years a friendly colleague sent me reprints of his interesting research publications on brain functioning, appending a brief note each time stating,

"Remember Joe, the brain thinks!" He was jokingly suggesting that I had nothing but a homunculus to offer in my teleological explanation of human thought. Postulating a little person within the brain to do its thinking was supposedly what I was doing in my predication modeling of human beings. In reply, I jokingly called him a rigidly narrow biological mechanist. After we got through the friendly denigration there was still an important issue here. The *scientific method* that he followed so religiously is grounded in the empirical observations of physical structures as well as manipulating events and predicting to some outcome. This way of proving things in scientific research (rigidly controlling and predicting) relies on material and efficient causation and therefore quickly absorbs association theories, which draw from the *same* causal descriptions. As a result, my friend had no use for additional causal terminology like *formal* and *final causation*. He was locked into a physical reality that never let him down because it was framed by the same causes that his method of validation relied on. Theory and method were essentially identical, a grand tautology that he confidently espoused.

I believed that the only way I could enlarge the narrow human image that my friend used was to argue for and conduct research myself that was clearly amenable to formal and final causation. At the very least, I would have to show that there was nothing in the research on brain functioning carried out by associationists like him that would preclude using telic concepts that I adopted such as predication, dialectical reasoning, transcendence, and reflexivity.[4] Does empirical observation and research have such facts to support my concepts? I think so.

To begin with, there are two types of cellular neurons in the brain's cerebral tissue forming synapses (connections) with other neurons. One type forms excitatory and the other inhibitory synapses.[5] Researchers have theorized that the nervous system may function on the basis of such "excite versus inhibit" oppositionality.[6] A large number of the brain's neurons—in the cortex roughly half—have *no axons* to input signals. They have only *dendrites*, which output signals. So there is no way in which the course of input-to-mediation-to-output takes place in these neurons. I recall feeling elated when I once heard a leading brain researcher say that "It's 'top-down' for much of the brain," with no bottom-up inputs directing thought at every turn. This suggests that the person can frame ideas independent of, in addition to, or in contradiction of what is being input from the external world and sent upward to a central processor acting as mediator. It may suggest other things to the associationist, but my point here is that such findings are surely not detrimental to theories of human agency.

The brain's corpus callosum has fibers joining brain halves that are mirror images of each other.[7] The brain is far from an organic machine churning out unilinear formulations in computer-like fashion. There seems to be an excessive amount of neural cells crisscrossing each other in brain tissue. For example, there are some 50 million cells per cubic centimeter in the human visual cortex and 10 million larger neurons per cubic centimeter in the motor field.[8] The estimated number of neurons in the entire brain is 100 billion. The organization of these nerve cells in the brain is modular, in which up to 10,000 of them are locked together by mutual connectives into a mind-boggling organization of zigs and zags that fire electrical impulses in patterns.[9] Once it is activated, each of these modules draws electrical power from other modules. A *conflict theory* of brain functioning has even been proposed in which it is suggested that adjacent modules of the brain compete for electrical energy with their neighbors.[10] The dendritic cellular network functions on the inhibitory side of processing brain signals.

Surely this clash and competition view of brain functioning is consistent with a theory of dialectical reasoning, and the patterned firing of the brain in these opposing modules is consistent with formal causation. Material causation cannot account for such patterning, and efficient causation has broken down completely in the findings on the neurons without axons. So it seems quite plausible to think of brain functioning in terms of formal causation. We also see such theories being advanced today in the study of vision, in which it is suggested that there are inborn patterns or schema that organize vision from the outset of life.[11] A predication model fits in here perfectly.

But what of final causation? Is there empirical evidence to support such a cause in human brain functioning? Work on the *readiness potential* (RP), in which electrical readings of brain function are taken from the scalp, provides us with this evidence. It has been shown in the human cortex that some 500 to 800 milliseconds (ms) before making a motion like bending a finger or twisting a wrist, a slow negative potential can be picked up off the cortex of a person's brain. This RP gradually peaks just prior to a person's making an overt movement, then shifts rapidly in the positive direction. About 50 to 150 ms before contraction of a muscle group, a more precise and brisk motion potential is observed over that part of the motor area belonging to the muscles called up for service. It is argued by some that the RP is an anticipatory volitional brain process, rising from unconsciousness to serve as an intentional motor command once consciousness has been reached.[12] This meets the qualification of a final cause assuming that it can be shown to reflect choice—that is, carrying out or not carrying out what the RP is signaling to be done.

It was then Benjamin Libet who next conducted researches in which he studied the RP measures taken from the scalp of his volunteer research participants in timed conjunction with *electromyogram* (EMG) measurements taken from their wrist and fingers.[13] The EMG records that a movement, no matter how slight, has actually taken place. After initially finding that an RP took place about 550 ms before the EMG showed that a motion occurred (i.e., the participant flexed a finger or twisted a wrist), Libet discovered that his research participants were capable of intentionally negating what the RP was signaling to occur. The participants became conscious of their impulse to move a finger or wrist approximately 200 ms before it took place and in this brief period could purposely negate it. Libet described this as a *volitional* process that either took place or was "vetoed."[14] It is this negating capacity that I argue is the source of free will making human agency possible (see Chapters 1 and 4). Thus, even though a prompting to do something like move a finger begins as an unknown impulse, once it reaches awareness, the person has the physical control to keep it from happening. In dialectical terms we might characterize this as a *thesis* (impulse to move) and its *antithesis* (reject the impulse).

IMAGING BRAIN FUNCTION

A much-studied area of brain functioning today is the limbic system and its relation to the prefrontal cortex. Research has proven that the prefrontal cortex is where reasoned judgments are formed, whereas the limbic system is involved with emotional reactions of all sorts, including fear and elation. When a person is engulfed by emotion, the sound judgments activated in the frontal region of the brain can restore temperamental balance. If for some reason the frontal lobes are functionally inadequate, the person continues to flounder in emotional release. Structurally, the prefrontal lobes are organized in reciprocal relation to the limbic system.[15]

One of the ways in which to study interactions in the brain like this is through *magnetic resonance imaging* (MRI). This technology involves taking pictures of an organ like the brain every 3 seconds or so to trace the electronic activation of its parts. Electrical activity "lights up" things in the region being activated.

Research has demonstrated that, when adults look at pictures of people expressing fright, both their prefrontal and limbic areas light up on the MRI. However, when looking at the same pictures, teenagers light up very little in the prefrontal cortex but quite a bit in the limbic region of their brain. Developmental studies have found that the prefrontal cortex matures at a slow rate, trailing the maturation of the limbic system. On the basis of such facts it is probably not surprising to read in the popular press that the idiosyncrasies of adolescents, such as moodiness, self-involvement, and complex love entanglements, are due to the fact that the correct equipment is not yet mature.[16] I do not want to disparage such theorizing, but there are surely questions I have concerning it. Assuming the facts that form the basis for the theorizing are correct, there is still plenty of room for psychological ramifications to take place. There are striking individual differences. Not all teenagers sulk into self-indulgence. Many enter into group activities or seek a smaller circle of very personal friendships, nurtured by the hour over the telephone.

More fundamentally, I find it interesting how readily brain imaging is presumed to be a measure of biological forces impelling and directing people along, effectively dismissing anything like personal control through free will. It used to be electrical stimulation of the brain that captured the imagination of those who think of people as biological robots. Wilder Penfield (1891–1976), who founded the field of electrical brain stimulation in the 1930s, never discovered evidence of mind control through such stimulation. He argued that the human mind would be proven to be under control only when the brain is stimulated to make a person believe something as if it were a personal selection. After many years of research, Penfield concluded that "There is no place in the cerebral cortex where electrical stimulation will cause a patient to believe or to decide."[17]

Belief and decision-making are obviously teleological actions. I do not think MRI findings are fundamentally different in what they suggest regarding the human mind than what Penfield's studies have suggested. Just because we can record electrical impulses taking place in our brains does not mean that these are the actual sources of thought—as my good friend insisted ("The brain thinks!"). Here again, these biological actions are patterned and not entirely amenable to efficient-cause explanation. Patterns in brain imaging could well be reflections of formal-cause actions being intentionally affirmed and extended in precedent-sequacious fashion rather than efficiently caused stimulations of the actions per se. Efficient causation may be involved as a mechanical instrumentality. We might be looking at the routes selected and followed in thought rather than the actual creative source of thought or the meaning being expressed. Indeed, the routes of patterned thought may involve more aspects of the body than simply the brain's neuronal network.

Eminent brain researcher Karl H. Pribram has demonstrated that the brain is continually involved as a total organ in the carrying out of visual and motor activity. Of particular interest is his finding that brain patterning is not fixed by specific neurons creating singular patterns of meaning. The same neuron can be active in a number of different (formal-cause) patterns. Pribram drew the analogy of a classroom of students who can be included when we group them variously according to gender, hair color, wearing eyeglasses or not, being left or right handed, and so on.[18] The same student can be re-grouped according to such diverse patterns. In like fashion, neurons in the brain partake of many different (formal-cause) patterns relating to different behavioral actions. If we now think of individuals who slice up their lives intentionally (final causation) according to subjective criteria (e.g., personally liked vs. disliked actions or objects), we can all be functioning in the same way at the biological level (process) and yet arrive at totally different patterns of meaning reflecting unique hence individualized predications (content). Recall in Chapter 1 the contrast of Scott and Suzy on this very point. Or, some of us can agree collectively, whereas only a small proportion find our way to individualistic outlooks departing from the group. Whatever the case, if Penfield is correct, we are never going to find such outlooks stamped into simple lock-step functioning by our biology.

GENES, DNA, AND CHOICE

The real boon to genetic theory occurred with the discovery of *DNA* (deoxyribonucleic acid), described popularly as the "stuff" of genes, heritable packets of information aligned along the chromosomes in the nucleus of a cell.[19] These DNA packets take the shape of a twisting staircase—the famous *double helix*. The two long strands of the helix are called *nucleotides*, and they contain huge numbers of subunits called *bases*, which are coded by certain letters. The "information" of DNA is found in the patterned arrangements of these lettered bases into what might be called a *coded signal* (formal causation again?). Each gene is thus a string of signaling "instructions" directing the cell's actions, such as to manufacture a protein aiding digestion or resist infection.[20] It is common to hear today that all the information needed to make a human being can be found in the ready-made signals of DNA. Claims are now being made that the genetic code has been broken.

Research on DNA has already been reported showing that not only organic malfunctions of the physical body like breast cancer, sickle-cell anemia, and osteoarthritis, but actual behaviors like good decision making, memory, novelty seeking, and anxiety management are subject to such genetic mapping. I do not want to give the impression that all scientists uncritically accept these research findings.

Critics have asserted that this work has not been sufficiently cross-validated (i.e., repeatedly tested). The challenge of determining causation for a behavior is particularly evident in the study of the biological basis of homosexuality. Is homosexuality a choice made by an intentional organism or a genetically determined, mechanistic behavior? Same-gender sexual preference in males has been traced in at least one laboratory to the DNA of the X chromosome, which is inherited from the mother.[21] The suggestion here is that the biochemistry involved subtly biases the direction taken by the person, so long as several environmental factors also fall into place. In other words, this is not simple efficient causation. Although not firmly established through studies in several other labs, the X chromosome finding was quick to stir controversy.

For the gay person, there is good news and bad news in such findings. The good news is that if homosexuality is genetically determined, then it follows that sexual preference is not a freely selected lifestyle as so many critics of the gay community contend. Teleology is therefore out of the question. But now the bad news here is that, if homosexuality is due to genetic factors on the chromosome, those who disapprove of it are free to define it as an abnormal physical development that might one day be corrected through chemical therapy of some sort.[22] Whatever the case may be, the possessor of this unique chromosome—the homosexual person—is likely to intentionally oppose those who would seek to change his or her gay lifestyle. Teleology thus sneaks back into the picture.

There is a group of psychotherapists who practice what is called *conversion therapy*, in which the claim is made that gay men and lesbians who have unwanted same-sex feelings of attraction can and do change their biological orientation through intentional therapeutic effort.[23] This controversial intervention cuts to the core of the mechanism versus teleology debate. Members of the homosexual community oppose it; others argue that such interventions are nothing more than helping individuals with problems in human intimacy regardless of their sexual orientation.[24] In 1995, a group of psychologists opposed to conversion therapy tried to have it officially discouraged (if not barred) by the American Psychological Association.[25] The grounds advanced for this action—which was never carried out—were ethical in nature. It was argued that, even if an actively gay person were to come to a therapist and ask for help to change her or his sexual orientation, the therapist should be morally forced to deny such assistance. The image of humanity favored by such practitioners clearly favors the mechanistic view and negates the choice one might make to undertake profound behavioral change— whether alone or with the aid of others.

To oppose conversion therapy, one must support the physical account of behavior. You cannot convert what you do not have—namely, choice. These psychologists are therefore highly unlikely to frame human beings as intentional organisms. Yet, in their legal disputes they are prepared to invoke telic conceptions such as ethics and morality. There are obviously two images of humanity involved here, one limited to efficient and material causation and the other open to formal and final causation. The life context determines which image will be used as a grounding assumption.

EMOTIONS OF LOVE AND LUST IN OUR TIME

A major source of biological influence derives from the realm of emotions like *love* and *lust* (or "sex"). Love is generally said to involve an idealization and sentimental attachment to the loved one over and above the strictly biological sexual prompting of genital lust. Love is presumably a more civilized expression of emotion than lust. It has been suggested that "Civilization does not repress human sexuality [i.e., lust], rather it humanizes it and marries it to love."[26] This humanizing would seem to start with the material and efficient causes in biological organs and move on to the formal and final causes of higher mental functions such as evaluation and idealization.

In recent times, thanks in large measure to the influence of feminist ideology, *sex* has also been distinguished from *gender*. *Sex* is viewed from this perspective as the biological aspect of male–female relations, whereas *gender* refers to the patterns of behavior "constructed" by the society, which dictates how males and females are to behave in the culture.[27] Note the suggested collective origin of a society rendering such demands. Thus, according to this Leviathan Assumption, masculinity and femininity are shaped into the person targeted, who could in theory be molded either way via cultural influence. Yet observations on the behavior of male and female children cast doubt on this belief. For example, in every known society we find boys generally playing more roughly and competitively than girls, no matter how early or how much social-shaping effort is applied to erase this difference.[28]

I can think of no sociocultural change that has been more sweeping and important than the revolution in sexual mores beginning in the 1960s and carrying forward to the present. The changes that I have lived through on this matter, dating back to the 1940s, simply boggle the mind. This revolution dramatically changed how we look at romantic courtship (if this concept has any meaning at all today!), the family structure, and countless other nuances in the area of gender relations (formerly known as relations between the sexes). After defining *love* as a willingness to sacrifice oneself for others, Bellah and his coauthors went on to distinguish between today's *Christian* and *therapeutic* forms of love.[29] Christian love is said to be founded on commitment and obligation, rooted ultimately in obedience to God's word. This form of love rests more on decision and action than on feelings, which occasionally may be denied consideration in carrying out God's will.[30] Therapeutic love, on the other hand, is modeled on what takes place in psychotherapy and is typified by liberating individuals through "helping them get in touch with their own wants and interests, freed from the artificial constraints of social roles, the guilt-inducing demands of parents and other authorities, and the false promises of illusory ideals such as love."[31] Therapeutic love holds that, before we can love others, we must learn to love our selves.[32] But this must be our *real self*, an authentic core of feelings on which the person can base a commitment to the loved one.

With its heavy emphasis on self-love, personal feelings, and a striving for freedom from social (including gender) roles as well as the guilt-inducing expectations of authority figures, we have the suggestion of individualism in therapeutic love. But it is also common for religious adherents to frame deeply personal contact with their deity, one that follows the word of God as they understand it no matter what the broader culture might say about this interpretation. This would surely produce an individual with great inner strength who might be expected to exhibit Christian love with a mate. I therefore see a range of individuality in those who might be classified as involved in either Christian or therapeutic love.

Bellah et al. advanced an intriguing interpretation concerning the practice begun in the 1960s of couples forming relationships in which they cohabit for some time. In earlier times this was called *shacking up* over short periods of time or *common-law marriage* for longer periods. The usual explanation for such arrangements today is that the participants are testing the waters to see how well their live-in partner meets their needs for a mate and vice versa. This is thought to be an advance over the old days, when lovers relied on "chemistry" to make their choices or even on an arranged union that was worked out by parents. Bellah et al. said in this context that "A deeply ingrained individualism lies behind much contemporary understanding of love. The idea that people must take responsibility for deciding what they want and finding relationships that will meet their needs is widespread"[33] ["Do the parts fit?"]. Yet it is not unusual today to know, as I have, a fine young couple who lived together for a few years, only to hear of them in divorce proceedings a few months after their formal wedding. As a matter of fact, studies have found that couples who live together before their first marriage have a higher separation and divorce rate over the first 10 years of marriage than couples who do not.[34]

Why is this? I think it reflects the need for teleological factors in the union such as meaning, wishful intention, and exertion of will. People who live together with the machine-like expectation that a successful marriage depends on a preliminary good fit among the parts are probably not expecting (i.e., intending) to adjust these parts when they first begin rattling. At least, the therapeutic lovers are not likely to have this expectation as they stand at the altar. Love in this case is more on the side of emotional gratification than building for the future. With the mindset of "when it's rattling it's broken for good," the course of action is clear: "Cut your losses!" No wonder that many unmarried young adults today find it hard to believe that permanent bonds between a husband and wife are truly possible.[35]

ADDICTION

Indulging in drugs, whether narcotics like marijuana, morphine, or heroin, or stimulants like cocaine, is another realm in which biology influences behavior. Addiction clearly has a physical involvement, one that would not seem to require teleological description. And yet, it is fascinating to observe the individual differences that occur in drug usage. Some people can take drugs recreationally on weekends and never become "hooked." Others become seriously addicted following the first few indulgences attempted. Some people can tell when to lay off taking their recreational drug and even face the discomforts of going "cold turkey" (i.e., with no special assistance), which they describe as similar to a case of the flu rather than the hell that others sink into when they lose their source for a "fix." Distinctions are drawn between *biological* and *psychological addiction.* The former explanations would rely totally on material and efficient causation, whereas the latter explanations would use formal and final causation as well.

Willful self-effort to manage addiction is well known and sometimes quite remarkable. A concrete example of this fact can be seen in the contrast of American surgeon William Stewart Halstead (1852–1922) and Sigmund Freud (1856–1939), both of whom in the late 19th century experimented with the anaesthetic possibilities of the then-little-known drug cocaine.[36] When Halstead administered self-injections of cocaine he found himself quickly falling prey to addiction, eventually extending his usage to other drugs like morphine. Despite heroic efforts on the part of friends to break his addiction, including being forcefully detained on a schooner that kept him isolated at sea for months, Halstead soon returned to drugs on reaching land. It was probably not a biological need that took him back to drugs. As one addict has summed it up so well, "Addiction is not a matter of sticking a needle in your arm. . . . Addiction is up here, in my head."[37] This strikes me as referring to intention and self-control as primary factors in the addictive habit. Halstead eventually settled on 180 milligrams of morphine daily, a level he could live with and successfully carry on his work as a surgeon. He developed original operation techniques in treating such illnesses as goiter, hernia, breast cancer, bladder disease, and aneurysms, as well as introduced procedures in the operating room that are standard practices today. He made efforts to "kick" the drug habit from time to time but was unsuccessful, carrying on with his daily dosage for the rest of his life. Even so, Halstead became famous in his lifetime and is now referred to as one of the fathers of modern surgery.[38]

Freud also took cocaine intravenously (0.05 grams) and described his physiological reactions in scientific detail.[39] But he did not become addicted to this drug. Indeed, Freud tells that he has

> taken the drug myself for some months without perceiving or experiencing any . . . desire for continued use of cocaine. On the contrary, there occurred more frequently than I should have liked, an aversion to the drug, which was sufficient cause for curtailing its use.[40]

However, Freud *was* addicted to nicotine. He began smoking at age 24, first cigarettes but soon exclusively cigars. He continued this addiction until his death. Freud said that he once had to give up smoking for a year and a half because of some concern over his heart, but he happily returned to his

> habit and vice, and believe that I owe to the cigar a great intensification of my capacity to work and a facilitation of my self-control. My model in this was my father, who was a heavy smoker and remained one till his 81st year.[41]

Despite these presumed advantages, Freud suffered for roughly the last two decades of his life from mouth and jaw cancer—the likely result of his heavy nicotine indulgence. He died in his 83rd year thanks to two doses of morphine (2 centigrams each) administered by his personal physician, Max Schur, who had agreed to this arrangement when Freud requested it due to the advancing level of his incurable cancer.[42]

And so here we have a concrete example of how two eminent men lived out their celebrated lives with addictions. Yet to fully understand them we have to consider not only the biological influence of their addictions but also what they did to adjust and even rationalize these vices as they enjoyed highly creative and productive careers. On a more common, noncelebrity level, Moynihan told of a young man heading for a life of heroin addiction in his teen years who willfully changed things around by putting himself in a different life context. He removed the drug-related influence of addicted friends by joining the U.S. Air Force, where he made new friends and sounder life choices with good success.[43] He could do so because he, as all human beings, has the capacity for agency (see Chapter 1). Association theory fails to capture the essence of such personal, self-directed life victories.

Another addiction is that of alcohol, a drug that presents a major social problem in America today. It is not hard to find teleological involvement here as in Alcoholics Anonymous (AA),[44] an organization that has successfully helped people stay "on the wagon" for years and often enough, for a lifetime. The teleology involved stems quite openly from spiritual precepts in that AA members first admit that they are powerless to stop drinking and therefore turn their lives over to God as each of them understands this deity concept. This succumbing to a personal deity has no distinctive theology behind it. These members are not proselytizing for "a" religion or, indeed, for religion per se. But there is this deeply sensed need, stemming in most cases from having "hit bottom" in life, that convinces each person to put his or her trust in a higher power. Although it can be, this is not necessarily a collectivist mentality taking over. We can just as easily have a parallel individualism at work. Human beings have spiritual urges that are tremendously influential in their lives both individually and collectively.

Addiction, whether psychological or biological, is a complex and often tragic phenomenon. However, as a concept it has been trivialized and extended to just about any behavioral pattern with obsessive features, so that today we hear of addictions to gambling, promiscuous sex, television viewing, overeating, specific tastes like chocolate, physical fitness, and so forth. Any kind of craving can be said to be an addiction, whether involving physical or psychological urges. Often both of these sources are involved ("I am addicted to gambling. I love it. It runs in my family"). This appeal to hereditary influence in a time when mechanistic explanations absolve one from personal responsibility can play a role in defending the person who is "addicted" against criticism. However, to give a complete picture of those who struggle with addiction, we often must reach beyond the strictly biological or mechanical to include the intentional and the great telic effort needed to change one's course.

RACISM

We come now to what is surely the most important and challenging social problem facing America today, the problem of *racism*. Almost by definition we seem forced to accept racism as traceable to the biological capacities of human beings. It is difficult to quarrel with the following suggestion: "No doctrine of racism is complete without a theory of biological superiority."[45] Martin Luther King, Jr. (1929–1968) always considered racism to be a belief in the congenital inferiority of certain people. And yet the most telling theories surrounding racial problems today do not strike me as heavily biological in nature, if we mean by this that they focus on things like chemistry, physical structure, or genetics. Even when skin color is put into the mix we do not find anything particularly physical involved, except as in the so-called "one-drop principle," which states that just one drop of African American blood in a person's constitution stamps her or him as a member of this race.[46] But there is very little left to address the real problems of racism if we frame things in this way.

Biologists may theorize and explain how color arises in the skin or how genes are involved in such pigmentation, but what racists (and nonracists) have in mind when they consider race today is almost always something else. Racist theory at present is more along the lines of character analysis, class conflict, or anomic decline of a subculture than it is a biological analysis of human beings. The biological aspects are still important as background, but the majority of racist criticisms today are *not* founded on them. Skin color per se is not as relevant as the value system and presumed attitudes that the minority group holds toward the majority value system (and vice versa). Class conflict is eclipsing segregation. Minority groups are themselves increasingly seeking to be segregated from the majority. I next turn to an analysis of the meaning of race.

What Is Meant by *Race*?

For many years the scientific grounds for identifying specific racial collectives were under debate. It seemed that the only unequivocal categorization by race was "human versus nonhuman."[47] Eventually, most scientists agreed that there are three broad racial groupings: *Caucasoid*, *Negroid*, and *Mongoloid*.[48] A garden-variety definition of *race* would be something like "a group that is socially defined but on the basis of *physical* criteria."[49] The most prominent characteristics examined in this classification were facial (e.g., prognathous) structure and skin color. The definition recognizes that race—and the racism to follow—is a cultural belief framed (process) by a social collective. The culture carries forward this belief as an aspect of its general knowledge (content). My goal here is not to analyze racism in detail, but rather to show how much the concept relies on telic-predicating assumptions. The discussion is limited to *African Americans* or *Black* people.

Just as soon as Black people are referred to, the concept of slavery is likely to be brought into the discussion. The equation of one meaning with the other is actually an accident of history. Vast numbers of Africans were sold into slavery and brought to America. With the founding of a government expounding freedom for all of its citizens, the embarrassment of holding slaves in America was all too evident. In time, disagreement over slavery as an aspect of states' rights led to the Civil War.

In the ancient world slavery had nothing to do with race as such.[50] Members of any racial group could be slaves. As a matter of fact, the word *slave* is derived from *Slav*, the name of Caucasian peoples who were taken as booty during ancient wars in Eastern Europe. Slavery is therefore related to economics in that the person becomes the property of the slaveholder and is then used in some kind of labor to turn a profit. People were even known to sell themselves into slavery to clear their debts—similar to a bankruptcy for life, or at least for a long (indentured) period. But gradually in America, due to so many Black slaves on plantations, a mixing and then virtual identification of the meaning "black" with "slave" took place even though not all Black people were slaves. Black people from different regions in Africa, living in different African tribes, were suddenly thrown together as if they were one social collective when they were not.[51] Culture shock was immense. Beliefs and patterns of behavior followed by these peoples for centuries were disrupted within a generation.

An interesting question here is why a slave owner in American colonial times would invest in workers considered inferior? The meaning of slavery has obviously shifted here from strictly economic considerations—Black people as profitable workers—to something more personal and characterological. What brought this shift about? According to Dinesh D'Souza, the fact that several of the drafters of the Declaration of Independence (1776), U.S. Constitution (1787), and Bill of Rights (1791) were slave owners demanded this shift in meaning. The assumption in these documents that all men are created equal forced these founders to dismiss Black people from the human race by suggesting that "blacks are not men, that blacks are lesser than men, inferior human beings, not entitled to the same rights as everyone else."[52]

Because it was White men in positions of power who framed such rationalizations, it is understandable that current social analysts like Beverly Tatum have defined *cultural racism* as "the cultural images and messages that affirm the assumed superiority of Whites and the assumed inferiority of people of color."[53] There is also an implied evolutionary theme that Black people have not quite reached the same level on the ladder of evolution enjoyed by White people. Not all of the early colonists believed in this racist justification, of course, including some who owned slaves. It offered a rationale for the inconsistency between the supposed equal rights of all human beings and the concomitant holding of slave labor. But it also seriously degraded the Black population in America.

A term we are likely to hear in discussions of racism is *ethnic*, referring to the categorization of people on the basis of cultural manifestations like customs, language usage, behavioral style, socioeconomic mores, and so on.[54] In other words, ethnic characteristics are not genetic or hereditary in origin but rather are learned through sociocultural contact. One group sharing racial identity with another could therefore be ethnically different from it in speech pattern (e.g., northern vs. southern White Americans).

These two aspects of human behavior are frequently confounded, so that we might ascribe ethnic styles of behavior to genetic influence when they are not actually biologically induced. Here is also a major source of stereotypy in human relations, which in turn invites various prejudices to be framed. A *prejudice* is a biasing predication that is acquired through cultural influence rather than firsthand experience. Prejudice leads to the practice of *discrimination*, which involves treating groups of people differently on the basis of biased assumptions.[55]

To appreciate our humanity we must be fully cognizant of the working of our predication process, for this is the key to understanding how stereotypes can be affirmed into existence and establish a context of meaning that we readily take as reflecting truth or reality. We do have the ability dialectically to deconstruct such biasing grounds for ongoing thought. The question of why some people do and some do not use this self-critical capacity to reflexively examine grounding assumptions is difficult to answer. We are likely to consider the latter people to be rigidly biased. It seems likely that the question of values would be involved here (see Chapter 7). Economic factors play a role as well. For example, White people who are poor and uneducated, living at the lowest socioeconomic levels, are the people most likely to be unyielding racists.[56] This suggests that, among other concerns, these White people evaluate Black people as an economic threat, occasionally reflecting a paranoia that suggests serious maladjustment.[57]

What Is the Notion of Racial Inferiority, and Where Does It Come From?

If racism has come down to a judgment of Black people being worthlessly inferior, on what basis is this charge being leveled, and what are the explanations accounting for this alleged difference between the races? Certainly anyone with an eye toward the performance of Black people in physical activities would have a difficult time making this claim across the board. It is not indulging in stereotypy to note that Black people have proven themselves on average to be superior to White people in such areas as performance and competitive physical activities. This does not appear to be an ethnic difference. Naturally, there is overlap between the two races so that when we compare a single White person against a single Black person such rank orderings do not always hold. Surely this understanding is common knowledge today.

A major area—probably "the" major area—of supposed inferiority confronting Black people has to do with intelligence deficits and related incapacities to excel in school or on certain jobs. For three-quarters of a century, African Americans have worn the albatross around their necks of being on average 10 to 15 IQ points lower in intelligence than White Americans.[58] This difference refers to the mean (average) score of the entire Black population compared with the entire White population. Once again, many individual Black test takers outperform White test takers within such group comparisons. Surveys show that Black students tend to study less and drop out of school more readily than White students. How do we explain these differences? There are numerous attempts to do so, and so far as I can judge the predominant strategy is to engage in ethnic analyses. Probably the major explanations draw on the continuing injustice of racial prejudice, which denies African Americans the opportunities open to White Americans through the built-in institutions of a racist society and culture. The tendency of some White people to avoid overt racism yet retain subtle biases of a racist nature due to such institutional influence is termed *aversive racism*.[59] Aversive racists purportedly experience ambivalence for they would like to be egalitarian but are sympathetic to ingrained racist positions on such practices as affirmative action.[60]

The notorious *Bell Curve*, a book written in 1994 by Richard Hernstein and Charles Murray and widely criticized by those who feel it is founded on racism or indirectly supports racist views, summarized research findings suggesting that the disparity in IQ between Black and White test takers may be partly due to heredity—a racial and not merely an ethnic difference.[61] This interpretation is based on the finding that White people perform better than Black people on tests of general ability, thereby suggesting that they are not as literal in reasoning as Black people and can thus better adapt to unique circumstances, abstract generalizations, or unexpected developments. One can teach specific steps to be taken on the job but cannot teach such higher-order reasoning ability, which would therefore suggest a genetic shortcoming. It follows that a White person is more likely than a Black person to be promoted to higher job levels, in which a more divergent style of reasoning is called for. The reply to such analyses varies, of course. Many critics reject the validity of IQ testing altogether. Others accept the scores reported but attribute them to cultural rather than biological differences.[62] To accept these scores as hereditary findings would be to suggest that the Black population is irretrievably inferior to the White population. To put it mildly, this is not a popular point of view among experts now investigating this issue. I concur in looking for cultural sources of the disparity and merely want to stress that this search will inevitably take us—at least partly!—out of the realm of biological explanation. There is plenty of room for the teleological considerations involved.

Issues and Developments in Anti-Black Racism

There have been other interesting issues taking place in the Black community that fuel the issue of racism but not in a clearly biological sense. At present we are finding Black people behaving in what can only be considered a dialectical manner, doing precisely the opposite of what White people do. For example, there are certain styles of speech, dress, and music considered authentically "Black" and which are therefore valued by the Black community, whereas other such ethnic manifestations associated with the White community "are viewed with disdain."[63] Some scholars have even termed this an "oppositional social identity."[64] The oppositional or dialectical impact on Black adolescents has been documented. Unfortunately, one of these influences is that "Doing well in school becomes identified as trying to be White. Being smart becomes the opposite of being cool."[65] Once again, not all Black students fail to work hard at their studies because of this desire to be cool and anti-White, but enough apparently do to make it a point of concern by those who wish to see Black school performance improve. For example, John McWhorter spoke of a self-defeating cult of anti-intellectualism in the Black culture.[66]

Some White people take the anti-White sentiment among some Black people to be a form of reverse racism. In reply, a number of Black activists have made the interesting claim that in one sense of the term, Black people cannot be true racists. Only White people are in a position to be racists of this ilk. According to this argument, to be a genuine racist, one must hold prejudiced attitudes and also have the power to do something about them, such as discriminate against the targeted group in some harmful manner.[67] Because this "prejudice plus power" duality is only true for people of European ancestry in America, it follows that they are the only group that can be genuinely racist. Black people may have racial prejudices of one sort or another, but because they lack the power to do anything about it in the culture, they are not entirely racist in their behavior.[68]

D'Souza, who believes that traditional racism is on the wane, has coined the phrase *rational discrimination*.[69] By this he means that much of what passes as racial discrimination is a rational estimate of the chances that harm will follow an encounter with a Black person—especially a young, Black man. Rational racial discrimination is thus a protective move on the part of White people. Newspaper and television reports continually remind us that, although African Americans make up only 12 percent of the national population, they represent 50 percent of the prison population.[70] Jesse Jackson, the celebrated political activist, affirmed this rational discriminatory view when he said that "There is nothing more painful for me to walk down the street and hear footsteps and start to think about robbery, and then see it's somebody white and feel relieved."[71] Reverend Jackson spoke here as a middle-class person, expressing fears over the actions of what might be termed an "underclass" person.[72] The Black community seems to have bifurcated in this fashion, and the separation is obviously not due to race but rather to educational factors and related economic advantages. A major problem in America today is the fact that poverty has itself become institutionalized.[73]

Robin D. G. Kelley argued that social science has helped erase the Black community's ethnic individuality.[74] Social scientists did not look at the inner-city African Americans as behaving individually, but rather from the very outset of investigating this group they assumed that the people they studied were acting solely according to "their unique cultural 'norms'."[75] The social scientists relied on associationist principles of explanation (my presumption), for Kelley said that they eventually turned ghetto residents into an "undifferentiated mass"[76] of "homogeneous humanity."[77] This is a cookie-cutter image of people that completely overlooks the individual differences and potentials of Black people. C. Mason Weaver agreed and added that problems which arise in the Black community are framed in such a way that they supposedly require "a government solution, not an individual one."[78] The result is that dependency is artificially forced on them as if it were a chosen way of life.[79] The Black person's confidence level is consequently weakened by feelings of induced inferiority and victimhood. Note that confidence level is a self-evaluation that is telic in origin, and the resultant good or bad biological feelings are effects and not causes (a point we covered in Chapter 5).

One of the more interesting analyses of past mistakes that have led to some problems now facing Black people is to be found in Shelby Steele's *A Dream Deferred: The Second Betrayal of Black Freedom in America*.[80] Steele argued that the great civil rights victory enjoyed by African Americans in the 1960s left them with more freedom but no real self-determination.[81] Collective identity took over individual identity as the Black community succumbed to the White people's needs to redeem themselves regarding the sins of slavery. In what Steele called a *redemptive liberalism*, the White community offered various forms of restitution, and the Black community accepted the role of victim, of needing help from the larger collective to solve their problems. In line with what I have noted earlier, Steele observed that African Americans "became essentially a *sociological people* with a sociological identity, a group moving from dehumanization of oppression to the deindividualization of the remedies for it."[82] The interventions made on their behalf tended to suppress the individual lifestyle for Black people. Steele observed, "So it is this collective black identity, not our individuality, that obligates white America to us."[83]

He further argued that all of the interventions made on behalf of the Black community reaffirm to these people that "their racial identity is the most important thing about them."[84] And this elevation of communal racial identity is occurring at a time when the Black person should be preparing to be a self-reliant, personally responsible individual rather than just another face in the crowd. To become such a person one must learn the strengths and weaknesses of the group. Steele believes that the collective is greatly threatened by individuals because they point up the insecurities of the group and offer alternatives that do not merely repeat the party line.[85] Finally, he refers to something I suspect he has experienced firsthand, namely "The defensiveness and rigidity of [the] . . . punitive stance toward individual blacks who openly dissent from the party line. For these blacks there is an excommunicative sanction."[86]

CONCLUDING COMMENT

In Chapter 6 I have clearly demonstrated that, even though there are extraspectively observable biological influences on behavior, and even though we find theories of a physical nature in social sciences like psychology, there is still plenty of room for introspectively framed teleological actions. More often than not these accounts are where important insights and understandings come from. It has been my observation that mechanistic theorists tend to rely informally on telic concepts like *choice, purpose, intention,* and *decision* to convey their formal theoretical notions—as when giving a talk on some topic of interest. They use the meanings of such concepts in analogies and metaphors just before they tell us (or write down) that it was all due to efficient and material causation after all. McCauley has noted how, in "unguarded moments," scientists have a tendency to "lapse into blatantly intentional and teleological talk when discussing the operations of complex systems."[87] This takes place unconsciously, of course. But there is also the aforementioned conscious use of analogy and metaphor to lighten the presentation— as when we might hear that the computing process is *careful, stubborn, very detailed,* or *unforgiving.* These phrasings make sense only because they are so familiar to us, not as merely illusions but as the actual way in which we humans function cognitively.

A common mistake in the use of teleology is trying to use it extraspectively. That is, some people understand the teleological theorist to be saying that purpose per se can be seen in events being carried along "out there," in the flow of efficient causation that we see taking place such as when the windstorm blows over a tree. And yet, as I have stated previously, telic description is exclusively introspective in nature. It is found in the point of view of an organism "coming at" experience to frame it and then to behave according to this predicated understanding. Although there are those who think otherwise, I believe it is best to see teleology as an exclusively introspective process.

Because efficient causation is exclusively extraspective in formulation, we cannot hope to resolve the basic difference between windstorms and brain-storms. Coming back to the friend I mentioned earlier in the chapter, the brain may think, but can it judge, choose, and self-analyze its thoughts both before and after things happen? I don't think so. . . .

7

VALUES AT EVERY TURN

In Chapter 7 I take up the concept of *value*, applying its relevance to such topics as religion and politics as well as examining the role that cultural relativism has to play in commitments to values. We have, of course, touched on such topics before (see Chapter 3), but I have a more detailed analysis in mind for this chapter. A basic assumption I make is that the human being is a valuing organism. It is very doubtful that any effort to capture the human image is possible without putting this evaluative capacity in the forefront. Everything that we have covered regarding human nature to this point must be grasped in light of this innate capacity to render ongoing evaluations that then influence what takes place.

VALUES AND VIRTUES

A *value* is a judgment of worth based on an evaluation pointing in either a positive or a negative direction. Values may be discussed in terms of process or content. The person evaluates (*process*) and comes up with a judgment along some dimension of more or less worth (*content*). This person can evaluate the need of a fading friendship or the sincerity of an enemy's promise. A value level can be more or less important in terms of what is under evaluation. Evaluating the worth of a pair of shoes is insignificant compared to evaluating the worth of a life commitment to a marital partner. We may follow Plato and speak of the *intrinsic* value of precious stones like diamonds or of the *instrumental* value of some action like knowing how to administer artificial respiration.[1] The role of affective assessment in human cognition captures the fact that we make a range of like–dislike evaluations concerning literally everything that we confront in life. Of course, I am commenting now as a predication theorist. If we adopt an association theory with its heavy reliance on mediation to explain behavior, values would come down to the number of positive and negative reinforcements or inputs given to the person in the past that then formed the value (e.g., positively reinforcing truthfulness shapes it into a value). Inherited tendencies to respond in a positive or negative way to different life events might also be relied on by the association theorist, such as innately preferring to pluck apples from trees rather than pull weeds from the garden.

The branch of philosophy dedicated to the study of values is called *axiology*.[2] Axiologists have divided value theories into two types: *subjectivist*, in which the level and direction of value depends on a person's feelings such as pleasure, desire, or interest, and *objectivist*, in which value stems from the more intrinsic essence of an object or idea, as in Kant's treatment of *duty*. He believed that every human being is prompted by a sense of duty, which is a positive feature of behavior.[3] This reflects the tendency in most estimates of value to frame them in a positive manner. The general meaning of the word *value* suggests something worthwhile, a good and not a bad object or action. Values can be considered from a negative perspective, of course, because they do take on dialectical alignments such as faithful–unfaithful, honest–dishonest, and so on.[4] But values are usually thought of from the positive perspective. A person may value using lies to get along in life, but no one would call this a value per se. If conveyed by stories, such as Aesop's fables, values are called *virtues*. The intent of such fables is to build strength of character, especially in children.

In *The Book of Virtues*, William Bennett described such character building as teaching "moral literacy."[5] I find it interesting that he appreciates how stories and poems are effective in character building because they engage the child's actual reasoning process. Thus, he noted that

> Today we speak about values and how it is important to "have them," as if they were beads on a string or marbles in a pouch. But these stories [in the book] speak to morality and virtues not as something to be possessed, but as the central part of human nature, not as something to have but as something to be, the most important thing to be.[6]

In our terms, a value like the Golden Rule is the content of a process of evaluative reasoning. What is needed to develop the child's moral literacy is practice in the actual processing that frames such moral content.

When Bennett referred to "something to be," he was referring to the person who processes—that is, who reasons actively to judge or decide—and not to a mechanism that relies on some kind of rote memory of value labels that are poured like marbles into a mental pouch as the associationists would have it. We must teach children that it is through personal acts of (e)valuation that they literally create values in their lives, or miss an opportunity to do so. Holding to values that are not actually created through affirmed judgments is holding a bag of wind. Instruction in such self-understanding results in what I have called the *authority within*, a recognition that one's behavior rests ultimately on moral or ethical self-evaluation.

Émile Durkheim, the 19th-century sociologist, proposed that the level of virtuous behavior in any society is somehow defined as a constant proportion of all the social behavior manifested. *Durkheim's constant,* as it is called, holds that the standards for judging behavior are raised or lowered to keep a proportionate balance intact rather than to greatly magnify or diminish the degree of virtuous behavior. Moynihan has suggested that Americans "have been redefining deviancy so as to exempt much conduct previously stigmatized, and also quietly raising the 'normal' level in categories where behavior is now abnormal by any earlier standard."[7] For example, using what used to be judged as vulgar language has been "defined down" so that to behave this way today is judged as normal. And the existence of so-called "street people" or the "underclass"[8] has been viewed by some as an alternative, hence normal, lifestyle brought about by a capitalistic economic system. Durkheim's theory is fascinating but, as an extraspective formulation, it cannot point to the way in which the people involved might intentionally change such behavior, a possibility that does exist when we ponder Aesop's fables. This is because Durkheim referred to contents (Bennett's marbles), whereas Aesop dealt predominantly in the evaluative process.

If people speak of values, it is usually the specific meaningful content that they are referring to. Just as people do not care about the brain processes that produce the contents of thoughts (ideas, etc.) so, too, they are rarely interested in the evaluation process that establishes the worth of a value. The actual value has no real existence.[9] It is known through its descriptive function as a preferred meaning. "Life is precious," "My word is my bond," "Blood is thicker than water," "No one is an island," "I can get it done myself." Values also are suggested when the person or group begins taking an interest in some object or action.[10] The object of this interest may be positive or negative. It is often said that the daily news is top-heavy with negative events. News reporters seem to look for bad things to report. This may be true, but if so it doubtless stems from the fact that the readership has lent an increased valuation—whether positive or negative—to these bad things. And this is what sells papers in the first place. It is not always easy to tell which direction the valuation takes. Some people are elevated by a story in which others have been injured or killed because they gratefully think, "I'm glad that wasn't me." Here we find a positive issuing from a negative, reflecting essentially dialectical reasoning.

RECEIVING VERSUS CONCEIVING VALUES

Values can be either *received* or *conceived*. To *receive* a value is to accept it unquestioned from other sources in one's social milieu (e.g., parents, teachers). Terms like *introject* or *input* have been used to describe this acceptance from others. To *conceive* a value is to affirm it following a personal examination of its meaning and the implications thereby. Terms like *vow* and *commit* capture the active role taken by the person who affirms a value and, in a sense, creates it for the first time. Receiving a value means it is acquired and accepted when such personal commitment is not necessarily involved. Affective assessment might enliven the influence behind the value reception ("People I love believe this"). Such affection is often mistakenly interpreted as emotion. It is, of course, quite possible to have emotional sensations during the expression of a value ("I love my country and would die for it"). Indeed, some people virtually identify values with emotions, so that a value is seen as what one likes to do or possess.[11] As I have suggested previously, emotion is not affection. The same emotion can be affectively assessed either positively or negatively depending on circumstances ("My hatred is righteous" vs. "My hatred is becoming self-destructive").

The predication theorist doubtless views value selection as intentionally conceived. Both transcendence and self-reflexivity are used in the theoretical account of just how this happens. From this perspective, a value is a belief having major significance for the person involved. This implies that the meaning of the value has been examined and evaluated from higher levels of abstraction (transcending evaluations). Assume that we were considering the value of *truth* and *falsehood*. We know what these words mean (level 1), but then we also know that the truth is usually better than falsehood (level 2). The latter evaluation has carried us up a ladder of abstraction that can be extended through successive evaluations to even higher levels—taking us eventually to the realm of *universal beliefs* that apply to everything known (e.g., sincerity, fairness, respect, acceptance). We might consider these highly abstract concepts our basic values. Although basic, such guiding lights always shine meaning from above.

When it comes to value formation, people do not rely on only one way to acquire them, either receiving or conceiving them. Both types of value formation doubtless take place over a lifetime. Although people can be influenced in value formation through identification with others (e.g., fellow church members, personal friends, a hero figure) in time they can take values on as personally conceived. A received value can therefore eventually turn into a conceived value due to personal effort, and one can gain increased conviction in personally framed beliefs through contact with others.

RELIGIOUS VALUES

I think it is possible to distinguish between *ethics* and *morals* by noting that the former has as its goal instruction in how one is to behave without invoking religion, and the latter has the same goal but relies on religious beliefs to support its teachings. I may be wrong in this distinction, but would like to use it so that we will not be mixing the contrasting meanings involved. Religion has many definitions. A frequently used definition suggests that *religion* is an attitude of devotion to something considered greater than the self. This definition focuses on the individual and would accept such things as the pursuit of great wealth or political power as religious manifestations. A more dramatic and explicit definition would be "true religion begins with the quest for meaning and value beyond self-centeredness. It renounces the ego's claim to finality."[12]

The central role that reflexivity in thinking plays in our moral understanding as individuals has often been cited. This self-reflexive ability to turn our attention inward is central to prayer and meditation.[13] As Taylor noted,

> We see here that the stress on reflexivity, on the inward path, is not only for the benefit of intellectuals, trying to prove the existence of God; the very essence of Christian piety is to sense this dependence of my inmost being on God.[14]

It is interesting to note that researchers on morality claim to have found that people are typically moved to behave in a moral fashion if they see a personal benefit resulting, especially in a society that is democratic, market-oriented, and esteems self-interest.[15] On the other hand, it has been suggested that people in such societies have become morally cynical over the fact that their elected leaders are interested only in serving personal interests and not in obeying universal moral principles, so why should they behave differently?[16]

Science relies exclusively on reason to guide belief and action. In contrast, religion relies predominantly on emotion and affect ("We must have faith"). As Martin Luther (1483–1546) said, "Reason is the greatest enemy that faith has. It never comes to the aid of spiritual things, but . . . struggles against the divine Word, treating with contempt all that emanates from God."[17] Reason is often said to search for the ultimate grounds on which an argument or belief is founded. This would be demonstrative (not dialectical) reasoning, of course. In science, such an emphasis takes us directly to empirical research. But this in turn brings about what is called the *criterion problem* in designing scientific experiments. This problem stems from the fact that a scale of measurement for an experimental test must be selected before we carry out our research data collection. We have to know what constitutes a positive or negative outcome on the basis of the criterion set for our experimental prediction—another manifestation of the fact that as predicating organisms we must know to know further (see Chapter 4).

For example, assume we tested our belief that "Living a moral life is good. Living an immoral life is bad." We design an experiment to test this hypothesis. In designing the experiment we will have to stipulate before proceeding what moral and immoral means and present a way of identifying these two patterns of behavior as our criterion measure (or standard). Even more difficult will be the task of measuring when this behavior leads to a good outcome and when it leads to a bad outcome. We have to stipulate good from bad before we begin. In selecting such criterion measures are we not relying on value-laden decisions that we decide on in advance regarding what is a "moral" action and what is a "good" pattern of behavior? We are indeed. There is no escaping this criterion problem. All attempts to validate moral (or ethical) issues are put in this position of deciding the measurement values beforehand of what they are out to test in a supposedly "objective" (noninfluencing) fashion.

Religions are therefore believed on spiritual grounds, on faith and not facts. But this does not mean that there is no room for personal evaluations of religious belief. Studies conducted on religious people show that they distinguish among moral, amoral, and even nonmoral religious rules, so that they do not follow every demand placed on them by their religion.[18] An example here might be the command to reject the practice of abortion. Not all religious people follow this command from their church. Even children do not take on religious teachings without making their own interpretations of the demands proffered by adults. This inability to cite empirically proven religious beliefs opens such devotees to criticism. Atheists and agnostics are frequently critical of what they take as pressing one's religious views on others. A devoutly religious person or church group may work to have a law adopted that would limit certain businesses from functioning in the community (e.g., a store selling pornographic magazines). The business person or persons affected may then ask, "This is a free country, so what right have you got pressing your personal religion onto me and my customers?" The religious person replies, "I am pressing my religious commands onto me, not you." The religious person has every right and even a duty to live out her or his religion actively. If we look at such issues from the perspective of a predication model, we can see that both sides actually rely on a precedent affirmation of a valued meaning that makes them equally "pressing" their views onto the lived reality of the other. That's life in a democracy!

I have already noted that an authoritophobia has taken hold in America (see Chapter 5). In line with this nonjudgmental attitude we find many devoutly religious people concurring that it is wrong to "throw the first stone" in judging others.[19] Yesterday's moral infractions are today's "no-fault" missteps. Gertrude Himmelfarb observed that we are currently suspicious of the very idea of morality: "Moral principles, still more moral judgments, are thought to be at best an intellectual embarrassment, at worst evidence of an illiberal and repressive disposition."[20] There are many sources of influence directing this nonjudgmental view. The traditional reason for avoiding judgment is probably religious. Only God judges. Of course, the truth is that a decision not to judge is itself a judgment. Pontius Pilate took this course of judging not to judge, undoubtedly exercising his dialectical reasoning capacity in the process. But I also think that a major, if not the primary, reason for the anti-judgment thrust today is the belief that, if no one judges others, everyone remains equal. Political correctness is at the heart of this effort to remove any stigma of blame, such as in blaming the victim.[21]

POLITICS

In this section I discuss a field of human thought and social organization known as *politics* as it relates to predication and the human image. I analyze the division of political beliefs into liberal and conservative, then move on to the one-sidedness of certain groups within our culture, and finally, the movement against *advantage* by some people in the United States.

Dialectics of Conservatism and Liberalism

A familiar definition of *politics* is as the "science and art of government." But we must acknowledge that competition over seizing the control of social policies is fundamental to any political party. Politics is therefore a power play.[22] Choice of ends is central here, so much so that politicians have been known to believe that the end justifies the means. The political dimension consists of opposing views known as *conservative* and *liberal*, concepts that have actually exchanged places over the centuries. Initially, liberalism was of a Jeffersonian variety that stressed individual liberty and a small national government[23] (see Chapter 5). Today this would seem to suggest a conservative position, although both modern liberals and conservatives claim to seek freedom in their political efforts. As I have suggested in Chapter 5, for the conservative this means being free from governmental control, whereas for the liberal this means being free to change traditional ways of doing things.[24] Today's liberals are generally open to governmental influence. Conservatives are likely to consider such influence an interference rather than an assistance. We see the hazy outlines here of a more individualistic attitude among conservatives and a more collective attitude among liberals.

In America, the liberal outlook is generally held by the Democratic Party and the conservative by the Republican Party. Is there a lesson to be learned from the fact that political views are readily sorted into pro and con on most matters of public policy? I believe there is, one that also answers the question of why expanding political parties in many countries tend to align themselves in directly opposing organizations. The reason is that this is an expected outcome of the dialectical nature of human reasoning. The more that a thinker learns about anything, the more detailed such knowledge becomes. This includes the oppositional specification of what is being grasped and also implied ("Why do you favor rather than reject that?"). As we have repeatedly seen, such opposed views need not be shaped by or taken in from the external environment, although these received valuations obviously occur frequently in any organization, political or otherwise.

There are those who express concern over the dominance of a primarily two-party system in a society, particularly when these two views overlap a good deal in their recommended solutions to social problems. Although I appreciate the concern, I do not think the coalescing into just two "loyal oppositions" will ever disappear in America. I believe that, ultimately, the most important issue here is the image of humanity being manifested in such political dualities. It all comes down to answering "Who are we?" and "What do we want to be?" questions that make sense only to an organism with agency. These are the moral and ethical concerns that we always find enfolding the political landscape.

The Role of Politics in One-sidedness and Cynicism

A concern expressed today is just how politicized the citizens of America are becoming. There appears to be a greater polarization taking place today than ever before in our history.[25] Both the academic community and the media are said to be extremely liberal and actively working to bring American values into the socialistic camp without benefit of seriously examining the opposing conservative arguments. This collectivist ideology is usually traced back to the notorious 1960s. Copeland has explained the development here as one of a federal bureaucracy seeing the poor not as neighbors but as clients, so that "instead of being leaders or representatives of poor communities, the bureaucrats became spokesmen and champions for the cause of the poor."[26] Once this advocacy had solidified, the upper socioeconomic class was defined as "the enemy." The strategy followed here is, of course, the Marxian argument.

It is reasonable to think that politics force people into collectives as they band together for a certain goal attainment. We all know that there is strength in numbers. However, there is an old saying, used by the Marxists and others, which holds that the political is also the personal.[27] The suggestion here is that political motivation must be felt deeply by each person involved for it to be a successful collective enterprise.

By teaching college students exclusively liberal attitudes it is difficult to see how they can learn to deal with life circumspectly. We should all be alert to this tendency of taking such a narrow approach to social issues, whether liberal or conservative in spirit (recall Jung's admonishments concerning living one-sidedly; see Chapter 2). The resulting unipredication of students makes for a low level of their consciousness (see Chapter 4). Young adults are especially vulnerable to identification with admired teachers. We are discussing mental contents now. What beliefs are the students processing at the moment? There is an even broader issue to consider, stemming from the fact that humans reason dialectically. If students become one-sided, they reason excessively in a demonstrative mode, turning themselves eventually into virtual robots. Higher education should be especially sensitive to the fact that learning from dialectically opposed directions does not confuse the student, it enriches his or her understanding. Such well-rounded, albeit at times contradictory, formulations encourage a sophistication and tendency to question, elaborate, and then to select a defensible position to guide behavior into the future—not as "the truth" but as "the best truth I can justify and live by so far."

Allan Bloom (1930–1992) called for an approach to higher education that effectively removed political biases from the picture as much as possible.[28] He recommended that students learn things from the point of view of an earlier historical era and not from the present looking backward in time. Seventeenth-century art is not to be genuinely understood through the eyes of the 21st century. Rather than narrowing students' outlook through today's political positions (as the "real" world), Bloom held that universities should engage them in the great debates of history on the nature of morality, truth, and beauty. Such ancient arguments transcend today's concerns to provide the student with contents that can be used as a predicating framework for any of a number of issues arising later in life. It is the process that we focus on here, learning how to analyze, self-criticize, and take a position. Bloom argued that modern (and postmodern) education was infected with the belief that only currently active events matter. He had an "Ivory Tower" understanding of education as transcending time so that the student might grow (e.g., intellectually, ethically, emotionally) on the basis of knowledge that is of eternal relevance.

I believe that the bias toward currency is due to the grip that efficient causation (ongoing action, mechanical thrust) has on the human imagination today—to be observed in the power emphasis of the Star Trek-like fantasies on TV and in the movies. Only that which is hot off the presses is considered significant. All else is to be tossed into yesterday's trash. There is an underlying conviction regarding progress at work here, founded on an assumption that the unidirectional motion of efficient causality moves civilization along like falling dominoes toward a perfection lying down the road of time (see Chapter 1). Life is thus a bull market! I think that we also see a comparable assumption of unidirectional influence in the interest and trust given to *opinion polls*. Instead of viewing the results of such polls as reflective of final causation (e.g., recording people's immediate intentions), they tend to be interpreted collectively, as efficiently caused forces moving beliefs along without true choice. Swings in the polls are construed as the result of new inputs (i.e., contents) that have manipulated the populace one way or another. Mere rethinking of ideas to change minds (i.e., process) is not given much credence in such collectivist orientations.

One-sidedness in belief tends to encourage *cynicism*. The cynic cannot believe that people are motivated by anything but selfishness. She or he thinks that everyone approaches life with the attitude of "What's in this for me?" A one-sided thinker is likely to doubt the sincerity of those who take alternative positions on issues. Such people would be drawn exclusively to what they want to get out of life at any point in time. Referring to America, Goldfarb believed that "cynicism dominates the assumptions of our political and cultural life."[29] He suggested that this cynicism has its roots in the view of cultural relativism, a topic we consider later in this chapter. He also believed that selfish forms of individualism promote cynicism.[30] If the person assumes that he or she already knows what is true and right according to the "one and only" worthwhile view of things, what need is there of listening to the "wrong" views of others?

It must be admitted that in this age of saturation with political propaganda through the media it is sometimes difficult to avoid cynicism. Political candidates have predrafted sound bite answers, which they offer even when the questions put to them are not quite addressing what these "canned" statements supposedly answer. An answer is an answer regardless of the question. There is a "spin" or manipulating bias for every fact pattern, designed to shape our premise affirmations in favor of the candidate. To be fair, we know that when a person is open and spontaneous with media representatives (reporters, etc.), the chances of being misquoted by taking a comment out of its context is better than even money. The motivation here is sensationalism, which invariably draws a crowd to provide financial rewards for the media concerned.

Sometimes a cynical attitude suggests political wisdom.[31] The cynic detracts—with a raised eyebrow—from every helpful suggestion made by a candidate for political office no matter how creative it may be. It is the competition engendered in political contests that invariably nourishes the cynical attitude. Initially in America an effort was made to keep political factions from getting out of hand. But by about the 1830s, all advocates in the political spectrum agreed that aggressive competition between political parties was good for a country's advance, especially one with democratic ideals.[32] In recent years, however, we have seen a return to concern over the nature of proper political behavior, as being unnecessarily mean spirited. This issue would seem to be a continuing one.

The Revolt Against Advantage

Traditional cultural revolts have been aimed at getting or allowing participation in advantages of one sort or another. The advantages include more than simply economic rewards for work done, although this is undoubtedly an important consideration. There are obviously other desirable advantages like obtaining an education, working in an occupation of one's choosing, living in a nice neighborhood, and participating in public activities. Distinctions in class level are the way that we identify the "haves" and "have nots" of the community. These formal distinctions in America today are identified as lower-, middle-, and upper-class levels, determined essentially by combining education with income level.

At present, thanks to the Marxian and various existential arguments that became popular in the 1960s, there seems to be an effort by some to revolt against advantages per se. The "street" philosophy of this period was to encourage a symbolic protest against the advantaged classes in such matters as attire, manners, sexual practices, work ethic, and language usage (as I have mentioned in earlier chapters). The liberals in America led this social criticism. I can recall when college students first began protesting materialism by wearing artificially tattered clothing (e.g., a shirt carefully ripped along the seam) and blue-denim "bib" overalls, with young women's hair being askew and young men needing haircuts and growing beards. These young adults were essentially walking demonstrations against the presumed materialism favored by the conservatives. Some went so far as to stop caring about personal hygiene (e.g., bathing, brushing teeth) in an apparent effort to identify with the presumably victimized unwashed masses. Traditional or conservative values were being discarded left and right. It got to the point that being sloppy literally signified a liberal political outlook.[33]

Of course, the 1960s through the 1970s did have a salutary effect on the nation in terms of ending an ignominious war and expanding civil rights. The so-called "hippie" blue-denim attire was co-opted by the broader culture in the sense that almost everyone wore and continues wearing denim clothes in work and nonwork (even "dress") situations. The truly remarkable aspect of this cultural change is the continuing revolt against advantage to be seen taking place in certain segments of the population. One naturally wonders about the sincerity in all of this. But there are too many examples of fairly wealthy communities seeking, inviting, and then actually helping disadvantaged minority groups to settle in their midst for this to be a phony expression of value.

That there is debate over some of these practices cannot be doubted. *Affirmative action* is a continuing source of such dispute. Affirmative action is aimed at providing reparative advantages to those who have been disadvantaged (e.g., various minorities, women of all races). Many White people who are no longer receiving such cultural advantages feel that affirmative action makes for an uneven playing field favoring minorities, and it is therefore an unacceptable (and illegal) practice. On the other hand, there are striking examples in which members of the advantaged group step back from certain advantages quite willingly. For example, we can find White American men who support African Americans and women of every race being given consideration *over* themselves in school admission or job promotions. These men consider this a proper corrective measure for past racial and gender injustices.

Some African Americans revolt against the advantages of affirmative action. Steele argued that achievement demands are not made on those being helped who are almost never expected to perform at the normal levels of other groups.[34] The Black person is consequently given the opportunity and even encouraged to assume a dependent role instead of openly competing to achieve on her or his own.[35] There is an insolvable paradox facing Black men and women who must now devalue their personal ability to help themselves as a way of eventually helping themselves.[36] They are pictured as victims of past repression and consequently unable to do without the help of others who effectively act as current repressors because they define African Americans as "damaged goods."

In reaction to such perceived degradation certain Black critics would like to see affirmative action terminated. Others would not agree, feeling that it is only selective racial bias that keeps such programs from working.[37] This is supposedly a more subtle form of racial bias (see Chapter 6). A Black analyst has also suggested that the emphasis being placed on responsibility and individual initiative is the most recent panacea for solving all of the problems of the Black community; however, this self-help emphasis is said to cloak an underlying belief in the moral inferiority of this community.[38] Finding the reality in all of this is surely next to impossible. It all depends on one's predication of the supposed facts. But, in the same breath, we can suggest that the differing perspectives to be found in such issues capture a different human being than the more robotic images projected in supposedly rigorous attempts to capture the human image.

CULTURE AS MULTI- AND RELATIVE

I turn now to an examination of *culture* as it relates to the predication model. In this section I analyze the concept of culture, how it is affected by relativism, and what multiculturalism means for American society.

The Concept of Culture

In previous chapters I have discussed the meaning of culture in relation to the concept of society, the relativistic nature of human thought as well as the culture that it draws on, and the combination of these factors leading to what is termed *cultural relativism* (see Chapter 3). *Culture* was defined as reflecting mental contents (meanings, knowledge), and society was involved with mental processing (reasoning, thinking). The process supposedly used by a society depends on the theorist accounting for such things, who draws from predications formed from either an association or a predication model. According to association theory, culture would be a special variant of mediation. The person under the mediating influence of one culture or another would be shaped by the stored contents available. Actually, *all* shaping is cultural on this view. In a farming culture the relative emphasis on shaping would be the planting, tending, and harvesting of crops. In a hunting culture the relative shaping emphasis would be on trailing, shooting, trapping, skinning, and so on.

According to the predication theory, relativism is always present in human reasoning because of the precedent affirmations of contextual meanings in this final-cause process (see Chapter 3). But this relativism can take two forms. We require a precedent meaning to be affirmed and thus sequaciously extended in ongoing thought.[39] The content of this precedent is likely to be influenced by cultural beliefs. This would be termed *cultural relativism*—relative to what is precedently affirmed as an assumption, conviction, bias, and so forth. But it is also possible for the person to concoct a unique belief—sound or unsound—and affirm it as a precedent to lend meaning to ongoing thought. This too is a relativism, albeit not actually cultural in nature. I call it a *personal relativism*. The cultural belief may be that all people are pretty much alike, but the person may predicate others as trustworthy or not depending on their nationality. The person frames this unique (and erroneous) belief without aid from the cultural lore. But it is still a relative mental processing, because how the person will behave is relative to the meaning affirmed in the predication processing.

As I have noted previously, the influence of culture on the social group is inherently collective. There are subcultures that form within the broader collective, as well as eccentric individualists who do not identify or interact with any collective (to the extent that this is possible). But, in the main, culture is a collective matter. It is therefore not surprising to find social scientists that specialize in collectives leading the field in the study of culture. The actual term *culture* was first used in Germany around the turn of the 20th century.[40] It was introduced to counter a political claim that German communal achievements were inferior to those of the French. The main point here focused on the relativism of standards and aspirations. German defenders argued that all societies have their unique way of organizing and doing things. Consequently, it is wrong to use a French standard as grounds for evaluating the style of Germanic culture. There is no transcending metric (*process*) that one can use to draw such culture-free evaluations of specific achievements (*contents*). There will always be the biasing influence of a culture's values clouding up the findings on such matters. Each culture must be judged *relative to its* own assumptions and expectations.

Culture and Behavior

Eminent anthropologist Franz Boas (1858–1942) is generally credited with bringing the concept of culture and cultural relativism to America early in the 20th century.[41] Boas was opposed to the predominant Darwinian view of society, which reduced all human behavior to biological development. Rather than attributing human behavior style to biological factors such as race (i.e., *nature*), he relied on the explanatory power of interpersonal relations such as learning by example or modeling (i.e., *nurture*). Boas's student, Ruth Benedict (1887–1948), then published her classic work *Patterns of Culture* in 1934, in which she referred to *cultural relativity* as a power that culture has to influence the actions of people.[42] Note that we are not forced into accepting a Leviathan Assumption because of this shift in behavioral explanation from biology to culture. As I have suggested previously, it is possible to think of cultural norms and values as personally affirmed beliefs held in common by a society's members rather than as an overriding manipulative force directing these members' behavior like puppets on a string. Final causation replaces efficient causation in this formulation. Norms are the contents framed by a predication process working through individuals.

Benedict did not interpret norms as mechanical mediators in the associationistic sense. She pointed to the spiritual nature of people, as when they petition a deity for help in resolving a problem. This was for her a proof that human beings are different from other animals in nature. It is not difficult to see a predicational model encompassing teleology in her image of humanity. The precise way that culture reached the individual was an important issue in the 1930s, a decade in which mechanistic behaviorism completely took over theorizing in the science of psychology. The era of the white rat was ushered in, and thousands of experiments including those of such luminaries as John Watson, Clark Hull, Edward Tolman, and B. F. Skinner were conducted to prove that people were blindly (i.e., sans intention) shaped by the environment.[43] The behaviorists found the arguments of the sociologists and anthropologists lacking a clear theory of how people learned cultural knowledge. They offered their mechanical views of behavior to correct the oversight.

The shaping environment fundamental to behavioristic theorizing now became the *social environment* and, quite often, the *cultural environment*. These latter concepts are used interchangeably. There is no real process–content distinction here for behaviorism. The content has no intrinsic meaning. It simply cues and thereby mediates the associative process, of which it is a part. Selecting whether a glass is half full or half empty is, as with everything else, simply a matter of reinforcing inputs that "happen" serendipitously to direct things without the person's intention. Choice is a mirage. If the person now believes that he or she is actually making choices, then all this means is that a further step in the shaping to bring about this illusion has taken place.

Almost from the first, the concept of cultural relativism was used to rationalize the "contradictory values and moral standards exhibited by different cultures."[44] In the styles of behaviorism, the responsibility for the action of individuals was assigned to the cultural environment. Hence, it was wrong to hold people responsible for their mistakes or misactions (e.g., sins). The person has two sources of behavioral direction: (a) the external environment in general and (b) the specific cultural values (e.g., moral, ethical) that he or she has input.

Multiculturalism in Identity Politics

As noted in Chapter 5, in America the metaphorical symbol of citizenry has traditionally been that of a melting pot. Although people came from every direction on the surface of the earth, once in the United States the goal was to meld into a common identity (while not forgetting one's ethnic roots, of course). This involved learning the English language, studying the history of the country (in special classes), and accepting the responsibility of voting as a person living in one country with binding values of freedom and equality for all. The slavery issue was decided through the horrors of a Civil War, and civil rights have been under debate and development through the years since this epic conflict. America is changing with the times, and it is in such changes that we find cultural relativity playing a new role. That is, the melting pot image placed emphasis on cultural uniformity. An ethnic group, living in ghetto circumstances, might form a subculture in which the people would pay homage to their roots by keeping their native language alive, enjoying certain national events, and so on.

The identity being pursued here is obviously not common to all; it focuses on the unique traditions and achievements of a delimited group. Admiration is continually expressed for the group's presumably superior capacities in some form or other. William Graham Sumner (1840–1910) named idealizing a group like this *ethnocentrism*.[45] People of all nations and for all historical time have carried out something of the sort to raise their collective morale through a distinctive identity. It is also possible to be ethnocentric about America even as one is also ethnocentric about an ethnic ancestry. Almost everyone can be identified as a member of some subgroup, providing thereby a potential rallying point to gather around when the circumstances call for it. But in the United States there is, or there used to be, this overriding sense of the one melting pot (see Chapter 5). I can recall during World War II when this unifying sentiment was especially strong. There is nothing like an external threat to pull people together!

In recent decades, an increasing number of small groups forming throughout America for specific purposes has come to be known as *identity politics*, with its arguments favoring multiculturalism. Identity politics *is* aimed at raising the opportunity for certain groups of people to take on more importance (recognition, acceptance, etc.) in the broader American culture than before. In doing so, the members of such groups will presumably raise their level of identity and thereby strengthen their self-esteem. We see a tie here with the self-esteem movement (see Chapter 5). The term *multiculturalism* emphasizes difference and not commonality. That is, multiculturalists call on the broader culture to properly recognize specific groups and to give them certain advantages that they may have been denied to date. Political correctness is also an aspect of such efforts to heighten self-confidence. Multiculturalism is viewed by some critics as a cover story for the underlying aim of political collectives. What I find fascinating here is that, whereas Boas viewed culture as an antidote to thinking about people in exclusively biological terms, the multiculturalist of today is an advocate for precisely these kinds of people, such as racial identities, people of color, women, and gay men and lesbians. These collectives are created and identified biologically (see Chapter 6). The concept of culture is now working for the "other side of the street" than what Boas had envisioned.

Multiculturalism has been tied to left-wing politics and roundly criticized by several scholars. Kilpatrick showed how, in its earlier forms, multiculturalism had advocates who viewed this in the older sense of everyone learning more about various minority groups in America.[46] No political agenda was being advanced. However, in time politics did enter as the term *multiculturalism* came to signify the rejection of Western culture in favor of all the other "equally" significant cultures that could be studied—as reflected in the chant of students at Stanford University in 1988: "Western culture's gotta go." And so it has indeed disappeared as an academic subject of study in many universities. Bork noted that, except for White, heterosexual males, multiculturalism urges all discernible citizen groups "to become or remain a separate tribe."[47] Horowitz traced its political origins to left-wing politics and added that multiculturalism is "the Left's latest assault on the American identity and a direct appeal to alienated minorities not to assimilate into the American culture."[48] A more detailed theory of where multiculturalism stems from today is found in the writings of such critics as Wrong[49] and Gitlin,[50] who have argued that multiculturalism is the ideology of identity politics, which is in itself "a reaction to the death of socialism."[51]

The suggestion here is that socialistic theorizing has dominated in intellectual and academic circles since early in the 20th century. But in the latter half of this century socialism has been losing its credibility in America and elsewhere. As a result, it is argued that a major countering strategy of the beleaguered leftists is to continue the attack on American institutions, hero figures, claims that civil rights are advancing, and so on. This effort retains the adversarial outlook toward capitalism in America that socialism had advanced. Some would even say that the current heroes of American culture are those critics of its government, from which spring the notorious ethical cynicism and disinterest in politics among our young adults.

The conflict here is no longer precisely a class warfare. It is more a *cultural warfare* that cuts across the traditional Marxian economic classes of proletariat and bourgeoisie. And so we find the multiculturalists arguing that racism is as active today in America as it has ever been.[52] The multiculturalist capitalizes on every opportunity to detract from historical precedents relevant to the presumed advances of American culture on such matters as racial prejudice. A running deconstruction takes place. Who can say that America is a suitable model for cultural improvement? Better to study some obscure (non-European) culture that had no discernible influence on America's development. All cultures are equally good anyway, relative to the values influencing their mores. Because America's culture is wretched, let's tear it down and replace it with something different.

One wonders from where the grounds for this assessment of America's wretchedness stem? Thanks to the multiculturalist's relativistic position, there is no basis on which to judge one culture's level of wretchedness in relation to any others. Note that the emphasis here is entirely collective. People supposedly change only by changing their cultural environment. At this point in history it would seem that the focus is completely on tearing down without much thought being given to what will follow. Or, maybe it is just that some hidden agenda (e.g., socialism) lying behind this assault on American culture has not yet shown its head. Doubtless right-wing conspiratorial theorists believe this to be the case.

CONFRONTING A "LEFT-WING CONSPIRACY" IN ACADEMIA?

Mentioning possible antisocialistic arguments always gives me pause because of the possibility that I might be considered an advocate of the great "right-wing political conspiracy" in suggesting that left-wing political machinations are about. It is not my intention to promote conspiracies, much less suggest that they actually exist. I am willing to admit that my political views—through no fault of my own, as best I can discern—have slowly moved to the right, away from the activist–leftist orientation I embraced many years ago. But that's another topic entangled in my personal predication of what left and right mean today as compared with what they meant in the immediate post–World War II period of my youth. All I can say for now is that there has been a dramatic reversal in what Jeffersonian liberalism—to which I subscribed—was all about (see Chapter 5).

Although I recognized over the years that academia was becoming increasingly politicized by left-wing views, especially in my profession of psychology, I never thought of the possibility that such developments might actually influence the potential acceptance of a teleological theory of humanity and the empirical data gathered in its support.[53] Like Bloom,[54] I, too, am an Ivory Tower academic who considers scholarship to be a dialectical affair in which all sides on an issue should not only be expressed but also understood in light of the proper historical context. Such transpredication is the goal of good scholarship. I have already suggested that politics polarizes instruction, reducing its level of conscious understanding through such unipredication. As I began in recent years to read more deeply into the question of political influence in human affairs, it began to dawn on me that there may have been more to the resistance of my academic colleagues to teleology than I realized.

I had always assumed that in suggesting people were intentional beings with free will, my views were considered by most of my colleagues as essentially nonscientific. They believed that a "real" scientist does not rest with explanations drawn in terms of formal and final causes. A real scientist brings such causes down to the efficient causation that always makes things happen. If politics was involved here, it would probably stem from the pro and con factions in a department of psychology on this point, with the supposed rigorous members ("real scientists") seeking to take control and restrict the teaching of psychology to association modeling, while the predication modelers tried to broaden the perspective. I hated such power struggles but accepted their inevitability and ignored them in my work as much as possible. At the five universities where I have taught there was little support for teleology in the psychology departments, but it is also true that there was little support for right-wing politics. Assuming that there is an influence stemming from a left-wing political faculty looking at a theory that is not acceptable to this political outlook, what would it mean for that theory?

If a field like psychology is to survive and grow, it should make a contribution benefiting humanity in some way. I think that providing an accurate human image encompassing agency meets this requirement. But claiming that people are free to behave according to their personal intentions can also be seen as working against a programmatic effort on the part of society to correct its problems en masse. One can easily see how this attitude goes along with a left-wing interest in large-scaled research projects such as those pursued by governmental agencies. To therefore argue in favor of personal agency is ipso facto to take a position in opposition to left-wing political views. Politics becomes entangled in what should be a disinterested pursuit of the truth.

There is another aspect of the concern by left wingers that has to do with shaping people to behave.[55] This fundamental conviction inevitably leads to the concurrent belief that it is external influence that shapes people and not personal choice. Personal choice has itself been shaped into the selection pattern it now manifests. There is an ethical or moral tone in such belief for it can then be said that people are not really responsible for their behavior as they would be if they were free agents. A theory assigning guilt to individuals is likely to be viewed (especially by scenarists) as mean-spirited, unfair, and even bigoted. The claim is made that such telic accounts blame the victim. Although to blame a person for life failures like not finishing high school, losing job after job for silly reasons, drinking to excess, and shoplifting may be technically correct, such judgments are said to unfairly overlook the dysfunctional home and social environment in which this person may have been reared (i.e., shaped).[56] As with multiculturalism, this no-fault argument holds that we are all equally manipulated in positive or negative directions by an environment. Because we are not responsible for this shaping, everyone is equal, and no credit or blame is to be assigned for resultant behaviors.

What is needed is a therapeutic approach to make up for past unhealthy shaping. At this point in such debates I always have the same feeling that deconstruction leaves me with. By deconstructing such meanings as guilt, blame, fault, and other such references to personal responsibility, we end up denying a significant aspect of human nature. This is a very dangerous game.

I have discussed this possibility of the influence of left-wing politics on the rejection of teleology with several of my colleagues over the years. Some of these academics dismiss the notion—as I would normally—as ridiculous. Others find it a plausible conjecture. Some colleagues frankly admit that teleological theory counters their hope that psychology will one day cure mental illnesses by controlling behavior. If people are free to do as they intend, they will never be satisfactorily controlled. Indeed, the great hope of psychology to one day predict the behavior of people will also be dashed. *Psychology* has often been defined as "the science of the control and prediction of behavior." To claim to have proven scientifically that people are free to be conditioned or not is to strike at the heart of such professional aspirations.[57]

Also, for the practicing clinical psychologist, belief in teleology does not provide any economic advantage as compared with the vast range of services in the treatment of emotional disorders that can be justified on mechanistic grounds, even if the actual cure relies on the unmentioned intentions and cooperation of those being shaped. Teleology just doesn't pay. There is another way in which economics enters the picture. Black critics of their own subculture (which is described as heavily left-wing in political commitment) have cautioned against placing complete confidence in leaders who make their living supposedly helping the Black community to survive. The charge here is that it might be in these leaders' best interest to keep Black people dependent, as unable to choose and reach goals for themselves.[58] If true, this would naturally work against placing faith in the individual's capacity to be self-responsible. As a matter of fact, the suggestion has now been floated that to emphasize the role of personal responsibility in the minority community is to express a subtle form of discrimination by attempting to foist a demeaning level of guilt on the minority for not meeting other people's standards.[59]

Finally, I should note that other of my colleagues have suggested that I am aiming my guns in the wrong direction. They believe that psychology is moving so rapidly into becoming a branch of biology that the real threat—to both behaviorism and teleology—is from this source. These biologically involved colleagues are said to be more dispersed as to left or right political commitment than the behaviorists or teleologists. I have my doubts on this score but have insufficient evidence to argue otherwise. Only time will tell. I do agree that biological explanations are rapidly increasing in psychology, due in large measure to the success of psychopharmacology. I also see this as a reflection of the growing service orientation in the rise of postmodernism. Biology plays a central role in efforts being made through medical research to increase levels of health as well as longevity. Whatever the case, I am hoping that politics will be de-emphasized or at least presented in a more balanced fashion in psychology's future.

CONCLUDING COMMENT

I cannot think of a better example of teleological behavior than what goes on in political activity. No other endeavor involves more mixing of behavioral patterns framed by conflicting goals, from positive to negative and back again. Political correctness puts a good face on things, even as the person following these admonitions knows full well the dark side to all of these corrective meanings. The person knows dark sides of all types due to his or her dialectical reasoning capacity. And when the chips are down, when failure seems to be imminent in some political contest, this darker side is likely to press for expression in overt behavior. The political contest becomes a war. The internal turmoil rises. Contestants must have a strong value system to survive as civilized human beings. Some meet the grade. Some do not. What a marvelous manifestation this is of the heights and depths of human nature. To think of organisms who behave like this as being moved solely by natural selection, biological structures, or mechanical forces is to rob the human spirit of its essence.

As we have found, the capacity to render valuations is central to human behavior, whether framed by the spontaneity of an affective assessment or the more directed judgments of the conscious mind (see Chapter 3). Positive–negative, true–false, good–bad, like–dislike, right–wrong, fair–unfair, and so on are the continuing evaluations rendered in human experience—often redundantly. To see people give up advantages in the name of religious commitment or simply through a desire to right past wrongs is almost beyond belief. But such adjustments and sacrifices do take place, promoted by a framing valuation of what ought to be done to set things straight. The *authority within* expresses itself at this point.

It is illogical in a behavioristic psychology to think that people will actually reject the positive reinforcements of life's advantages. To account for such behavior it is necessary to concoct an intricate reinforcement history in which those who decide to reject advantage have been somehow positively reinforced for such rejections in the past. How does one get positively reinforced for rejecting something positive unless there is some transcendent sense of good and bad framing things in the first place? To truly understand such behavior we must think of human beings as able to choose their own grounds for the sake of which they opt to behave one way rather than another (i.e., dialectically). Predication is therefore a recurring choice point.

Fundamentally, there is no real difference between the processing of an individual relativism and cultural or collective relativism. To speak of cultural relativism is to refer to the meaning that is already available to and endorsed by one's culture (its collective knowledge contents). The person situated within that culture is likely to endorse this meaning as well (as in a received value). He or she may be cognizant of the obverse of this valued meaning. Those who cannot separate themselves from the generally held belief can be described as thinking collectively, whereas those who can do so can be described as individualists or parallel individualists. In either case, the general acceptance of the valued meaning (e.g, "Justice plays no favorites") makes it out to be a cultural belief, but it is of course created and sustained in the minds of persons, many of whom are individualistic in their worldview.

There is a significant clash in values between the melting pot and the multicultural images of American citizenship. The melting pot springs from the people to the political structure of the society. People work to become "one" above all else, keeping their ethnic identities secondary to their identities as American citizens. In the case of multiculturalism, this order is reversed; the ethnic identity is considered primary, and American citizenship is secondary. This is why critics of multiculturalism see it as an ideology for prompting ethnic minorities to oppose assimilation into the American society and culture. Whatever the case, I personally hope that we Americans retain—or is it regain?—the melting pot image and practice tolerance and fair play in the future. To go in the opposite direction is to toy with a weakened American identity that has harmful cultural ramifications. This is not something that will come about through some external force shaping us into doing the right thing. This is a task calling for personal choice and active effort to attain a worthwhile end in human relations.

8

THE HUMAN IMAGE IN POSTMODERN AMERICA

In this final chapter I want to specify the exact differences between collective and individual thinking (reasoning, etc.) and then assemble a profile of the likely personality and family dynamics in the postmodern (or postindustrial) era. As I have noted previously, behaviorist psychology in the 20th century effectively took the *person* out of consideration in favor of a *biological automaton* under the direction of impersonal natural laws (see Chapter 2). This was well suited to the industrial stage of that period, during which rigidly mechanical machines of a strictly material- and efficient-cause variety provided the model for human behavior. But a human image drawn on this form of machine is totally out of character for a postmodern era, when a new concept of the machine has been introduced, one that adds formal- and final-causes to its process by way of the programmer, who must repeatedly add his or her mental contribution to the mechanical process. Thus, with the arrival of computer technology, we must now deal with the human image as reflected in the logic of the software rather than exclusively in the machinery of the hardware.

To be more precise, I should say this involves the logic of the program writer as well as her or his dialectical reasoning capacity. Computers do not write their own executive programs. These higher-level programs are capable of "writing" lower-level programs, but the way in which they accomplish this is by following the steps written into their basic machine language. Such machine writing of programs is therefore limited to demonstrative reasoning, whereas the creation of executive programs relies in large part on the dialectical reasoning capacities of the programmer, who must render judgments of "this versus that" in arriving at a finished product. In other words, the full range of human reasoning cannot be separated from the computing machine process. We are therefore required to take this human being—the program writer—into consideration as a vital aspect of the machine process. As we noted previously, postmodern machines have shifted from people aping machines to machines aping people. And people require all four causes if they are to be fully captured by a theory.

This chapter begins with a summary of two forms of thinking that we have examined in previous chapters: collective versus individual. Next I describe what human personality will probably be like in the postmodernism now descending on America, carrying this over to the family and child-rearing cultural practices in this form of society. I am not speaking of an impersonal group shaping here but rather of an affirmation of a certain style of being that the great majority of people will predicate in common. I then move to a consideration of postmodernism as featuring collectivism or individualism and take up various measures to correct the human image for the postmodern era. I carry out a deeper analysis of relativism, including such themes as the anti-intellectualism it has seemed to encourage in certain groups. The ultimate value of relativism is clarified. The chapter (and volume) ends with summarizing comments concerning the imperfections of and improvements to the current human image.

COLLECTIVE VERSUS INDIVIDUAL THINKING

If one is willing to accept the possible existence of *collective* (group, etc.) *thinking*, it would have to be conceived as limited to demonstrative reasoning. There may be opposing sides expressed by different portions of the collective, but there is no ongoing dialectical reasoning taking place by either side. The association process determines the direction of such mechanical thinking. The emphasis is completely on the content of thought. Process takes a back seat. The collective has no capacity to transcend and conduct a self-analysis or self-criticism. It never reasons *for the sake of* anything but only *in response to* things and events. It relies on unipredication and is therefore operating at a low level of consciousness or actual unconsciousness. This makes it vulnerable to emotional displays as can be seen in the spontaneous reactions of crowds and mobs. I also suspect that the unconscious feature of collective thought is what makes advertising successful in various media. At the group level brief bits of unipolar information (including pictorial items) can be accepted uncritically, similar to what occurs under hypnotic suggestion. Changing minds is easily accomplished in the collective mode of thought.

Individual thinking stresses process, which encompasses meaning creation through framing experience dialectically, hence, alternatively. Contents known as *beliefs* are easily brought into question and denial due to the self-reflexive capacities of this predication process. Transpredication is utilized so that level of consciousness is frequently high. Frustrations are readily brought under control thanks to the ability to evaluate, critically examine, and anticipate ongoing life events. The dialectical aspects of this form of thinking explain concepts such as agency and free will.

Collective thought is simply another way of referring to cultural concepts or contents, which have meaning and can be repatterned into creative innovations by successive individuals who bring the predication process of reasoning to them. We do have some indications today of a collectivist tendency in practices such as political correctness, in which ground rules for verbal expression are decided by certain members of the collective and then pressed onto others. But I believe there will always be people resisting such collective efforts due to the fact that they can, because of their dialectical reasoning capacities, grasp what is occurring here and object to such group manipulation if it is seen as going too far. I also believe that the Jungian view of increasing dialectical meanings concocted as a reaction to previous one-sided thinking in the demonstrative mode will not easily disappear in America now that it has broken through to group consciousness. We are in for a continuing run of people trying dialectically to turn culture on its back, deconstruct its hallowed views, and introduce nonsense in the name of creative diversity. On the other hand, we can, and I hope that we will, become more aware of what is taking place and set in motion counter-measures to boost our level of critical thinking in a truly individual way that seeks genuine diversity, clarity, and honesty instead of mere political advantage and related forms of one-sidedness.

THE POSTINDUSTRIAL OR POSTMODERN PERSON

If we were to sketch an outline of the postindustrial individual's personality and lifestyle, what would she or he be like? From many sources I have put together the following profile.[1]

The *postmodern person* is quite sensitive to emotional feelings and resultant affective assessments, trying as much as possible to be relaxed and flexible ("cool") at all times. Emotional release is considered important, but there is also significant affinity with a disinterested science from which we all gain the benefits of a better and longer life. Such longevity is just naturally expected. This is an active person who enjoys physical exercise more for the health benefits than the competition that sporting events provide. This person is more oriented to being a spectator than a participant in sports. One wonders if this is not the result of being forced into organized sports during childhood (see later in this chapter). Attending various types of musical concerts is a favorite recreation.

Immediate gratification is preferred to holding off pleasure for long periods of time. Purchases of desirable items are quickly made on credit without great concern. Spontaneity is treasured. Time moves rapidly, and speed in getting tasks done is a major goal for the postmodern person. The rapidity of computer processing is a major source of satisfaction. Overemphasis on rapid completion of tasks sometimes results in a hurried performance in which background data are not fully assessed. This person has the attitude of *live and let live*, is reluctant to judge others and prefers that others do the same. The attitude toward using recreational (illegal) drugs is likely to be tolerant. Retaining a youthful outlook is important, so that sometimes this person finds it uncomfortable assuming traditionally mature behavioral patterns of the culture. This might be in part a reaction to the fact that he or she has had childhood cut short (see later in this chapter). Postmodernists are invested primarily in their own lives, but they have been repeatedly instructed in school to share thoughts and actions with others (via the existentialistic theme that "we are all alike"). So, although their private lives come first, they are not averse to helping others, particularly when there are no long-term strings attached. They are easily encouraged to participate in demonstrations for some good cause, such as environmental preservation or the rights of various minority collectives. Arguments favoring the development of diversity and multiculturalism are vigorously supported.

Education is seen as important in the postindustrial stage because job opportunities increasingly require advanced skills and specialized knowledge. Unskilled jobs are drying up, except in certain low-grade services (e.g., flipping hamburgers). The greatest opportunity for higher level job advancement in the postmodern era would seem to be in service areas such as research and development, finance, communications, and high-tech positions of all types. As the need for various services increases, so does the person's desire to be a party to such advances. On the other hand, long-standing traditions and loyalties such as entering into formal marriage, specific church membership, or active participation in political parties are not easily adopted. When in doubt, this person readily looks to others for answers. Sharing knowledge and information is sensed as rewarding. In political matters, the trend seems to be to focus on what a certain group favors and disregard all other matters. Single-issue political voting is what frequently results.

THE POSTMODERN FAMILY

Postmodern family life centers on sharing, acceptance, and minimal old-fashioned discipline. The ideal number of offspring is usually believed to be two. We do not find the traditional hierarchical organization of the family with parents—and especially father—at the top. Paternal authoritarian rule is avoided if at all possible. Feministic values continue to be influential. When problems arise in the family they are discussed, friends may be consulted, and some mutual agreement is eventually reached by all family members. If the family problem is intractable, there is no great reluctance to seek professional assistance beyond the usual church contacts (ministers, etc.). Church attendance is not primary but is not ignored either, especially on certain occasions like holidays. Both husband and wife are likely to be employed outside the home. Parents encourage children to participate in various supervised group activities suitable for their age. Family vacations are highpoints of the year. Every family member has the right to recommend the kind of vacation taken, and the final choice is made by a family vote.

There is an interesting admixture here of both individual and collective motivations. One can see grounds for suggesting a selfish individualism in the postmodern person (a point we return to later), but also there is a seeming desire to encourage freedom and equality—as in the family structure. The light treatment given to discipline of offspring has been criticized as supposedly avoiding a parental duty. The so-called "old-time" practice of spanking children has been greatly reduced and even dropped altogether in many postmodern families, where it may be equated with brutality. Actually, the meaning of spanking is unclear. It can mean anything from a few pats on the posterior to an out-and-out physical beating. The former has *not* been found to damage a child for life (as some fear), and the latter is, of course, totally unacceptable. Expert commentary on the roots of authority suggests that "to be perceived accurately, authority must be located at the center of [i. e., within] the individual."[2] This turns our attention to the introspective perspective, where it is probably being hoped that the child will see the necessity of punishment for certain familial infractions.

I have called this introspectively framed personal sense of right and wrong the *authority within* (see Chapter 7). I believe a good thing about postmodern treatment of familial authority is that it encourages verbal exchange among the family members, which in turn has everyone evaluating and expressing reasoned preferences—hopefully, stipulating the grounds on which such decisions are to be made. Is there logic involved, or simply affective assessments and resultant selfishness taking place? This puts the emphasis on process and is not restricted to content as in blind rule following. Children seem to have an innate sense of equity that can be addressed. They readily place themselves in the other person's shoes (introspectively) to judge (i.e., process) what is fair (see Chapter 3 on evaluation in thought). The willingness in the postmodern family to discuss things, and to give everyone a chance to actually influence the course of household rules, is surely a good practice.

But the goal here should not be to defer all power in decision making to the child. There are certain decisions that only the parents make (e.g., bedtime hour, flu shots, nourishing diet). The child who is used to receiving equity in the family will readily understand that certain decisions must be left to adults. Such ground rules set limits on the child, who usually expects and wants such clarity in any case. Many therapists have noted that so-called "brats" are children who do not really know where they stand in the family scheme of things. They disrupt, nag, and have temper tantrums out of the resultant sense of identity frustration.

There are families who ignore the predication capacities of their children altogether, pressing rule-contents on them as non-negotiable inputs. Why do such parents think it wrong to let the child question and contribute to rules of the household? I think it is because of a misguided belief that the child's evaluative processes are irrelevant to the "mechanism of socialization."[3] There are admittedly times when children are to be seen and not heard, but there are other times when children are to be heard in using their evaluative capacities, both affectively and intellectually. This is practice, not shaping! Processing is what should be cultivated here, not the rote associations of one-sided, often hurriedly framed, and redundant contents. I think the postmodern family orientation is in the right direction, even as there are the dangers of being too loosely organized so that the child may develop brat-like behavior in an effort to intentionally test and define those limits that the parents have left dangling. This is actually a formal- and final-cause issue, a failure to provide the child with the "that" (pattern) "for the sake of which" behavior is subsequently carried out (via final causation). If we think of our children as predicators rather than mediators, we can more readily adopt this kind of family relationship.

There is another parent–child issue in postmodernism that can be traced in part to the participation of children in setting household rules. I refer here to the fact that children seem to be increasingly forced into adult-like concerns before their time (as portrayed today in so many television and movie plots where children know best, replacing father and mother know best). Of course, to be perfectly honest, no one can say that rapid maturation of children is necessarily a bad thing. We think of the genius at this point, someone like Mozart, who while still a child can perform skillfully at the level of a gifted adult. The skill (in Mozart's case, music) draws our admiration to the child in terms of adult standards. Of course, we can ask, "How many Mozarts are there?" Few children are of his ilk. Nevertheless, I am among the growing number of critics who would like to have "children be children" for a longer period than the rush of postmodernism appears to be making possible. Postmodern parents of the middle class tend increasingly to place their children in the best preschools available, hoping to "quick start" their intellectual development.

The next step is participation in group organizations, especially team sports. Both the intellectual and physical levels can then be hurried along and measured as to their progress in such organized activities. Many children enjoy team competition, but some do not, and I suspect that all of them would like to have a choice in the matter of playing or not playing after school on any particular day. But when the team has a schedule their lives become a schedule. They have adult-like responsibilities to show up, practice, and then compete. And the evaluations of their performance on the soccer or baseball field are rarely sugarcoated if the coach and the parents really want a winning team. The result is that children must adapt to an adult world earlier than was the case a few generations ago.

There are other examples of the nurtured maturity of postmodern children. Sexual education and drug education in the early school grades would qualify as such. I do not think anyone can deny that such instruction must necessarily force children in the direction of quasi-adulthood. This does not *necessarily* mean that it should be cancelled or delayed. But the quick-paced tempo of postmodernism makes such educational developments plausible and even desirable, particularly in social contexts where these adult-like activities are being modeled for the children on the television and elsewhere. The sexual revolution carried out by adults in the 1960s had much to do with this. In my "old-fashioned opinion," one of the more regrettable losses in all of this is that, with the great emphasis on the physical apparatus of man and woman taught in sex education classes, there appears to have been a concomitant loss of romantic sentimentalism in the "hearts" of postmodernists. With sexual partners changing from one to another, it is hard to see how an old-fashioned romanticism is possible. Idealization of the sexual partner as a beloved human being seems out of the picture. Lust has replaced love (see Chapter 6).

One even sees this loss manifested in some of the music that postmodern teenagers favor. Not too many of the rock (and other) songs in recent times remind us of the romantic love song of yesteryear, either in tempo or lyrics. Indeed, such sentimentalized music (derogatorily referred to as "elevator music") is considered horrendously unsophisticated and out of touch with the times. I realize that disagreement over songs between the old and the young is a generational conflict to be expected. But the present dispute strikes me as something more than this traditional disagreement. For example, sexual violence is becoming increasingly common in music, leading some critics to call it outright depravity.[4] The startling positions taken in certain adolescent "dances" today in which the rhythm is tied more to the ongoing mutual masturbation of the partners—aping copulation—than keeping in time with the music, is another example of this depravity.

I think that childhood should be a time of great sentimentality, of seeking make-believe happy endings and truthful love and commitment from significant adults. Sigmund Freud aside, lust is just not the driving force in prepubertal emotional ties that it is in later years. The sense of love nurtured early in life can be retained for many years as romanticism, but this requires intention, commitment, and the expectation of growing satisfaction in long-term bonding with another human being. I believe that the decline of manners and morals in America could be corrected to some extent through an increase in romantic sentimentalism in human relations. Of course, it is difficult to be sentimental about a family structure that has disintegrated, with father gone (or unknown) and mother struggling unsuccessfully to keep food on the table.

I doubt that sex education before puberty helps to develop sentimental attachments to future sex partners. If one defines physical sexual release as an expression of love, I fear that such love will be narcissistic and therefore readily succumb to boredom with the love partner. As noted previously, lust is a physical awareness relying on the mechanics of our body, but love is a telic awareness that relies on mental processing like imagination and idealization. Lust draws on raw feelings, whereas love draws on mood-instilling affections. For a complete and well-rounded love life, it would seem that both aspects must be given equal emphasis. I think that in this regard postmodernism is somewhat one-sided.

We can continue to expect marriage rates to be low and divorce rates to be high in the postmodern world as the biologically oriented lover repeatedly searches for a new partner. This lover's narcissistic satisfaction, derived from lust, must necessarily decline without the offsetting romance from love. I could, of course, discuss the developmental problems that arise in the case of divorce, the challenge of one-parent child-rearing, and so forth—problems that will be well known to adults in the postmodern era. We cannot say for certain, but it may be that rather than a "problem" such changes in the family structure simply herald a new pattern of adult living. There is no formula apparent in postmodern living that will change things for the better. For the marriage commitment to improve, I would suggest that we need a changed understanding of who we are as human beings. We are agents who must value the marital union and anticipate the problems that always arise when such life commitments are made. A good marriage is a work in progress and not a done deal. Divorce is a quick fix with seriously negative implications for the offspring of the union.

POSTMODERNISM AS INDIVIDUALISM OR COLLECTIVISM

In pointing out earlier that postmodernists are self-oriented and not suited to long-term interpersonal commitments with others, it might appear that they favor individualism. As Tocqueville noted, although an enlightened self-interest has great merit, an excessive emphasis on individualism drawn from the equality of democracy can slide into egoism that "sterilizes the seeds of every virtue."[5] I have touched on this issue of melding egoism with selfishness previously, in which I acknowledged that some but not all forms of individualism are prompted by selfish motives (see Chapter 5). We must also not forget that collectively oriented people can be selfish, too.

Recall from Bell's theory that the postindustrial stage was an "intellectual technology."[6] No longer is work dominated as in the industrial stage by the manufacturing of goods. The major goals of postindustrialism are the advance of knowledge and information in a service economy, which in turn demands heavy use of telecommunications and computers.[7] Bell then made it crystal clear that "Knowledge is a *social* product"[8] and "Information is by its nature collective."[9] People are now in the position of making ongoing contact with others. As a result, in the postindustrial stage, "persons have to learn how to live with one another."[10] Work becomes primarily a game between persons, in which we have the consumer and the service provider competing, negotiating prices, and conducting various contractual arrangements.[11] This heavy emphasis on interpersonal activity suggests a collective life orientation in the postmodern society. Indeed, Bell flatly said that "The postindustrial [postmodern] society . . . is . . . a 'communal' society in which the social unit is the community rather than the individual."[12] Industrialism favored individualism, but postindustrialism favors collectivism.

But what sort of collective is this? Is it to be pictured in terms of the Leviathan Assumption, as people being associatively manipulated into thinking collectively? Or, is it to be pictured as consistent with the predication model of the person, who might agree with several others in daily contact and thereby create what is then considered a collective (actually, a parallel individualism)? I think we can find an answer here in the fact that Bell said knowledge "is a function of the categories we use to establish relationships. . . ."[13] Recall from Chapter 3 that *category* has roots in the Greek word meaning "to predicate." This suggests to me that Bell is thinking of a predication form of human reasoning process—which frames or conceptualizes through such categories—rather than an association reasoning process. He recognized that a postmodern society is organized in large measure for the purpose of social control, but he did not view such control as if it were directing the fate of robots.[14] As I have noted previously, this was the model for influencing people in the industrial society in which the concept of the engineer was born. Engineers designed and directed things, whereas the unskilled labor force provided the muscle to carry out their plans.[15] But in the postindustrial society a shift to services is accomplished, including amenities such as health, education, recreation, and the arts.[16] Bell also noted that a major problem for the postindustrial society is finding an adequate number of trained professionals and technicians to carry out the research and services.[17]

One wonders what role the Internet might have on this question of collectivism versus individualism. Surely we must expect to see the Internet continuing to flourish in the postmodern era. I have heard leading authorities claim that the Internet will promote individualism because it has no directing power over those who convey their ideas on this communication marvel. There is great freedom here for individuals to speak their minds. On the other hand, I have heard other authorities make the reverse point based on the fact that there is so little emphasis placed on checking sources to validate what is being claimed on the Internet. It seems more likely that people will be taken in en masse by such unreliable claims as we find prominently in rumor and gossip. Such misinformation is tailor-made for adoption by the collective. So, what will the influence of the vaunted Internet be in the future? No one can say with certainty but, as I do not believe that people are as original or creative as they think they are, my bet is on collectivism getting a greater boost from the Internet's information than will individualism.

THE ROLE OF OPPOSITION IN THE POSTMODERN IMAGE OF HUMANITY

Bell failed to recognize the problem of retaining the industrial image of human beings as quasi-machines when the postmodern stage has opened up the possibility of understanding them as agents with free will. I have shown in Chapter 5 how deconstruction helps provide for an understanding of agency through oppositionality in human reasoning. This telic image of humans is not merely possible today, it is essential to the advancement of a higher civilization. Yet, after giving opposition a major role in their theorizing, the postmodernists failed to see its full potential. It is as if they had discovered the dialectical nature of thought through predication but interpreted this solely as a content rather than a process as well. Postmodernists equate the meanings of both opposite and non-opposite words therefore as contents, as a collection of letters with signals affixed to them.

Postmodernists fail to grasp the fact that predicational reasoning brings a dialectical process to bear in the creation of meaning. Words defining opposite meanings are not created separately and then joined, as in first naming left, then naming right, and finally joining the two as opposites. This may be how the association theorist sees things. It is said of some people that they cannot tell their left hand from their right hand. This is true in the sense of content but not true in the sense of process. These people know full well that their hands are opposite in relation to each other. They process such knowledge correctly. But on occasion they get mixed up on the content names assigned to the opposite ends of the relation.

We can have content words naming classes of opposition such as contradictions, contraries, and negations. We can refer to content words representing specific oppositions like *tall* versus *short, hot* versus *cold,* and *rich* versus *poor.* But the source of oppositionality here is provided by a process stipulating a unique relation between two items. The word meanings listed (e.g., contradiction, negation, cold, tall, poor) do not create the opposition.

This formal-cause patterning is fashioned by the human reasoner's ongoing thought process. Contrast this with the supposed process of association, which also patterns, but in a demonstrative, efficient-cause manner. We might be said to learn salt and pepper associatively because these are condiments that are presented in tandem on meal tables. Mention salt and one thinks of pepper and vice versa. It is all a matter of associating one item with another. Learning tall versus short is no different.

I reject this association explanation. It is from the intrinsic opposition of human reasoning that we find a rationale for human agency. Where the postmodernist theorists have sold the human image short is in their claim that meaningful conversations are carried on solely by texts, and the author of such meaningful discourse is superfluous or irrelevant.[18] But texts never reason oppositionally, as people always do! In reifying language and throwing away the human element in discourse they have made it impossible for me to theorize about human reason introspectively. I am left with extraspection and thus cannot refer to the thinking human being from the truly personal perspective of the I, me, or myself. This is where intention, purpose, and choice are born, thanks to the oppositionality that I no longer can use in my explanations.

I noted in Chapter 2 that conditioning theorizing in behaviorism, which is now essentially being replicated by computer modelers, ignores the proven fact that, to shape (manipulate, condition, etc.) the behavior of a person, two preliminary requirements are necessary:[19] (a) The person under shaping must know what is taking place in the procedure, and (b) even when aware of the procedure, the person must be willing to comply with what is called for (see Chapter 2). As dialectical reasoners, people can and do "just say no" to what is being implied by experimental instructions.[20] I have experienced this at first hand. This ability is without question a reflection of teleology in the thinking and resultant behavior of human beings. It has been said in a humorous vein that this negation by an experimental subject leads to a reversal in the shaping because each time the subject ignores the instructions, the experimenter is noticeably redder in the face. The shaper has become the shaped (or vice versa).

THE CHALLENGE OF RELATIVISM

It seems to me that a continuing problem for the future in psychological study and explanation is *relativism*, both of a cultural and a personal variety (see Chapters 3 and 7, where this concept was visited previously). This is a long-standing problem—first confronted in ancient discussions of morality—but it seems to have mushroomed in recent decades, propelled by the influence of existential philosophies (as presented in Chapter 4). Never before have so many people been awakened to the realization that there are no certain truths that stand without the aid of biasing assumptions framing them in the first place ("Perception is everything"). Universal beliefs are difficult or impossible to identify. In my own exhortation to recast human beings as intentional organisms, I too am advancing an image of humanity in which the person is said always to be reasoning relative to the meanings of framing predications that influence the meaning extensions to follow in what might be seen in an arbitrary manner.[21] Much of our mental activity is essentially analogical, relying on what are formally called *metaphors, similes, allegories,* and so on. We use what we already know to learn more, as for example, "A brain is a sponge," "Time is money," "That stuff is as hard as a rock," and "He is like a flat tire."

We have seen in previous chapters that personal evaluation is an essential aspect of choice. Associationists do not assign personal responsibility to people under shaping, except possibly on the assumption that people will select certain rewards or reinforcers over others because they taste better, provide warmth in the cold, stimulate their emotions or calm them down, and so on. Such evaluations are more like physical reactions than actual judgments. It is quite difficult—probably impossible—to capture judgment in material- and efficient-cause terms. According to associationistic doctrine, a person's favorite choice is one that has been shaped into existence in the first place. As such, it is not really a choice because the alternative possibility is not open to selection.

Over the years I have observed two negative reactions to the awareness of relativism in human affairs. The first is the depression and demoralization that follows when people realize that relativism robs them of the assurance that they either have or can obtain absolutely certain truth. This is when we may hear defeatist statements like "Nothing can be counted on," "Every belief can be proven either true or false," "An excuse can be found for doing anything wrong," "There is no point in searching for justice," and so on. The second harmful outcome of realizing that relativism is inevitable is that it tends to weaken scholarship and the desire to excel. Although relativism has the external appearance of mental sophistication, actually it invariably detracts from the postmodern ideals of seeking the highest levels of knowledge and information. Relativism can be anti-intellectual.

I mean by this that those postmodernists who embrace an unyielding relativism sometimes claim that all scholarship is equal in value. Or, put another way, it is impossible to discern excellent from mediocre scholarship. If a scholar takes her or his subject matter too seriously and claims that "My views on this matter are the only ones that are true," this might be interpreted as akin to a totalitarian act of suppression, an effort to keep others from being recognized or appreciated.[22] As a result of this attitude, in some postmodern circles a scholar's work is considered a personal indulgence, an "ego trip" or "doing your own thing," which has no more legitimacy or contribution to make to knowledge than any other scholar's work regardless of how menial the latter may be. The pursuit of excellence and the distinction that results is viewed as a selfish display to be discouraged when it arises.

This anti-intellectual attitude detracts from the subject matter under study as well as the depth of scholarship pursued in creating it. The mentality of "one size fits all" now extends to "one idea equals all." I do not really see this as a prevalent attitude in science, where recognition is still given to scientists for their uniquely creative ideas and discoveries. I have tended to see this lowering of ideals occurring in the primary and secondary school years, when it has become politically incorrect to compete or excel in the classroom. Parents and even the children may want to excel, but the academic atmosphere discourages—or at least does not pointedly encourage—such efforts. This is not instruction in humility but an outright effort to minimize difference founded on the relativistic argument that all scholarship is equal when considered in relation to the framing assumptions in which it is grounded. Hence, on the basis of some culture–free, universal judgment, it cannot be greater or lesser than other scholarship (an argument the German apologists used in framing cultural relativism to begin with; see Chapter 7).

There are certain concepts that go under other names but can be seen as relating to relativism. Take the concept of *diversity*, for example. It refers to collectives, but with a relativistic intonation regarding the fact that different beliefs exist in diverse groups that, when combined into a single culture, enrich the lives of everyone. Presumably, there is no higher or lower level of culture in the mix. On the basis of personal experience, I have come to the conclusion that it would be nice if diversity were limited to relations between individuals. We meet another person and come to know him or her over time and the diverse predications that he or she affirms thanks to a certain cultural perspective differing from our own (so-called *multiculturalism*). This person also learns about such things from our biasing perspective. Diversity is working in a situation like this.

Unfortunately, too often because of eventual social concerns and policies, we do not relate with individuals as much as we do with collectives. This happens because, in the eyes of many—especially group leaders—to have a small number of people from another cultural milieu living in one's community does not constitute a truly diverse cultural unit. It is considered tokenism. We need a suitable number to make such minorities feel comfortable and even welcome in the established community. And before individuals on both sides of the cultural identities know it, we have other collective issues swamping the diversity such as relative grade school practices, voting procedures, or various environmental and residential concerns. Not that such matters are unimportant, but it seems that the group leaders are so ready to do things for their constituency that they—often unintentionally—create "sides" in society rather than a mixed diversity. The issue of minority status is so huge that it apparently cannot be easily reduced to the very human "one-on-one" kind of friendship that a few of us have been lucky enough to experience in the American culture.

The question that is taking form in all of this is, "What do we do, if anything, to resolve the fact that our belief system is relative to the assumptions we draw individually (*relativism of process*) or take collectively from our cultures (*relativism of content*)?" It seems to me that human beings have the capacity to understand and adapt to relativism without losing confidence in their convictions. I have touched briefly on this issue in Chapter 7 and now return to it because it is so important to our final understanding of human nature.

WHAT IS THE BASIC FUNCTION OF RELATIVISM?

The dispirited person who thinks that relativism must be somehow obviated at every turn is proceeding on an erroneous assumption. This person assumes that meaning can ultimately find its way to unipolarity in an unquestionable truth and that this truth has no necessary tie to its opposite meaning in the form of a contradiction, contrariety, or negation. Relativism stands against this simplistic view of reasoning, which ever searches for its opposite meaning to enrich understanding. I think the need to erase relativism stems from the fact that we learn in life experiences that some beliefs are truer than others. We can think of a hierarchy of truth in which the contradictions are more obvious at the lower than the higher levels of abstract thought. It follows therefore that we expect the contradictions to disappear entirely at the apex of this meaningful array.

Unfortunately for such reasoners, this eclipsing of opposition in meaning never occurs. About the only satisfaction for those seeking the universal in human reasoning takes place in processing not in content. As was pointed to in Chapter 3, there is *no* transcending certainty of a universal nature due to the relativism of cultural contents (which always imply their opposite meanings), but there *is* a common or universal *process* at work to make things happen in the same way. Universality is found in the fact that all people process thinking alike.

Of what value is this universal process of human reasoning if it does not provide us with absolute, singular certainty in meaning? I do not want to begin speculating on the role of natural selection in human evolution, but it does seem to me that if humanity had settled on one set of beliefs for all time it would have dropped dialectical reasoning altogether and descended into an unyielding unconsciousness due to the resultant unipredications of all thought. Association theorists never confront this issue because they describe people as unipredicators in any case. However, if we believe people to be predicators with a transcendental capacity to change things around through dialectical reasoning, we surely do not want them to forego this magnificent capacity to consciously generate alternatives, bring various injustices to light, and stretch the very nature of reality to conceptualize what is supposedly not there for conceptualization.

There are obviously both positive and negative implications of relativism in thought. As I have noted previously, an occasional or limited unconsciousness would not necessarily be a bad thing. Something would be held universally true, and discussion or debate would be closed. No one would even think to question the belief that we all assume to be absolutely true. We can all nod in satisfaction over how nice it is to have everyone agree with our beliefs, which could then be acted on to the benefit of all. Elevated concepts like truth, justice, and equality now spring to mind as examples of such universal beliefs. But what of other beliefs like morality, responsibility, guilt, and punishment? Here the chances of total agreement among people are less likely—making them more relative than other meaningful concepts. One suspects that, even in a heavenly existence, such meanings would be far less likely to achieve universal agreement. If such uniformity (or conformity) in belief were possible, would it not be a horrendously boring existence, not to mention dangerously rigid, in outlook? Could a deity want to destroy the relativistic reasoning capacities like this, particularly because they are so often the source of characterological improvement? In fact, the very foundation of a moral intellect would seem to issue from a dialectically generated relativism, magnificently exhibited by Hamlet in his famous soliloquy as he wrestled with his authority within.

THE DEFEAT OF BLIND RELATIVISM

I think it is wise to believe that, although our thought contents may be relative to their framing meanings—as suggested by the predication model—the process by which we reason per se is not relative to anything. It is what it is. Additionally, as we dispute the precedent contents framing our ideas we invariably find our line of thought becoming increasingly abstract. For example, a dispute over the right a woman has to choose an abortion as opposed to the fetus's right to life necessarily relies on highly abstract universals such as the meaning of life or the nature of human rights (see Chapter 7). Depending on the position taken at this abstract level, which gives precedent meaning to the issues being targeted below, one can virtually predict the course of the argument to follow.

As a predication theorist, I think it would be constructive if the disputants could take the introspective perspective of their opponents and thereby transcendentally examine the abstract assumptions being affirmed by them, from their point of view ("Is this what you think?"). This helps prevent the frequent tendency to argue without actually trying to understand specific principles guiding the disagreement, which results in irrelevancies or a string of ad hominems. Once a clear understanding of the abstract principles (universals, etc.) has taken place on both sides, I think that it would be easier to achieve either a solution or a sense of tolerance. We come to realize that, in the final analysis, people are all identical in the process by which they accomplish reasoning. Everyone must take a position (i.e., predicate) to reason to some end. If the person has no precedent, then it is likely that she or he is merely mouthing what others have said. The precedent is "What I have heard others say." People naturally differ in what the predicational process affirms as its framing assumption. Knowing our assumptions helps us to grasp their influences on our line of thought, as well as to appreciate that we could just as well be on either side of the point at issue. Neither we nor our opponents have certainty, although either of us may have stronger or weaker arguments in the debate.

If we make the framing meanings clear, we are no longer under a blind shaping to believe that we have the only belief possible. Our view may be defensible and strike us as certain, but we know that such convictions flow from the framing assumptions that we take on to begin with. It is probably true that everything begins in a sense of faith or conviction. Moreover, we appreciate that we can willfully negate these assumptions. We are not shaped into how this transcending evaluation unfolds. Should we go on with our present position, or move it toward the opponent's view a little or a lot? Possibly there are alternative assumptions on the matter under dispute. At this point, we have defeated blind relativism! We are in charge, responsible for what will take place next. We can select from a number of possible alternatives that our new position allows us to consider. Dialectical reasoning is the main vehicle for such transpredication, and consciousness is our reward. What frequently passes as cultural relativism is really a kind of personal relativism in which one senses that her or his position hangs by an assumptive thread, one that could snap in half to turn things around in the blink of an eye. As already mentioned, when such possible alternatives become clear, a sense of tolerance is much easier to adopt. We can tolerate disagreements with others and even see how we might think as they do, if we have a good understanding of how capable of change our mental processing is.

Finally, there are disagreements within a culture that cannot be blamed on cultural relativism at all. Indeed, many individuals who formerly held one view now hold its opposite. It was not culture that shifted meanings here, but the thinker, who dialectically reversed the grounds involved. At least, this is how the predication theorist views things. Associationists would not concur because every belief and action is always traceable to some kind of external manipulation.

I do not mean to suggest that dialectical reasoning necessarily brings about an adaptable intelligence, ready to concede to other viewpoints without question or resistance. Dialectical strategies can be used to manipulate and obfuscate as well as to do the right thing. The early dialecticians of Western Europe were the Sophists, well known for their ability to twist a person's words into undesirable accusations, such as in the humorous line "Have you stopped beating your wife?" Either a "yes" or a "no" puts the husband in a bad light.[23] But it is also true that dialectical reasoning has much to teach us if we are only willing to take it seriously rather than viewing it as a source of sophistical insincerity and error.

THE IMPERFECT HUMAN IMAGE

We all realize that we are not perfect organisms, and we never will be perfect. But if we know our true natures, the limits and possibilities we have as human beings, it is preferable to pretending that we are well-tuned robots. Mechanism neither directly suggests nor accounts for the many human attributes that we have covered in this volume. Free will is probably the most important of these. Free will does not mean that we can do anything we intend to do, although many such intentional goals can be brought to the light of day through personal will power—that is, exerting the effort to achieve some desired end. Another important insight is that relativism in reasoning does not equal nihilism or provide us with an excuse for avoiding the responsibility to think and decide. Because thought is intrinsically evaluative it cannot be carried on without leveling various judgments of what is being conceptualized. Biased reasoning is not the sole province of bigots. Everyone is subject to a harmfully biasing influence from time to time, thanks to one-sided judgment. Individual humans make mistakes and are clearly selfish on occasion. Human groups make comparable mistakes and are also selfish at times.

But we humans have the capacity to improve. In taking an honest look at who we *are* there invariably develops an implied who we *ought* to be. This comes from the dialectical beginnings of our thought process and the setting of goals for the sake of which we behave. For any negative attribution made of our behavior we can "spin" a dialectically generated positive attribution, falling back on the relativism of thought. This insincere tactic can keep us from actually looking into our darker side and thereby prevent any improvement from taking place. We thus "hustle" our way through life instead of maturing. I have no list of suggestions to improve the human image. Anyone can make up such lists. They have probably been drafted millions of times. What I am hoping is that human beings will finally reject the mechanistic, robotic, non-intentional characterizations of the process by which their minds work. Surely the brain, or large portions of it, relies on a biological mechanism of some sort. But when we speak of the mind, of thought, of meaningful choices that humans select, we have left mechanism behind and require a new model. This new image of humanity I can and do offer and have tried to present in covering the many topics of this book.

CONCLUDING COMMENT

In this book I have strolled and stumbled along many diverse and interlocking pathways of understanding having to do with the human image. But all of the directions taken have led me back to one and the same endpoint—teleology! A critic can rightfully charge that this was foreordained because I had intentionally predicated this endpoint from the outset—often actually stating what I was after. There is no doubt that I had this agenda in mind at all times. I obviously cannot deny such assessments of my work but am delighted by the predicational analysis used to level it (i.e., assigning agency to me). No one shaped me to do what I did. I obviously wanted to encourage analyses and empirical investigations of human beings as dialectical reasoners, who sometimes refuse to take what is offered by biology and past environmental influences in favor of redirecting things oppositionally to suit themselves. I think that significant credit should be given to the fact that teleology made so much sense. The mechanistic accounts did not even come close to providing meaningful insights like this. They were narrow, simplistic, and repetitive in explanatory power.

People care about the topics covered in this volume for they know themselves to be as depicted—agents with meanings and intentions orienting them to ongoing life. There is ample evidence proving the final-cause actions of human beings, assuming the scientist who confronts these data is open to such a theoretical possibility.[24] Unfortunately, there are psychologists who persist in using efficient-cause terminology as a form of pseudoteleology, even if the evidence favors a genuine final-cause account.[25] I believe that such one-sided efforts are mere skirmishes in the continuing decline of behavioristic explanations.

As I have noted several times, it is becoming increasingly clear that modern civilization is finding various character problems dramatically increasing. Whatever one traces this to—drugs, divorce, poverty, poor education, lack of interesting work, prejudices of one sort or another, DNA, and so on—the important fact is that there is serious concern today over rapidly deteriorating character structures. Because we humans are still being pictured as efficiently caused machines by a large majority of psychologists, it remains easy to leave the inwardly directing person out of things and assign complete responsibility to hereditary and environmental forces. But such nontelic approaches have failed to capture what is really taking place. And clearly, most psychologists—especially the mechanists—have not yet grasped the implications for the human image that computers, with their programmer's continued assistance, have for the changing human image in postmodern times. Teleology has arrived and it is here to stay. What I find amusing is that the mechanistic psychologists, rushing to paint their teleologically oriented colleagues as hysterical—probably right-wing—fanatics, reveal in such denigration what can only be called a highly motivated, intentional effort to repress them. The mechanists are unquestionably acting "for the sake of" planned strategies as was said of me in foreordaining the ubiquitous presence of teleology in my investigations. When the opponent makes our case in this fashion, how can we teleologists be worried about the future? We can't help but eventually win this dispute over human nature, can we? Well, maybe to speak of *winning* is too strong a word. But surely we should find our characterization of the human condition gaining support, for as has been demonstrated in the present volume, there is no known place of relevance to human experience, knowledge, or activity that is without room for some type of teleological understanding and explanation.

AFTERWORD

I completed the manuscript for this book before the horrendous destruction of the Twin Towers in New York City; the Pentagon building near Washington, DC; and the plane crash in Pennsylvania had taken place on September 11, 2001. An event this shocking may be expected to have a lasting effect on American citizens, over and above the precautions taken to prevent or minimize such terrorist attacks in the future. There may well be significant personal changes taking place at this time. For example, it has been reported that many Americans have now opted to spend more time with their families than previously. There is a kind of slowing down by some people, who are now aware of how suddenly their lives may be snuffed out. Obviously, such changes in lifestyle might well influence what I have had to say about the postmodern personality and family. Only time will tell. Even if such noticeable changes do come about, I am certain that my basic contention concerning teleology will not be adversely affected. In the future, it will not be robots rebuilding and revitalizing the United States of America. It will be human beings, with determination and dreams, choosing goals and seeing to it through hard work that they are realized as intended. This is the humanity that we must understand and explain during the postmodern era.

NOTES

CHAPTER 1: BEING HUMAN
COLLECTIVELY AND INDIVIDUALLY

1. Rychlak, J. F. (1994). *Logical learning theory: A human teleology and its empirical support*. Lincoln: University of Nebraska Press. See p. 319 on process: "A discernible, repeatable course of action on the basis of which some item(s) under description are sequentially patterned." See p. 311 on content: "An ingredient that is produced, conveyed, or otherwise employed by a process."

2. Aristotle. (1952). *Physics*. In R. M. Hutchins (Ed.), *Great books of the western world* (Vol. 8, pp. 259–355). Chicago: Encyclopaedia Britannica.

3. Whitehead, A. N., & Russell, B. (1963). *Principia mathematica* (3 vols., 2nd ed.). Cambridge: The University Press.

4. Hume, D. (1952). *An enquiry concerning human understanding*. In R. M. Hutchins (Ed.), *Great books of the western world* (Vol. 35, pp. 447–509). Chicago: Encyclopaedia Britannica. (Original work published 1758). p. 467.

5. Aristotle. (1952). Metaphysics. In R. M. Hutchins (Ed.), *Great books of the western world* (Vol. 8, pp. 495–626). Chicago: Encyclopaedia Britannica. p. 565.

6. Rogers, C. R. (1963). Learning to be free. In S. M. Farber & R. H. L. Wilson (Eds.), *Control of the mind: Conflict and creativity* (Vol. 2, pp. 268–288). New York: McGraw Hill. pp. 271–272.

7. Skinner, B. F. (1974). *About behaviorism*. New York: Alfred A. Knopf. p. 168.

8. Hobbes, T. (1952). *Leviathan*. In R. M. Hutchins (Ed.), *Great books of the western world* (Vol. 23, pp. 49–283). Chicago: Encyclopaedia Britannica. (Original work published 1651)

9. For a critical analysis of Bandura's "reciprocal interaction" on this point see: Rychlak, J. F. (1981). *Introduction to personality and psychotherapy: A theory-construction approach* (2nd ed.). Boston: Houghton Mifflin. pp. 778–784.

10. Rychlak, J. F. (1992). Morality in a mediating mechanism? A logical learning theorist looks at social constructionism. In D. N. Robinson (Ed.), *Social discourse and moral judgment* (pp. 43–60). San Diego, CA: Academic Press.

11. Hobbes (1952). Hobbes' reliance on efficient causation to describe human actions in mechanical fashion is to be seen in Chapters XI and XII, pp. 77–79. Invariably, in British philosophy the collective process is understood extraspectively in terms of efficient causation.

12. James, W. (1943). *Pragmatism*. New York: The World Book. pp. 202–203. (Original work published 1907)

13. For an in-depth explanation of how predication functions from birth, as well as evidence for infant predications see Rychlak (1994), pp. 48–49.

14. Horowitz, D. (1997). *Radical son: A generational odyssey*. New York: Free Press.

15. Horowitz, p. 205.

16. Horowitz, p. 205.

17. Horowitz, p. 257.

18. Horowitz, p. 282.

19. Horowitz, p. 347.

20. Horowitz, p. 347.

21. Aristotle. (1952). *Topics*. In R. M. Hutchins (Ed.), *Great books of the western world* (Vol. 8, pp. 139–223). Chicago: Encyclopaedia Britannica. p. 143.

22. I am referring to the law of contradiction or law of non-contradiction here, which holds that A is not non-A. This law underwrites demonstrative reasoning, and is fundamental to the binary logic of today's computers. I will have more to say about it when we consider the computer model in Chapter 4.

23. Rychlak (1994), Chapter 7. Presents evidence that human beings continually evaluate experience affectively.

CHAPTER 2: PERSONALITY THEORIZING AS DESCRIBING INDIVIDUALS OR COLLECTIVES

1. McGuire, W. (Ed.). (1974). *The Freud/Jung letters: The correspondence between Sigmund Freud and C. G. Jung*. Bollingen Series XCIV. Princeton, NJ: Princeton University Press. pp. 115–116.

2. Cameron, N. S., & Rychlak, J. F. (1985). *Personality development and psychopathology: A dynamic approach* (2nd ed.). Boston: Houghton Mifflin. See Chapter 4 for an in-depth analysis of Freud's conflict with the medical establishment and his strategy to resolve the problem by appearing to be a drive reduction theorist when he was actually nothing of the sort.

3. Cameron & Rychlak, p. 34.

4. Freud, S. (1953). *Three essays on the theory of sexuality*. In J. Strachey (Ed.), *The standard edition of the complete psychological works of Sigmund Freud* (Vol. 7, pp. 125–243). London: Hogarth Press. (Original work published 1905). p. 235.

5. Freud, S. (1962). The claims of psycho-analysis to scientific interest. In J. Strachey (Ed.), *The standard edition of the complete psychological works of Sigmund Freud* (Vol. 13, pp. 163–190). London: Hogarth Press. (Original work published 1913). p. 184.

6. McGuire (1974), p. 488.

7. Adler, A. (1958). *What life should mean to you*. New York: Capricorn. p. 59.

8. Ansbacher, H. L., & Ansbacher, R. R. (Eds.). (1956). *The individual psychology of Alfred Adler*. New York: Basic Books. p. 57.

9. Ansbacher, H. L., & Ansbacher, R. R. (Eds.). (1964). *Superiority and social interest*. Evanston, IL: Northwestern University Press. pp. 34–35.

10. Adler, A. (1964). *Social interest: A challenge to mankind*. New York: Capricorn. p. 285.

11. Ansbacher & Ansbacher (1956), p. 177.

12. Jung, C. G. (1956). *Symbols of transformation*. In H. Read, M. Fordham, & G. Adler (Eds.), *The collected works of C. G. Jung* (Vol. 5). Bollingen Series. New York: Pantheon. p. 58.

13. Jung, C. G. (1958). *Psychology and religion: West and east*. In H. Read, M. Fordham, & G. Adler (Eds.), *The collected works of C. G. Jung* (Vol. 11). Bollingen Series. New York: Pantheon. p. 258.

14. Jung, C. G. (1946). *Psychological types*. London: Kegan Paul, Trench, & Trubner. New York: Harcourt Brace. p. 377.

15. Jung, C. G. (1961). *Freud and psychoanalysis*. In H. Read, M. Fordham, & G. Adler (Eds.), *The collected works of C. G. Jung* (Vol. 4). Bollingen Series. New York: Pantheon. p. 11.

16. Jung, C. G. (1954). *The practice of psychotherapy*. In H. Read, M. Fordham, & G. Adler (Eds.), *The collected works of C. G. Jung* (Vol. 16). Bollingen Series. New York: Pantheon. p. 6.

17. Jung, C. G. (1959). *The archetypes and the collective unconscious*. In H. Read, M. Fordham, & G. Adler (Eds.), *The collected works of C. G. Jung* (Vol. 9I). Bollingen Series. New York: Pantheon. p. 349.

18. Jung (1961), p. 337.

19. Watson, J. B. (1924). *Behaviorism*. New York: Norton. p. 216. Italics in original.

20. Watson, J. B. (1913). Psychology as the behaviorist views it. *Psychological Review*, 20, 158–177.

21. Meyer, M. F. (1922). *Psychology of the other-one: An introductory textbook of psychology* (rev. ed.). Columbus: Missouri Books. See also: O'Donnell, J. M. (1985). *The origins of behaviorism: American psychology, 1870–1920*. New York: New York University Press. p. 72.

22. Hull, C. L. (1952). *A behavior system*. New Haven, CT: Yale University Press.

23. Skinner, B. F. (1974). *About behaviorism*. New York: Knopf. p. 168.

24. For core research relating to the findings on awareness and willingness to cooperate in conditioning experiments, see: Brewer, W. F. (1974). There is no convincing evidence for operant or classical conditioning in adult humans. In W. B. Weimer & D. S. Palermo (Eds.), *Cognition and the symbolic processes* (pp. 1–42). Hillsdale, NJ: Erlbaum; De Nike, L. D. (1964). The temporal relationship between awareness and performance in verbal conditioning. *Journal of Experimental Psychology*, 68, 521–529; Dulany, D. E., Jr. (1961). Hypotheses and habits in verbal operant conditioning. *Journal of Abnormal and Social Psychology*, 63, 251–263; Page, M. M. (1969). Social psychology of a classical conditioning of attitudes experiment. *Journal of Personality and Social Psychology*, 11, 177–186.

25. Mackintosh, N. J. (1983). *Conditioning and associative learning*. New York: Oxford University Press. See p. 20, where conditioning is defined as "the process whereby when an animal is exposed to certain relationships between events, representations of those events are formed, and associations established between them, with the consequence that the animal's behaviour changes in certain specifiable ways." This definition confounds the experimental procedure (method) with the construct tested (theory). Forming representations before associations are established could easily involve predication. What is more, the representations would frame meanings that make the so-called associations superfluous.

26. Rogers, C. R. (1951). *Client-centered therapy*. Boston: Houghton Mifflin.

27. Rogers, C. R. (1959). A theory of therapy, personality, and interpersonal relationships, as developed in the client-centered framework. In S. Koch (Ed.), *Psychology: A study of a science. Study I. Conceptual and systematic. Vol. 3: Formulation of the person and social context*. New York: McGraw-Hill. pp 184–256, p. 191.

28. Rogers (1951), pp. 484–486.

29. Rogers (1951), p. 522. Italics in original.

30. Rogers (1959), p. 200.

31. Rogers (1959), p. 200.

32. Rogers (1951), p. 493.

33. Rogers, C. R. (1969). *Freedom to learn*. Columbus, OH: Charles Merrill. p. 73. Italics in original.

34. Rogers, C. R. (1970). *Carl Rogers on encounter groups*. New York: Harper & Row. p. 44.

35. One good example of such writings concerning changes taking place in science is: Prigogine, I., & Stengers, I. (1984). *Order out of chaos: Man's new dialogue with nature*. New York: Bantam Books. See p. 73 on formal causation as primary.

CHAPTER 3: COLLECTIVE THEORIZING
IN THE THIRD MILLENNIUM

1. Moynihan, D. P. (1996). *Miles to go: A personal history of social policy*. Cambridge, MA: Harvard University Press. p. 62.

2. Gingrich, N. (1995). *To renew America*. New York: Harper Collins. pp. 7, 52–53.

3. Bell, D. (1973). *The coming of post-industrial society: A venture in social forecasting*. New York: Basic Books. p. 76.

4. Bell, p. 36.

5. Bell, p. xxiv.

6. Bell, p. 20.

7. Bell, p. xii.

8. Bell, p. 116.

9. Bell, p. 394.

10. Bell, p. 29.

11. Bell, p. xvi.

12. Bell, p. 146.

13. Bell, p. 127.

14. Bell, p. 128.

15. Bell, p. xviii.

16. Bell, p. 159.

17. Bell, p. 364.

18. I am taking some liberty here. Bell does not specifically state the litigious aspect, but I do think it is implied in what he does say. See especially p. 364.

19. Bell (1973), p. 9.

20. Yartz, F. J. (1984). *Ancient Greek philosophy: Sourcebook and perspectives*. Jefferson, NC: McFarland. p. 147.

21. Beginning about here I took some material on postmodernism and social constructionism from chapter 9 of an earlier book of mine: Rychlak, J. F. (1997). *In defense of human consciousness*. Washington, DC: American Psychological Association. Copyright © 1997 by the American Psychological Association. Adapted by permission of the publisher.

22. Culler, J. (1982). *On deconstruction: Theory and criticism after structuralism*. Ithaca, NY: Cornell University Press. p. 18.

23. Culler, p. 19.

24. Rosenau, P. M. (1992). *Post-modernism and the social sciences: Insights, inroads, and intrusions*. Princeton, NJ: Princeton University Press. p. 29.

25. Palmer, R. E. (1969). *Hermeneutics: Interpretation theory in Schleiermacher, Dilthey, Heidegger, and Gadamer*. Evanston, IL: Northwestern University Press. p. 34.
26. Palmer, p. 24.
27. Palmer, pp. 17–18.
28. Derrida, J. (1981). *Positions* (A. Bass, Trans.). Chicago: University of Chicago Press.
29. Rosenau (1992), p. xiv.
30. Culler (1982), p. 86.
31. Derrida (1981), p. 41.
32. Derrida (1981), p. 116.
33. Bauman, Z. (1990). Philosophical affinities of postmodern sociology. *The Sociological Review*, 38, 411–444. p. 427.
34. Gergen, K. J. (1989). Social psychology and the wrong revolution. *European Journal of Social Psychology*, 19, 463–484. p. 479.
35. Gergen, p. 472.
36. Harré, R. (1987). Enlarging the paradigm. *New Ideas in Psychology*, 5, 3–12. pp. 4–5.
37. Sampson, E. E. (1993). *Celebrating the other: A dialogic account of human behavior*. San Francisco: Westview. p. 4.
38. Gergen, K. J. (1991). *The saturated self: Dilemmas of identity in contemporary life*. New York: Basic Books. p. 157.
39. Berger, P. L. (1963). *Invitation to sociology: A humanistic perspective*. New York: Doubleday Anchor.
40. Berger, P. L., & Luckmann, T. (1966). *The social construction of reality: A treatise in the sociology of knowledge*. New York: Doubleday Anchor. p. 106. Italics in original.
41. Berger & Luckmann, pp. 60–61.
42. Berger & Luckmann, p. 83.
43. Berger (1963), p. 133.
44. Berger (1963), p. 142.
45. Stace, W. T. (1955). *The philosophy of Hegel*. New York: Dover. p. 22.
46. Hegel, G. W. F. (1952a). *The philosophy of right*. In R. M. Hutchins (Ed.), *Great books of the western world* (Vol. 46, pp. 1–150). Chicago: Encyclopaedia Britannica. (Original work published 1821). p. 53.
47. Hegel, G. W. F. (1952b). *The philosophy of history*. In R. M. Hutchins (Ed.), *Great books of the western world* (Vol. 46, pp. 151–369). Chicago: Encyclopaedia Britannica. (Original work published 1857). p. 182.
48. Hegel (1952b), p. 190. Italics in original.
49. Marx, K. (1952a). *Capital*. In R. M. Hutchins (Ed.), *Great books of the western world* (Vol. 50, pp. 1–393). Chicago: Encyclopaedia Britannica. (Original work published 1867). See especially p. 372.
50. Marx, K. (1952b). *Manifesto of the communist party*. In R. M. Hutchins (Ed.), *Great books of the western world* (Vol. 50, pp. 413–434). Chicago: Encyclopaedia Britannica. (Original work published 1847). p. 424.
51. Marx (1952b), p. 428.
52. Marx (1952b), p. 423.
53. Marx (1952b), p. 426.
54. Wilson, E. (1940). *To the Finland station: A study in the writing of history*. Garden City, NY: Doubleday. p. 188.

55. Hook, S. (1962). *From Hegel to Marx*. Ann Arbor: University of Michigan Press.

56. Marx (1952b), p. 423.

57. Chaplin, J. P. (1985). *Dictionary of psychology* (2nd rev. ed.). New York: Bantam Doubleday Dell. p. 113.

58. McLuhan, M. (1962). *The Gutenberg galaxy: The making of typographic man*. New York: Signet. p. 28.

59. Lonner, W. J., & Adamopoulos, J. (1997). Culture as antecedent to behavior. In J. W. Berry, Y. H. Poortinga, & J. Pandey (Eds.), *Handbook of cross-cultural psychology* (2nd ed., pp. 43–83). Boston: Allyn and Bacon. See p. 61, where it is claimed that culture can shape virtually any aspect of human behavior.

60. Rychlak, J. F. (1994). *Logical learning theory: A human teleology and its empirical support*. Lincoln: University of Nebraska Press.

CHAPTER 4: A MISSING LINK IN THE HUMAN IMAGE

1. Turing, A. (1950). Computing machinery and intelligence. *Mind, 59*, 433–460.

2. Weizenbaum, J. (1976). *Computer power and human reason: From judgment to calculation*. San Francisco: Freeman.

3. Shannon, C. E., & Weaver, W. (Eds.). (1962). *The mathematical theory of communication*. Urbana: University of Illinois Press.

4. Shannon, C. E. (1938). A symbolic analysis of relay and switching circuits. Master's thesis, Massachusetts Institute of Technology; published in *Transactions of the American Institute of Electrical Engineers 57*. pp. 1–11.

5. McCulloch, W., & Pitts, W. (1943). A logical calculus of the ideas immanent in nervous activity. *Bulletin of Mathematical Biophysics, 5*, 115–133.

6. For a more detailed analysis of Boolean logic as it relates to computer programming, see: Rychlak, J. F. (1997). *In defense of human consciousness*. Washington, DC: American Psychological Association. pp. 195–198.

7. Rosenblueth, A., Wiener, N., & Bigelow, J. (1943). Behavior, teleology, and purpose. *Philosophy of Science, 10*, 18–24. First to advance this argument for agency in a machine via negative feedback.

8. Rosenblueth et al., p. 19.

9. Rosenblueth et al., p. 19.

10. Rosenblueth et al., p. 18.

11. Rosenblueth et al., p. 24.

12. Skinner, B. F. (1957). *Verbal behavior*. New York: Appleton-Century-Crofts. p. 457.

13. Skinner, p. 458.

14. Wright, R. (1996, March 25). Can machines think? Maybe so, as Deep Blue's prowess suggests. *Time*. p. 50.

15. Kasparov, G. (1996, March 25). The day I sensed a new kind of intelligence. *Time*. p. 55.

16. Kasparov, p. 55.

17. Levy, S. (1997, May 19). Big Blue's hand of God. *Newsweek*. p. 72.

18. Krauthammer, C. (1997, May 26). Be afraid. The meaning of Deep Blue's victory. *The Weekly Standard*, pp. 19–22. See p. 19.

19. Krauthammer, p. 21.
20. Crevier, D. (1993). *AI: The tumultuous history of the search for artificial intelligence.* New York: Basic Books. p. 180.
21. Hayes, P. J., Fork, K. M., & Adams-Webber, J. R. (1992). Human reasoning about artificial intelligence. *Journal of Experimental and Theoretical Artificial Intelligence, 4,* 247–263. p. 251.
22. Hayes et al., p. 251.
23. Lowrie, W. (1961). *A short life of Kierkegaard.* Garden City, NY: Doubleday. pp. 71, 144.
24. Kaufmann, W. (1950). *Nietzsche: Philosopher, psychologist, antichrist.* New York: Meridian.
25. Kaufmann, p. 134.
26. Lowrie (1961), p. 103.
27. Rychlak, J. F. (1997). *In defense of human consciousness.* Washington, DC: American Psychological Association. pp. 2–3, 6, 66.
28. Farthing, G. W. (1992). *The psychology of consciousness.* Englewood Cliffs, NJ: Prentice-Hall. p. 6.
29. Spielberger, C. D. (1962). The rise of awareness in verbal conditioning. In C. W. Eriksen (Ed.), *Behavior and awareness: A symposium of research and interpretation* (pp. 73–101). Durham, NC: Duke University Press. p. 76.
30. Baenninger, R. (1994). A retreat before the canon of parsimony. *Contemporary Psychology, 39,* 805–807. p. 806.
31. Aristotle. (1952). *Topics.* In R. M. Hutchins (Ed.), *Great books of the western world* (Vol. 8, pp. 143–223). Chicago: Encyclopaedia Britannica. p. 143.
32. Rychlak (1997), pp. 53, 307.
33. Rychlak (1997), pp. 205, 208, 210.

CHAPTER 5: THE SELF TAKES OVER

1. Markus, H., & Wurf, E. (1987). The dynamic self-concept: A social psychological perspective. *Annual Review of Psychology, 38,* 299–337. On p. 299 the self is described as a mediator. On p. 301 the self is said to be a node in the memory network.
2. Rosenthal, P. (1984). *Words & values.* New York: Oxford University Press. pp. 9–11.
3. Mecca, A. M., Smelser, N. J., & Vasconcellos, J. (Eds.). (1989). *The social importance of self-esteem.* Berkeley: University of California Press. p. xii. Rogers is considered by many to be a self theorist, but it is his accepting, nondirective attitude toward others that has primarily influenced the self-esteem movement in education (and human affairs generally).
4. Vasconcellos, J. (1989). Preface. In A. M. Mecca, N. J. Smelser, & J. Vasconcellos (Eds.), *The social importance of self-esteem* (pp. xi–xxi). Berkeley: University of California Press. p. xii.
5. Bork, R. H. (1996). *Slouching towards Gomorrah: Modern liberalism and American decline.* New York: Regan Books.
6. Smelser, N. J. (1989). Self-esteem and social problems: An introduction. In A. M. Mecca, N. J. Smelser, & J. Vasconcellos (Eds.), *The social importance of self-esteem* (pp. 1–23). Berkeley: University of California Press. p. 15.

7. Scheff, T. J., Retzinger, S. M., & Ryan, M. T. (1989). Crime, violence, and self-esteem: Review and proposals. In A. M. Mecca, N. J. Smelser, & J. Vasconcellos (Eds.), *The social importance of self-esteem* (pp. 165–199). Berkeley: University of California Press. p. 172.

8. Schneiderman, L., Furman, W. M., & Weber, J. (1989). Self-esteem and chronic welfare dependency. In A. M. Mecca, N. J. Smelser, & J. Vasconcellos (Eds.), *The social importance of self-esteem* (pp. 200–247). Berkeley: University of California Press. p. 234.

9. Wattenberg, B. J. (1995). *Values matter most.* Washington, DC: Regnery. p.195.

10. Freeman, M. (1993). *Rewriting the self: History, memory, narrative.* New York: Routledge. p. 148.

11. Freeman, p. 49. Italics in original.

12. Freeman, p. 223.

13. Fromm, E. (1939). Selfishness and self-love. *Psychiatry, 2,* 507–523.

14. Riesman, D. (1955). *Individualism reconsidered.* Garden City, NY: Doubleday Anchor.

15. Arieli, Y. (1964). *Individualism and nationalism in American ideology.* Cambridge, MA: Harvard University Press. p. 192.

16. Arieli, p. 63.

17. Arieli, p. 38.

18. Clinton, H. R. (1996). *It takes a village: And other lessons.* New York: Touchstone. p. 15. Gingrich, N. (1995). *To renew America.* New York: Harper-Collins. p. 40. Although Clinton (liberal) and Gingrich (conservative) are on opposite sides of the political spectrum they both attest to the importance of personal responsibility in achieving the rewards that American citizenship has to offer.

19. Bernstein, R. (1995). *Dictatorship of virtue: How the battle over multiculturalism is reshaping our schools, our country, our lives.* New York: Vintage. p. 243.

20. Bernstein, pp. 243–244.

21. Martin, G. (1996). Speaking properly: The need for a shared vocabulary. pp. 75–83. In D. Anderson (Ed.), *Gentility recalled: "Mere" manners and the making of social order.* London: The Social Affairs Unit. p. 83.

22. O'Hear, A. (1996). Knowing your place: Manners between the generations. In D. Anderson (Ed.), *Gentility recalled: "Mere" manners and the making of social order* (pp. 87–94). London: The Social Affairs Unit. p. 87.

23. Kennedy, E., & Charles, S. C. (1997). *Authority: The most misunderstood idea in America.* New York: Free Press. p. 43.

24. Himmelfarb, G. (1994). *The de-moralization of society.* New York: Vintage. p. 51.

25. Himmelfarb, p. 39.

26. Freud, S. (1961). *The ego and the id, and other works.* In J. Strachey (Ed.), *The standard edition of the complete psychological works of Sigmund Freud* (Vol. 19). London: Hogarth Press. (Original work published 1923). p. 36.

27. Gaylin, W., & Jennings, B. (1996). *The perversion of autonomy.* New York: Free Press. p. 30.

28. Gaylin & Jennings, p. 6.

29. Didion, J. (1961). *Slouching towards Bethlehem.* New York: Dell. See pp. 162–163 for an example of someone who would reject all moral imperatives.

30. Gaylin & Jennings (1996), p. 78.

31. Gaylin & Jennings (1996), p. 229.

32. Horowitz, D. (1997). *Radical son*. New York: Free Press. p. 385.
33. Gaylin & Jennings (1996), p. 205.
34. Gaylin & Jennings (1996), p. 206.
35. Gaylin & Jennings (1996), p. 210.
36. Gaylin & Jennings (1996), p. 211.
37. Gaylin & Jennings (1996), p. 208.

CHAPTER 6: BIOLOGY AND BEHAVIOR

1. Cameron, N., & Rychlak, J. F. (1985). *Personality development and psychotherapy: A dynamic approach* (2nd ed.). Boston: Houghton Mifflin. See pp. 8–14 for a discussion of Freud's views on biological reductionism.
2. McGuire, W. (1974). *The Freud/Jung letters: The correspondence between Sigmund Freud and C. G. Jung*. Bollingen Series XCIV. Princeton, NJ: Princeton University Press. pp. 115–116.
3. McGuire, p. 374.
4. Rychlak, J. F. (1991). *Artificial intelligence and human reason: A teleological critique*. New York: Columbia University Press. pp. 144–160; Rychlak, J. F. (1994). *Logical learning theory: A human teleology and its empirical support*. Lincoln: University of Nebraska Press. Chapter 8.
5. Eccles, J. C. (1977). In K. R. Popper & J. C. Eccles (Eds.), *The self and its brain* (Part 2, pp. 225–421). London: Springer International. See p. 232.
6. Granit, R. (1977). *The purposive brain*. Cambridge, MA: MIT Press.
7. Eccles (1977), p. 241.
8. Granit (1977), p. 41.
9. Mountcastle, V. B. (1975). Modality and topographic properties of single neurons of cat's somatic sensory cortex. *Journal of Neurophysiology, 20*, 408–434.
10. Eccles (1977), p. 234.
11. Pribram, K. H. (1991). *Brain and perception: Holonomy and structure in figural processing*. Hillsdale, NJ: Erlbaum; Neisser, U. (1991). The development of consciousness and the acquisition of skill. In F. S. Kessel, P. M. Cole, & D. L. Johnson (Eds.), *Self and consciousness: Multiple perspectives*. Hillsdale, NJ: Erlbaum. p. 6.
12. Granit (1977), pp. 7, 9, 165.
13. Libet, B. (1985). Unconscious cerebral initiative and the role of conscious will in voluntary action. *Behavioral and Brain Sciences, 8*, 529–566. See p. 532.
14. Libet, pp. 536–537.
15. Eccles (1977), p. 349.
16. Brownlee, S. (1999, August 9). Inside the teen brain. *U.S. News & World Report*, 44–54.
17. Penfield, W. (1975). *The mystery of the mind*. Princeton, NJ: Princeton University Press. p. 77.
18. Pribram, K. H., & Drake, S. D. (1999). Conscious awareness processing in the synaptodendritic web. *New Ideas in Psychology, 17*, 205–214.
19. Shreve, J. (1999, October). Secrets of the gene. *National Geographic*, 42–75.
20. Shreve, pp. 42–75.
21. Nash, M. (1998, April 27). The personality genes. *Time*, 60–61.

22. Thompson, L. (1995, June 12). Search for a gay gene. *Time*, 60–61. For an example of this suggestion to repair the presumed genetic defect of homosexuality see the comments of the Rev. Louis P. Sheldon on p. 61.

23. Edwards, R. (1996, September). Can sexual orientation change with therapy? *Monitor*, p. 49.

24. Edwards, p. 49.

25. Edwards, p. 49.

26. Leoussi, A. S. (1996). Keeping up appearances: Clothes as a public matter. In D. Anderson (Ed.), *Gentility recalled: Mere manners and the making of social order*. London: The Social Affairs Unit (pp. 97–106). See p. 104.

27. Bork, R. H. (1996). *Slouching towards Gomorrah: Modern liberalism and American decline*. New York: Regan. p. 197.

28. Bork, p. 199.

29. Bellah, R. N., Madsen, R., Sullivan, W. M., Swidler, A., & Tipton, S. M. (1985). *Habits of the heart: Individualism and commitment in American life*. Berkeley: University of California Press. pp. 101–102, 195, 197.

30. Bellah et al., p. 97.

31. Bellah et al., pp. 101–102.

32. Bellah et al., p. 98.

33. Bellah et al., p. 108.

34. Vos Savant, M. (2000, June 11). Is there a connection between divorce and living together? *Parade Magazine*, p. 8. A study conducted at the Center for Demography and Ecology at the University of Wisconsin found that the rate of separation or divorce in the first ten years for those couples who cohabit is 36% and for those who do not is 27%.

35. Kass, L. R. (1997, February 9). Courtship's end: Men and women are paying a high price for their individualism. *Chicago Tribune Magazine*, pp. 20–23.

36. Gray, M. (2000). *Drug crazy: How we got into this mess and how we can get out*. New York: Routledge. p. 54; Freud, S. (1974). *Cocaine papers*. New York: Stonehill. p. 255.

37. Auletta, K. (1999). *The underclass* (2nd ed.). Woodstock, NY: Overbook. p. 45.

38. Gray (2000), p. 53.

39. Freud (1974), p. 86.

40. Freud (1974), p. 173.

41. Schur, M. (1972). *Freud: Living and dying*. New York: International Universities Press. p. 62.

42. Schur, p. 529.

43. Moynihan, D. P. (1996). *Miles to go: A personal history of social policy*. Cambridge, MA: Harvard University Press. p. 205.

44. Alcoholics Anonymous. (1976). [3rd ed.]. New York: AA World Services.

45. D'Souza, D. (1995). *The end of racism: Principles for a multiracial society*. New York: Free Press. p. 422.

46. D'Souza, p. 204.

47. Tatum, B. D. (1997). *Why are all the black kids sitting together in the cafeteria, and other conversations about race*. New York: Basic Books. p. 16.

48. D'Souza (1995), p. 468.

49. Van den Berghe, P. L. (1967). *Race and racism*. New York: Wiley. p. 14. Italics in original.

50. D'Souza (1995), p. 38.

51. The American Indian (or Native American) population suffered from the same misunderstanding, in which tribes with significant cultural differences were treated by American settlers as if they were one people.

52. Lemann, N. (1996, February/March). The end of racism? An interview with Dinesh D'Souza. *American Heritage*, pp. 93–105. See p. 95.

53. Tatum (1997), p. 6.

54. Tatum (1997), p. 16.

55. D'Souza (1995), p. 160.

56. Sniderman, P., & Piazza, T. (1993). *The scar of race*. Cambridge, MA: Harvard University Press. pp. 46–50.

57. Bernstein, R. (1995). *Dictatorship of virtue: How the battle over multiculturalism is reshaping our schools, our country, our lives*. New York: Vintage. p. 193.

58. D'Souza (1995), p. 475.

59. Dovido, F. F., Mann, J., & Gaertner, S. L. (1989). Resistance to affirmative action: The implications of aversive racism. In F. A. Blanchard & F. J. Crosby (Eds.), *Affirmative action in perspective* (pp. 83–102). New York: Springer-Verlag. p. 86.

60. Dovido et al., p. 92.

61. Hernstein, R., & Murray, C. (1994). *The Bell curve: Intelligence and class structure in American life*. New York: Free Press.

62. D'Souza (1995), pp. 475–476.

63. Tatum (1997), p. 61.

64. Tatum (1997), pp. 60–61.

65. Tatum (1997), p. 62.

66. McWhorter, J. (2000). *Losing the race: Self-sabotage in black America*. New York: Free Press.

67. Horowitz, D. (1999). *Hating whitey and other progressive causes*. Dallas: Spence. p. 28.

68. Tatum (1997), p. 10.

69. D'Souza (1995), p. 287.

70. D'Souza (1995), p. 282.

71. D'Souza (1995), p. 267.

72. D'Souza (1995), p. 540.

73. Copeland, W. R. (1994). *And the poor get welfare: The ethics of poverty in the United States*. Nashville, TN: Abingdon Press.

74. Kelley, R. D. G. (1997). *Yo' mama's disfunktional!: Fighting the culture wars in urban America*. Boston: Beacon Press.

75. Kelley, p. 23.

76. Kelley, p. 42.

77. Kelley, p. 22.

78. Weaver, C. M. (1996). *It's OK to leave the plantation: The new underground railroad* (J. Reeder, Ed.). Bonsall, CA: Reeder. p. 115.

79. Weaver, p. 115.

80. Steele, S. (1998). *A dream deferred: The second betrayal of black freedom in America*. New York: Harper Collins.

81. Steele, p. 48.

82. Steele, pp. 58–59. Italics in original.

83. Steele, p. 61.

84. Steele, p. 61.

85. Steele, p. 71.
86. Steele, S. (1990). *The content of our character: A new vision of race in America.* New York: HarperCollins. p. 73.
87. McCauley, R. N. (1998, September). Comparing the cognitive foundations of religion and science. *Emory Cognition Project (Report #17).* Atlanta, GA: Emory University, p. 10; See also Dennett, D. C. (1987). *The intentional stance.* Cambridge, MA: The MIT Press.

CHAPTER 7: VALUES AT EVERY TURN

1. Reese, W. L. (1980). *Dictionary of philosophy and religion: Eastern and western thought.* Atlantic Highlands, NJ: Humanities Press. p. 604.
2. Frondizi, R. (1963). *What is a value? An introduction to axiology.* LaSalle, IL: Open Court Books. p. 4.
3. Becker, H., & Barnes, H. E. (1952). *Social thought from lore to science (Volume 1): A history and interpretation of man's ideas about life with his fellows.* Washington, DC: Harren. p. 486.
4. Frondizi (1963), p. 8.
5. Bennett, W. J. (1993). *The book of virtues: A treasury of great moral stories.* New York: Simon & Schuster. p. 11.
6. Bennett, p. 14.
7. Moynihan, D. P. (1996). *Miles to go: A personal history of social policy.* Cambridge, MA: Harvard University Press. p. 144.
8. Auletta, K. (1999). *The underclass* (2nd ed.). Woodstock, NY: Overlook Press.
9. Frondizi (1963), p. 8.
10. Frondizi (1963), p. 44.
11. Kilpatrick, W. (1992). *Why Johnny can't tell right from wrong: And what we can do about it.* New York: Touchstone.
12. Smith, H. (1991). *The world's religions* (2nd ed.). San Francisco: Harper. p.19.
13. Thornton, B. S. (1999). *Plagues of the mind: The new epidemic of false knowledge.* Wilmington, DE: ISI Books. See p. 100 for a recognition of reflexivity.
14. Taylor, C. (1989). *Sources of the self: The making of modern identity.* Cambridge, MA: Harvard University Press. p. 139.
15. Bandura, A. (1991). Social cognitive theory of moral thought and action. In W. Kurtlines & J. Gewitz (Eds.), *Handbook of moral behavior and development* (pp. 45–103). Hillsdale, NJ: Erlbaum; Kohlberg, L. (1976). Moral stages and moralization: The cognitive-development approach. In T. Lickona (Ed.), *Moral development and behavior: Theory, research and social issues* (pp. 31–53). New York: Rinehart & Winston; Vallegas-dePosada, C. (1994). A motivational model for understanding moral actions and moral development. *Psychological Reports, 74,* 951–959.
16. Goldfarb, J. C. (1991). *The cynical society: The culture of politics and the politics of culture in American life.* Chicago: The University of Chicago Press. p. 18.
17. Rosenblatt, R. (1984, November 12). Defenders of the faith. *Time,* 112.
18. Wainryb, C., & Turiel, E. (1993). Conceptual and informational features in moral decision making. *Educational Psychologist, 28,* 205–218.
19. Schlessinger, L., & Vogel, S. (1998). *The Ten Commandments: The significance of God's laws in everyday life.* New York: HarperCollins. p. 210.

20. Himmelfarb, G. (1996). *The de-moralization of society: From Victorian virtues to modern values.* New York: Vintage. p. 240.
21. Ryan, W. (1971). *Blaming the victim.* New York: Free Press.
22. Copeland, W. R. (1994). *And the poor get welfare: The ethics of poverty in the United States.* Nashville, TN: Abingdon Press. p. 95.
23. Horowitz, D. (1998). *The politics of bad faith: The radical assault on America's future.* New York: Free Press. p. 8.
24. Copeland (1994), pp. 73, 85.
25. Bork, R. H. (1996). *Slouching towards Gomorrah: Modern liberalism and American decline.* New York: Regan. p. 54.
26. Copeland (1994), p. 36.
27. Horowitz, D. (1997). *Radical son: A generational odyssey.* New York: Free Press. p. 89.
28. Bloom, A. (1987). *The closing of the American mind: How higher education has failed democracy and impoverished the souls of today's students.* New York: Simon and Schuster.
29. Goldfarb (1991), p. 2.
30. Goldfarb (1991), p. 18.
31. Goldfarb (1991), p. 22.
32. Goldfarb (1991), p. 48.
33. Fernandez, J. (with Underwood, J.). (1993). *Tales out of school: Joseph Fernandez's crusade to restore American education.* Boston: Little Brown. p. 95.
34. Steele, S. (1998). *A dream deferred: The second betrayal of black freedom in America.* New York: Harper Collins. p. 100.
35. Weaver, C. M. (1996). *It's OK to leave the plantation: The new underground railroad!* (J. Reeder, Ed.). Bonsall, CA: Reeder Publishing. p. 87.
36. Steele (1998), p. 49.
37. Tatum, B. D. (1997). *"Why are all the black kids sitting together in the cafeteria?" and other conversations about race.* New York: Basic Books. pp. 121–122.
38. Kelley, R. D. G. (1987). *Yo' mama's disfunktional: Fighting the culture wars in urban America.* Boston: Beacon Press. pp. 84–85, 91.
39. Scalia, A. (1997). *A matter of interpretation: Federal courts and the law.* Princeton, NJ: Princeton University Press. The precedent-sequacious process of reasoning clarified by Logical Learning Theory can be seen in Judge Scalia's analysis of legal practices. See especially p. 39.
40. Berlin, I. (1992). *The crooked timber of humanity.* New York: Vintage. pp. 20, 70; see also: Finkielkraut, A. (1995). *The defeat of the mind.* New York: Columbia University Press.
41. Boas, F. (1932). *Anthropology and modern life.* New York: Norton.
42. Benedict, R. (1934). *Patterns of culture.* Boston: Houghton Mifflin.
43. Hull, C. L. (1937). Mind, mechanism, and adaptive behavior. *Psychological Review, 44,* 1–32; Skinner, B. F. (1938). *The behavior of organisms: An experimental analysis.* New York: Appleton-Century-Crofts; Tolman, E. C. (1932). *Purposive behavior in animals and men.* New York: Appleton-Century-Crofts. Watson, J. B. (1924). *Behaviorism.* New York: Norton.
44. Wrong, D. H. (1997). Cultural relativism as ideology. *Critical Review, 11,* 291–300. See p. 294.
45. Sumner, W. G. (1940). *Folkways.* New York: Mentor Books. pp. 27–28.
46. Kilpatrick, W. (1992). *Why Johnny can't tell right from wrong and what we can do about it.* New York: Simon & Schuster.

47. Bork (1996), pp. 298–299.

48. Horowitz (1997), p. 406.

49. Wrong (1997), p. 298.

50. Gitlin, T. (1995). *The twilight of common dreams: Why America is wracked by culture wars*. New York: Metropolitan Books. pp. 166–169.

51. Wrong (1997), p. 297.

52. Kilpatrick (1992), pp. 123–128.

53. For my personal contribution to such teleological theorizing see: Rychlak, J. F. (1994). *Logical learning theory: A human teleology and its empirical support*. Lincoln: University of Nebraska Press.

54. Bloom (1987).

55. Clinton, H. R. (1996). *It takes a village, and other lessons our children teach us*. New York: Touchstone. p. 97.

56. Fernandez (with Underwood) (1993), pp. 77–78. This attitude has relevance up to a point. But, as Fernandez suggests, we must recognize that sociopathic behaviors are also up to the person who must take responsibility for them. Such a view is consistent with a teleological understanding of human behavior.

57. Rychlak (1994), Chapter 2 presents basic concepts for a telic image of human nature.

58. Weaver (1996), p. 83; see also Steele (1998), pp. 35, 60.

59. Satel, S. (2001, January). The indoctrinologists are coming. *The Atlantic Monthly*, 59–64. See esp. p. 60 where Rodney Clark, a psychologist at Wayne State University, is quoted as expressing this view of personal responsibility.

CHAPTER 8: THE HUMAN IMAGE IN POSTMODERN AMERICA

1. Rosenau, P. M. (1992). *Post-modernism and the social sciences: Insights, inroads and intrusions*. Princeton, NJ: Princeton University Press. p. 53. I have taken such information from many sources to gain my overall impression.

2. Kennedy, E., & Charles, S. C. (1997). *Authority: The most misunderstood idea in America*. New York: Free Press. p. 205.

3. Gaylin, W., & Jennings, B. (1996). *The perversion of autonomy: The proper uses of coercion and constraints in a liberal society*. New York: Free Press. pp. 79, 91, 93.

4. Samuels, A., Croal, N., & Gates, D. (2000, October 9). The rap on rap. *Newsweek*, pp. 56–67. As expressed in this article, it is no longer a question of merely sex and violence as themes for today's music. Musical themes have sunk to depravity in some misguided deconstructive effort to shock an audience. Who can say what sort of emotions are being prompted in such an atmosphere?

5. Tocqueville, de. A. (1966). *Democracy in America* (J. P. Meyer, Ed., & G. Lawrence, Trans.). New York: Harper Perennial. p. 507. (Original work published in four volumes, 1835–1840).

6. Bell, D. (1973). *The coming of post-industrial society: A venture in social forecasting*. New York: Basic Books. pp. 27–33.

7. Bell, pp. 27–33.

8. Bell, p. xiv. Italics in original.

9. Bell, p. xviii.

10. Bell, p. xvii.

11. Bell, p. 127.

12. Bell, p. 128.
13. Bell, p. 9.
14. Bell, p. 20.
15. Bell, p. 127.
16. Bell, p. 127.
17. Bell, p. 232.
18. Ellis, J. J. (1989). *Against deconstruction*. Princeton, NJ: Princeton University Press. p. 116.
19. Brewer, W. F. (1974). There is no convincing evidence for operant or classical conditioning in adult humans. In W. B. Weimer & D. S. Palermo (Eds.), *Cognition and the symbolic processes*. Hillsdale, NJ: Erlbaum. pp. 1–42. A historic paper that proved a major factor in the weakening of conditioning theory in psychology.
20. Page, M. M. (1972). Demand characteristics and the verbal operant conditioning experiment. *Journal of Personality and Social Psychology, 23*, 372–378.
21. Rychlak, J. F. (1994). *Logical learning theory: A human teleology and its empirical support*. Lincoln: University of Nebraska Press. pp. 21, 312.
22. Rosenau (1992), p. 128.
23. Rychlak, J. F. (Ed.). (1976). *Dialectic: Humanistic rationale for behavior and development*. Basel, Switzerland: Karger AG. p. 6.
24. Rychlak (1994), p. 50.
25. Kirsch, I., & Lynn, S. J. (1999). Automaticity in clinical psychology. *American Psychologist, 54*, 504–515. These authors explain what I would consider teleological behaviors in terms of what they call "response expectancies." This oxymoron is an effort to retain traditional mechanical terminology in a telic context. A response to a stimulus is an *after-the-fact* effect in an efficiently caused sequence. An expectancy is a *before-the-fact* anticipation, presumption, or estimation of what is likely to take place in a formal–final cause sequence. Trying to turn them into efficient causes is not only a mistake, it is flatly impossible. Nevertheless, look for such efforts to continue in psychology because the old machine models of human beings will continue to hold sway for some time.

AUTHOR INDEX

Numbers in italics refer to listings in the references.

SUBJECT INDEX

Adams, S., 73
Addiction
    biological vs. psychological, 92
    Freud vs. Halstead, 93
    over-extended concept, 94
Adler, A., 18, 22, 49, 72, 83
Aesop, 104–105
Affective assessment, affection
    based on dialectical reasoning, 15
    difficult to change, 49
    important in forming self-esteem, 72
    influence direction of thought, 49
    not emotion, 15
    value formation, 194
Affirmation
    committing to a belief, 13
    in framing a major premise, 14
Affirmative action
    rejection of, 114
    repairing losses of disadvantaged, 113
Agency
    deciding to act for oneself, 6, 10
    human, 13
Alcoholics Anonymous
    teleological emphasis, 94
    willful intention of alcoholic, 71
Anthropomorphize
    in a "competition" with computer, 59
    of computer processing, 53
Aquinas, T., 78
Archetype as primordial image, Jung, 22
Aristotle, 6, 19, 37, 42
Association model
    efficient causation in, 6
    mechanistic nature of, 6, 25
    mediation in, 6
    of consciousness, 65
Authoritophobia
    cannot assume or relate to authority, 77
    no judgment makes all equal, 109
    taken hold in America, 108
    turns anti-authority into a moral victory, 77
Authority within
    recognizes moral basis of behavior, 105, 129

source of guilty feelings, 77–78
Autonomy
    self-rule, 78
    suggests individualism, 79
Axiology
    objectivist value theory, 104
    subjectivist value theory, 104

Behaviorism
    efficient causation is basic, 24
    paramount in social construction, 40
    study of intentionless responses, 24
Bell, D., 33, 49, 134
Bell's 3-stage theory of society
    preindustrial, industrial, postindustrial, 34
Bennett, W. J., 105
Berger, P., 44, 49
Biological reductionism
    limited use in Freudian theory, 19
    plus teleology in Adlerian theory, 21
Biology
    extraspective accounts dominate, 83
    furthers robotism, 125
    one drop principle, 95
    taking over psychology, 122
Boas, F., 118
Brain
    imaging of, 87–89
    structure, 84–87
British philosophy dominated in rise of science, 8
Burke, E., 78

Category is from the Greek meaning "to predicate," 36
Cathexis of libido is seen to be intentional, 20
Cause(s), Causation
    Aristotelian theory of, 5–6
    as "responsible for," 5
    –effect, 39
Choice impossible in Association model, 90, 117, 136
Clark, R., 160

Class warfare is turning into cultural warfare,
119
Client-centered
early approach to therapy in Rogerian
theory, 28
reliance on the individual, 28
Collective
association process is basic to, 10
–consciousness, Jung, 22
content vs. process in, 126
exclusively demonstrative reasoning in,
126
gathering of people into a group identity, 10
Collectivism
content of a process, 10
definition of, 4
individual submerged within group, 10
theory, favors association model, 9
Collectivist holds person to be indivisible
from group, 4
Communism
bourgeoisie vs. proletariat, 44
revolutionary ideology, 11, 43
Computer
hardware and software of, 52
"information" lacks meaning, 52
input v. output of, 54
logic of is demonstrative, 53
matches rather than predicates, 53
has ability to "think" dialectically, 53
Conditioning
as operant responding, 26
conditioned reinforcement, 25
requirements of, 27
Conscious, consciousness
as awareness, 65
class, 43, 46
collective vs. personal, Jung, 22
enlightened, 42
smaller circle within larger, Jung, 22
vs. unconscious, 19
Construct can mean assembling or framing,
40
Content
culture as, 45
emphasized in association model, 47
not to be confused with process, 11
produced by a process, 4
vs. process explanations, 71
Creative power
compensates for human weakness, 21

will power, 21
Culture
arises via shaping, 116
as variant form of mediation, 115
content produced by societal processes,
45
coined in Germany, early 20th century,
115
does not produce, 46
inherently collective, 45
nature vs. nurture dispute, 46, 116
print vs. oral form of, 45
relativism in, 46, 115–116

Deconstructionism
definition, 38
example of, Nietzsche, 38–39
founder of school, Derrida, 38
intertextuality, 39
reflects a dialectical aspect, 38
text and trace in, 38
Deep Blue
and negation of chess moves, 60
and virtual dialectical reasoning, 61
computer that G. Kasparov opposed,
58–59
Demonstrative reasoning
in collective thought, 126
processing meaning is unipolar, 14
self-contradiction as meaningless, 14
takes affirmations to be primary and
true, 14
Derrida, J., 41, 42, 49
Dialectical reasoning
people can "just say no," 135
relies on oppositionality, 14
takes affirmation to be bipolar, 14
Discrimination
flows from prejudice, 97
rational-, 99
Drive
–reduction, 25
stimulus, 25
D'Souza, D., 96
Durkheim, É., 40, 105
Durkheim's constant in social judgments, 105
"Duty" was a major concept for Kant, 104

Efficient cause reflects motion, force, or sig-
nals, 5
Ego
Freudian concept, 19

rational aspect of mind, 19
   vs. Shadow, Jung, 23
Encounter groups employ collective process,
   29
Engels, F., 44
Ethnic refers to socio-cultural factors, 97
Ethnocentrism idealizes a collective identity,
   117
Evaluation
   in personal responsibility, 74
   intrinsic to human thought, 141
   in value formation, 103
Existentialism
   basis of "street smarts" today, 62
   challenges convention and authority, 62
   denies possibility of certainty, 64
   founders: Nietzsche & Kierkegaard, 63
   furthers negation, 64
   people encouraged to control future, 36
   popular philosophy in USA, 36
   pro forma view of mind, 62
Extraspective perspective
   favors association modeling, 8
   in biological explanations, 83
   third-person description, 8
   vs. introspective perspective, 8

Feedback
   frequently misunderstood, 55
   output returning as input, 54–55
   positive vs. negative forms of, 54
Final cause
   always involves formal cause, 5
   primary cause of free will, 56
   purpose, reason, intention in events, 5
Formal cause relates to patterning, 5
Free will, freedom of the will
   behave otherwise in same circum-
     stances, 56
   belief in self-determination and purpose,
     6
   is not without limitations, 141
   negated by robotic theory, 31
   via negative feedback in computers, 54
Freud, S., 18, 20, 22, 24, 83, 93–94, 131

Halstead, W. S., 93
Hegel, G. W. F., 42
Hegelian dialectic
   ideas imply their contradictions, 42
   thesis, antithesis, synthesis, 42

Hermeneutics
   broadened to any textual organization,
     38
   conveying hidden messages, 38
Homeless
   coined by Snyder and Hombs, 81
   vs. normless, 81
Hombs, M. E., 81
Homosexuality
   and conversion therapy, 90
   as genetically determined, 89
Homunculus as little person in the brain, 85
Horowitz, D., 13–14
Human image
   and teleology, 67
   eccentricities of, 57, 61–62
   must change in postmodern era, 66–67

Id
   Freudian concept, 19
   as total hedonism of mind, 19
Identity politics
   favors multiculturalism, 118
   raise opportunity for certain groups, 118
Individual
   employs predication process, 10
   refers to a single being, 3
   thinking emphasizes process, 127
Individualist likes ideology of individualism,
   4
Individual psychology
   Adler's theory, 21
   holds individual responsible for self, 21
Individualism
   an ideological belief (content), 4
   definition, 4
   equated with difference, 76
   myth of, 76
   rugged, 63
   solitary vs. parallel, 4
Intention
   in meaning expression, 7
   in teleology, 5
Introspective perspective
   favors predication modeling, 8
   first-person description, 8
   vs. extraspective perspective, 8

Jackson, J., 99–100
Jefferson, T., 73
Jung, C. G., 18, 20, 83, 111

"Know to know further" is based on predication, 57, 108, 136
Kant, I., 104
Kasparov, G., 56, 58, 65, 67
Kerouac, J., 63
Kierkegaard, S., 63
King, M. L., 95

Lenat, D., 61
Leviathan Assumption
    as group mind, 10
    in shaping behavior, 91
    believing collectives can think, 9–10
    used in Jungian theory, 22
    used in later Rogerian theory, 30
Libertarian says the state exists for the individual, 4
Libido
    as general life energy, Jung, 20
    fixation of, 19–20
    in personality development, 19
    is not biological, 84
    psychical desire for sex, Freud, 19
Life Plan is a major guiding premise (Adler), 20
Love
    as self-love, 91
    Christian vs. therapeutic varieties of, 91
    idealizing loved one, 90
    sacrificing self for others, 91
    vs. lust, 90
Luther, M. L., 107

Marriage
    common-law, 92
    teleological factors in, 92
Marx, K., 42, 45
Marxian Argument
    based on a collective ideology, 13
    class-linked individuality, 44
    definition, 44
Marxian dialectic
    a presumed law of nature and history, 43
    ideas are shaped results not causes, 43
Material cause is the substance of things, 5
Meaning
    as "to intend," 7
    essential to introspective theories, 8
    lacking in mediation theorizing, 6
Mechanism
    efficient cause explains all, 6

opposite of teleology, 6
Mediation
    identical to association model, 6
    language as a mediator, 41
Moral (s), Morality
    an intellectual embarrassment today, 109
    –literacy, 104
Mozart, W. A., 130
Multiculturalism
    America now a salad not a melting pot, 75
    as diversity, 137
    holds that all cultures are equal, 119
    tied to left wing politics, 118

Negation
    fundamental to free will actions, 87
    in performance of Big Blue, 60
    major dialectical outcome, 57
    of a physical prompting, 87
    prominent in modern behavior, 64
Nietzsche, F., 38–40, 63
Norm(s)
    in Black community, 100
    as predications held in common, 46, 73

Oedipal complex in questioning authority, 78
One-sidedness
    encourages cynicism, 112
    in collegiate political education, 111
    in Jungian theory, 23
    of current behavior in America, 67
Operant conditioning
    reinforcement, 26
    response, 26
    Skinner's theory, 26
Opposite, opposition
    goes unnoticed in science, 63
    in dialectical reasoning, 14, 43, 58
    in views of Derrida and Nietzsche, 41
    play of, in all things, Jung, 23
    social identity, 99
Organismic valuing process, 28

Parallel individualism
    in Adlerian theory, 21
    vs. solitary, 4
Penfield, W., 89
Personal freedom via loss of manners, 58, 76
Personal responsibility
    based on self-evaluation, 74, 121

demands a conscious examination, 75

Personality
    type vs. trait theories of, 18
    vs. character, 18

Phenomenal field defines subjective reality, 28

Pilate, P., 109

Plato, 104

Politics
    as the science and art of government, 109
    Democratic vs. Republican parties, 109–110
    divided into liberal vs. conservative, 109
    heavily laden with teleology, 122
    involves seeking power, 109
    the political is also the personal, Marx, 110

Political correctness (PC)
    if no judgments made, everyone is equal, 109
    often tied to diversity and multiculturalism, 74
    well-intentioned defense of the needy, 74

Political structure in America
    liberals (left) vs. conservatives (right), 79
    opposing interpretations of freedom, 80

Postmodern person
    highly involved with lust, not love, 132
    not sentimental, 131
    sensitive to affection and emotion, 127

Postmodernism
    also named poststructuralism, 37–38
    Bell's postindustrial society as, 36
    decline in romanticism, 131
    dialogue is never ending, 38
    family, 128–132
    favors collectivism, 133
    find it impossible to know the truth, 38

Predicate is extending meaning to a target, 7

Predication
    as logical meaning extension, 7
    major premise in, 13, 20

Predication model
    as leading to selfishness, 72
    recognizes that all thought is relative, 48
    relies on formal and final causation, 8
    uses one concept to frame another, 6–7
    view of consciousness, 65

Prejudice
    a biasing predication learned culturally, 97
    leads to discrimination of others, 97, 99

Process
    active causation producing content, 4
    emphasized in predication model, 47
    not to be confused with content, 11
    society as, 45
    vs. content difference in explanation, 71

Pro forma
    archetypal themes, Jung, 22
    as personally forming meanings, 14
    basic to predication process, 22

Programmer must be given recognition, 125–126

Psychoanalysis founders Freud, Adler, and Jung, 18

Race
    defining a collective via physical criteria, 95
    as oppositional social identity, 99
    three racial groupings, 95

Racial inferiority
    questions concerning, 97–99
    traced to cultural influences, 98

Racial prejudice
    based on assumed superiority of Whites, 96
    the issue of civil rights, 97

Racism
    and values, 97
    aversive-, 98
    a belief in congenital inferiority of people, 95
    cultural-, 96

Rational discrimination, 99

Realism is also called essentialism, 37

Reflexive, self-reflexive
    examining personal thought for alternatives, 15
    relies on process of transcendence, 15

Reinforcement can be positive or negative, 11

Relativism
    always occurring in thinking, 47, 115
    as conditioned bonding in collectives, 46
    as transpredication, 66
    can be anti-intellectual, 136

content emphasis in association model, 47

cultural, 45, 115, 135

negative reactions to, 136

of process vs. content, 138

via comparing contents of two cultures, 47

Religion

begins in quest for meaning and values, 107

believed on spiritual grounds and faith, 108

criterion problem in proving, 107–108

devotion to something greater than self, 107

emphasis is placed on morality, 107

importance of faith over reason, 107

Responsibility

personal, 73–74

personal, as existentialist tenet, 36

Robot relies on program to carry out "acts," 6

Rogers, C. R., 8–10, 70

Scenarist

lecture others based on imagined scenarios, 58

seek to protect the disadvantaged, 58

take on a "righteous" attitude with others, 58

Self

as mediator or predicator, 70

as uniqueness of person, 69–70

–consciousness in communistic revolution, 43

–determinism in Adlerian theory, 6, 21, 93–94

–formation, Jungian theory, 23

real-, 91

Self-esteem

appreciation of one's being, 70

as a quasi drive, 71

as coming from achievement, 73

association vs. predication interpretations of, 71

influenced by affective assessment, 72

Self-reflexivity aids in keeping tabs on self, 70

Sequacious

meaning flows from a precedent 37, 47–48, 115

meaning extends via necessity of logic, 37

Shape, shaping

depends on knowledge and cooperation, 27

in social constructionism, 40

of overt behavior, 26–27, 44

Signal is efficiently caused, 40

Skinner, B. F. 8–10, 56

Slave derives meaning from "slav," 96

Snyder, M., 81

Social constructionism

holds that people shaped 100% by society, 40

objectify and internalize, Berger, 41

individuals can create social beliefs, 41

Social interest

Adlerian concept, 21

brought to bear individually, 21

Society

as a process, producing cultural contents, 45

various classes in, 35, 113

Solitary vs. parallel individualism, 4

S–R psychology

as behaviorism, 24

efficient-cause nature of, 24

Stereotypes act as guides in human thinking, 49

Structuralism

also called idealism, 37

deny authorship of a speaker's ideas, 37

Students for a Democratic Society (SDS), 63

Superego

conscience; moral aspects of mind, 19

Freudian concept, 19

Taine, H., 78

Teleology

and negative feedback, 54–55

exclusively introspective theory, 8, 101

from the Greek "telos" or "end," 5–6

human, 44

in Adlerian theory, 20

in Freudian theory, 20

in Jungian theory, 22

opposite of mechanism, 6

rejected by some postmodernists, 40

Theory can be confounded with method, 85

Three stage theories

Bell's theory used in this book, 34

common in history of ideas, 34
Tolerance is based on understanding, 140
Transcendence, transcend
    enables self-examination, 15
    process of rising above to see all, 15
Transpredication as consciousness, 65
Turing test simulates a person, 52–53, 61

Unipredication as unconsciousness, 65
Universal (s)
    an authoritative believe or concept, 77, 106, 140
    moral rules as, 79

Value(s)

as such, is a content, 104
can be defined down, 105
conceived, 106
created via the predication process, 105
emotions, involved, 106
judgment of worth, 103
received, 106
received can be developed into conceived, 107
when conveyed by stories are "virtues," 104
Virtual reality of the computer program, 62

Whitehead, A. N., 56–57

ABOUT THE AUTHOR

Joseph F. Rychlak, PhD, is Professor Emeritus at Loyola University, Chicago. In addition to teaching for 44 years at five universities, Dr. Rychlak has distinguished himself as a psychotherapist, author, theorist, and scientific researcher. He is a fellow of both the American Psychological Association (APA) and the American Psychological Society. He has twice been elected president of the APA Division of Theoretical and Philosophical Psychology. Rychlak is known as a rigorous humanist because he submits his nonmechanistic theoretical claims to the traditional scientific test. His wife Lenora, to whom this book is dedicated, continues to assist him, and they both take great pleasure in their eight grandchildren.